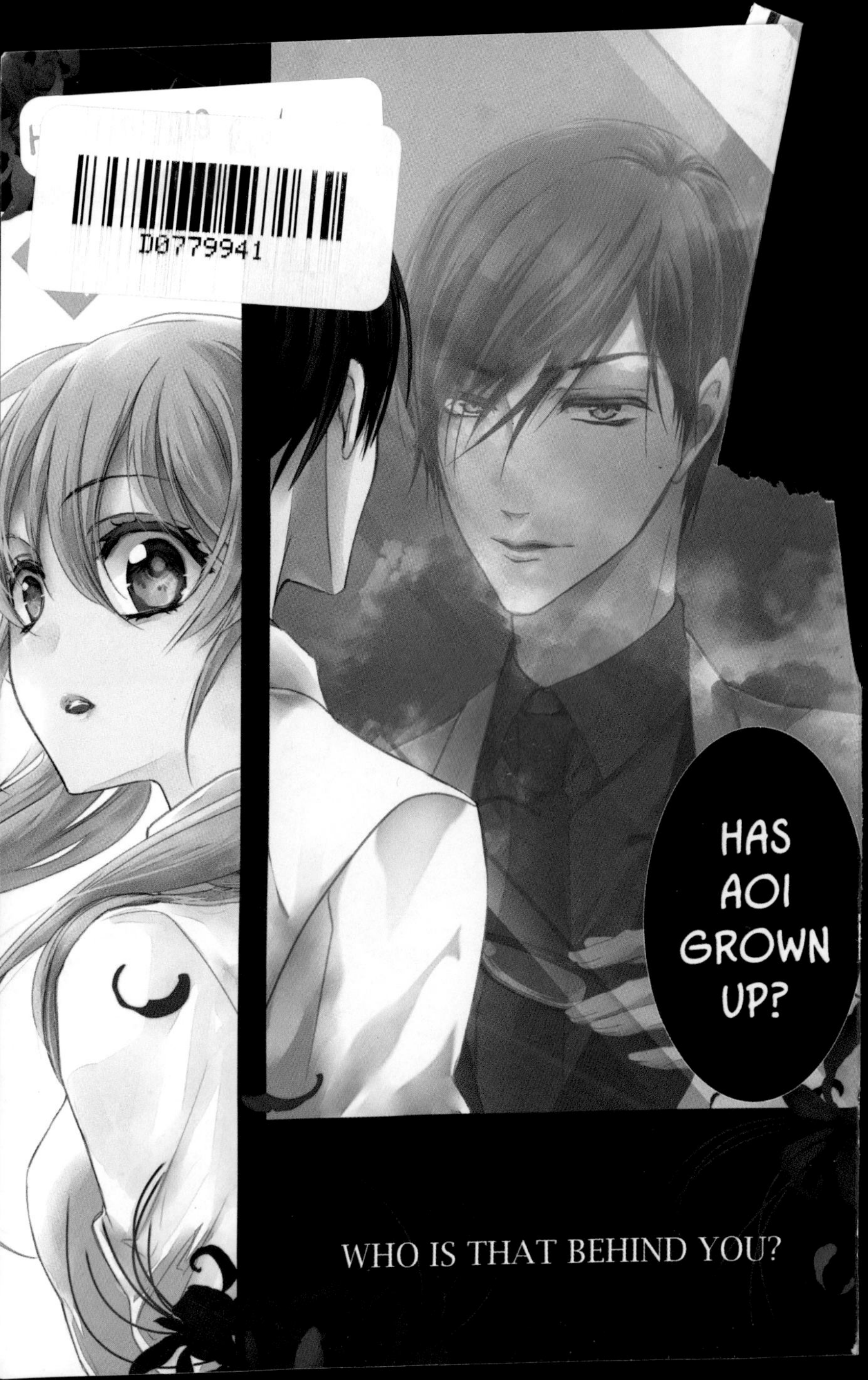
HAS AOI GROWN UP?
WHO IS THAT BEHIND YOU?

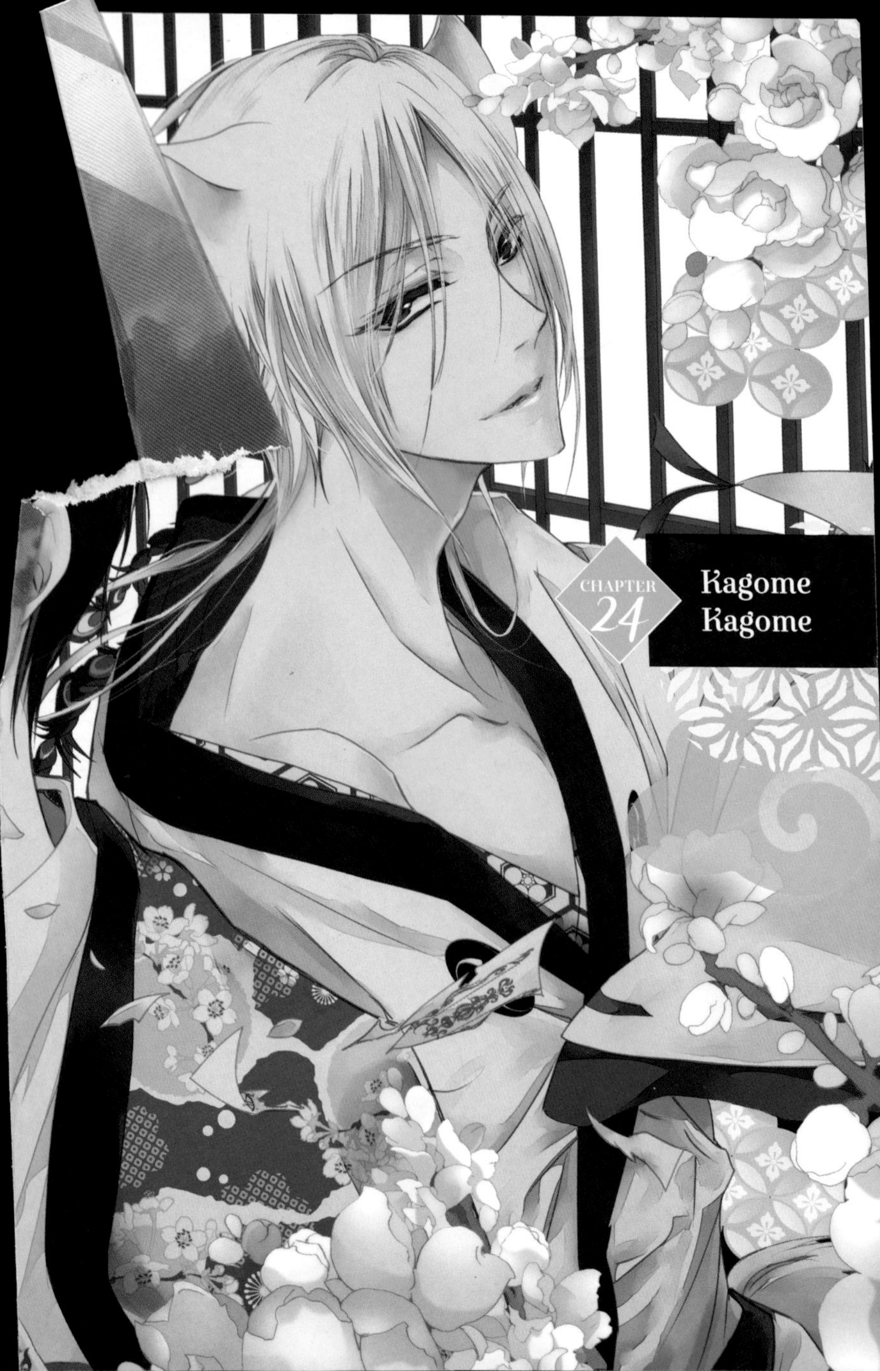
CHAPTER 24
Kagome Kagome

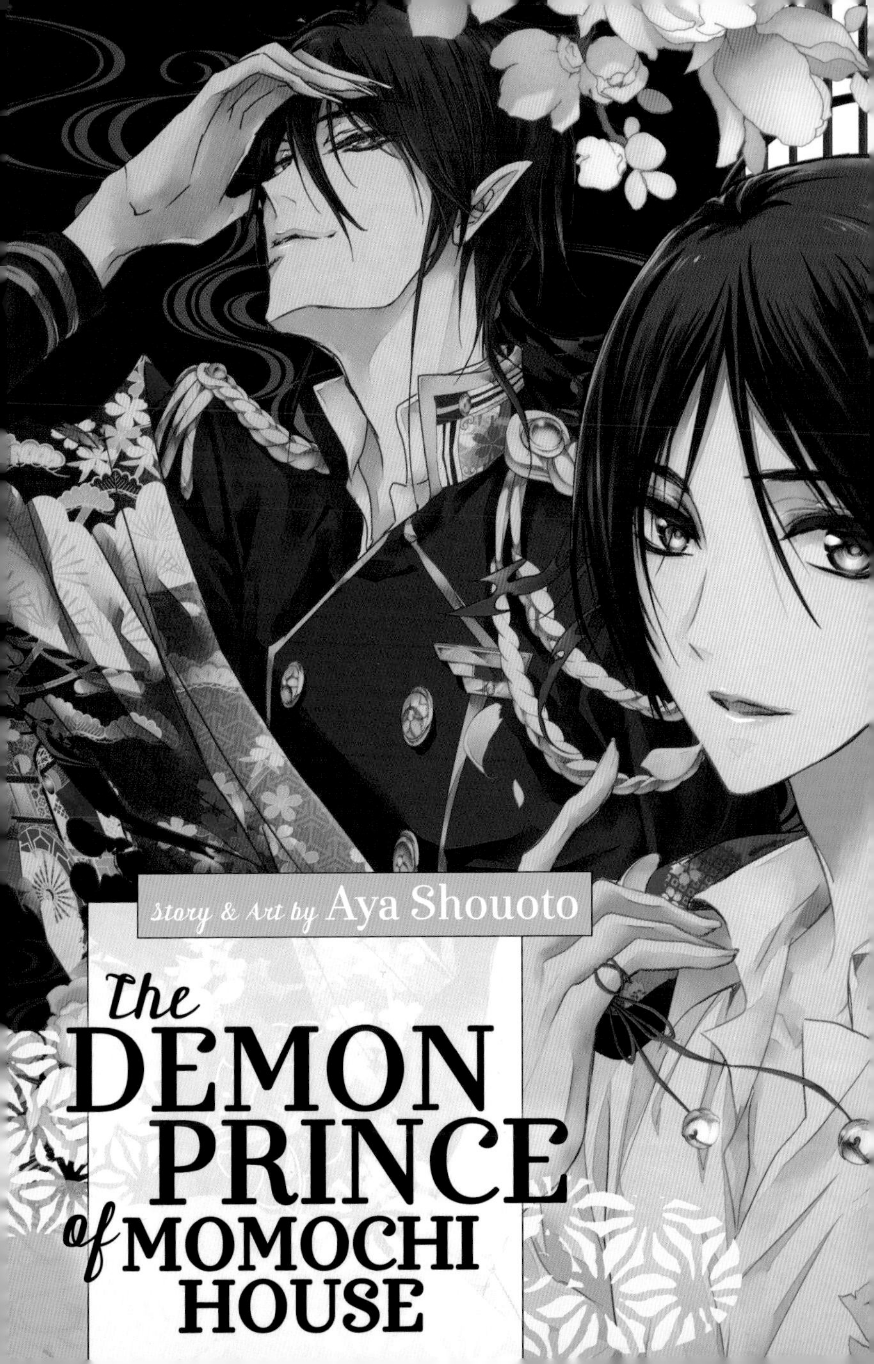
Story & Art by Aya Shouoto
The DEMON PRINCE of MOMOCHI HOUSE

The DEMON PRINCE of MOMOCHI HOUSE

7

Contents

The Mysterious Residents of Momochi House

Aoi Nanamori

When he was 7 years old, he wandered into Momochi House and was chosen as the Omamori-sama. He transforms into a nue to perform his duties, but it seems this role was meant for Himari.

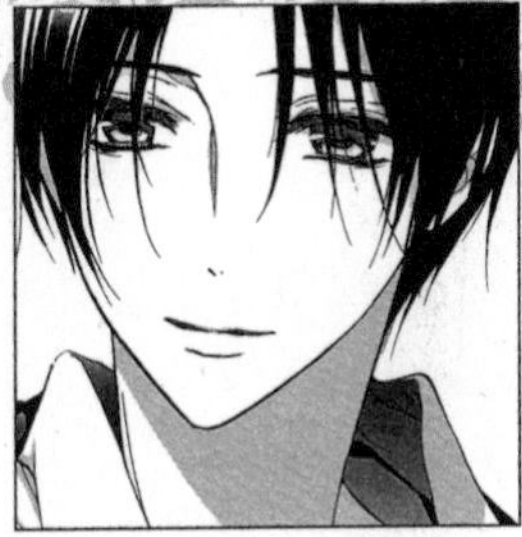

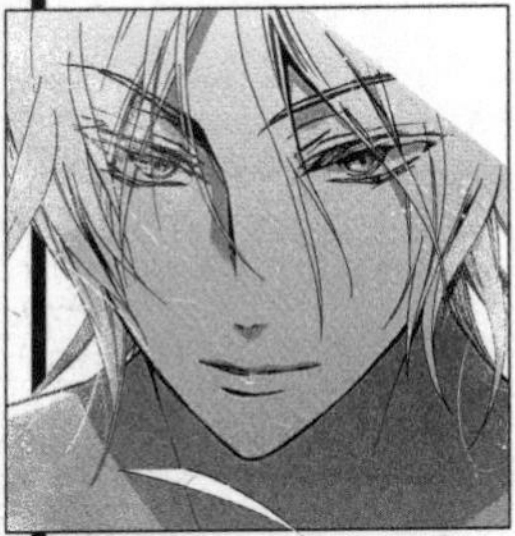

Omamori-sama (Nue)

An ayakashi, or demon, with the ears of a cat, the wings of a bird, and the tail of a fox. As the Omamori-sama, the nue protects Momochi House and eliminates demons who make their way in from the spiritual realm.

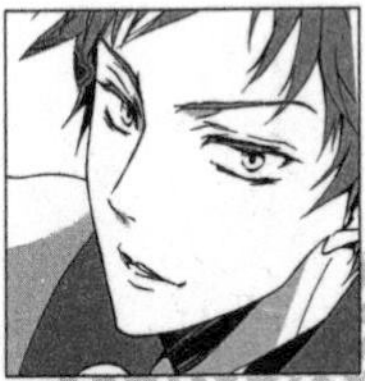

Ise

One of Omamori-sama's shikigami. He's an orangutan.

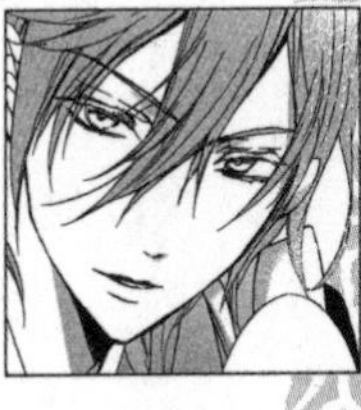

Yukari

One of Omamori-sama's shikigami. He's a water serpent.

Lesser Yokai

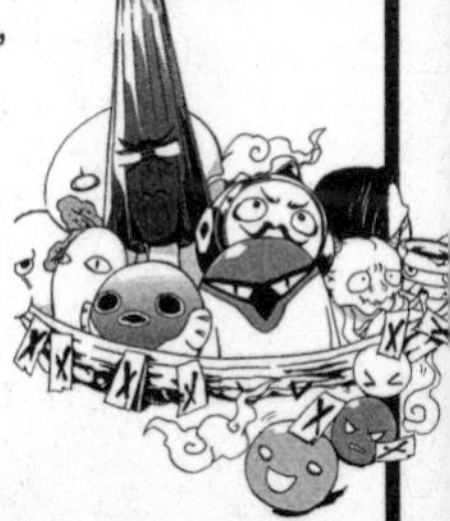

Himari Momochi

A 16-year-old orphan who, according to a certain will, has inherited Momochi House. As rightful owner, she has the ability to expel beings from the house.

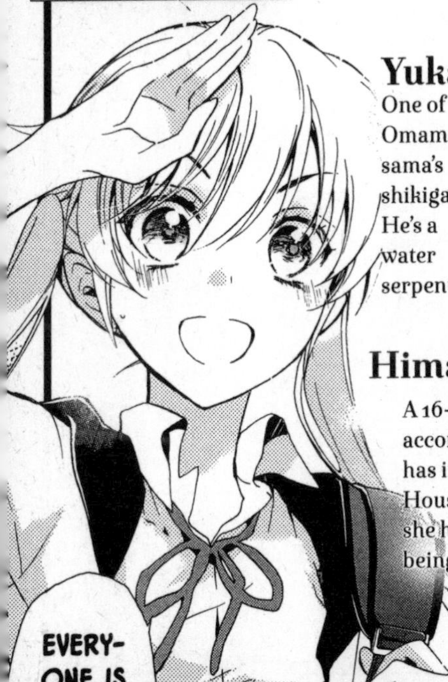
EVERY-ONE IS

Momochi House: Story Thus Far

Himari is depressed after being rejected by Aoi, and she doesn't understand why he's more affectionate than usual. Himari meets the new substitute teacher at school named Takamura Nachi, who is an occult fanatic. He gives Himari the "Seeing Mirror" that transports her inside it. The mirror makes the sorrow in one's heart disappear. Himari's interactions with Aoi and the nue in the mirror world cause her to reevaluate her feelings. Despite being rejected, Himari resolves to do whatever she can to free him from Momochi House, but Aoi has fallen into a slump. Aoi's old friend Nekobaba comes to Momochi House and tries to get Aoi back to normal, but nothing seems to work. Himari follows Nekobaba's advice and investigates Aoi's family. She uses Mr. Nachi's old town map to find the Nanamori house...

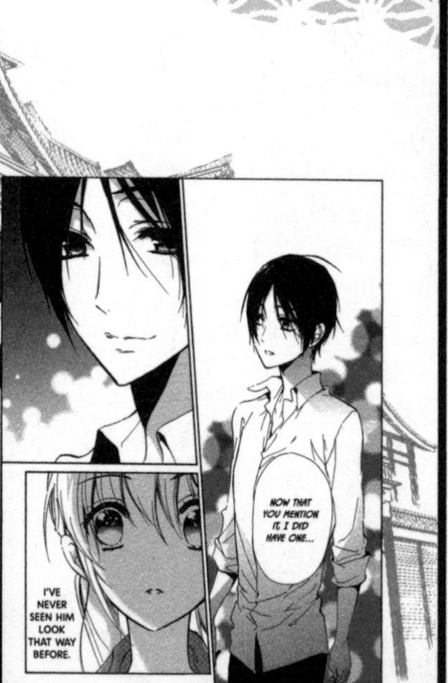
NOW THAT YOU MENTION IT, I DID HAVE ONE...
I'VE NEVER SEEN HIM LOOK THAT WAY BEFORE.

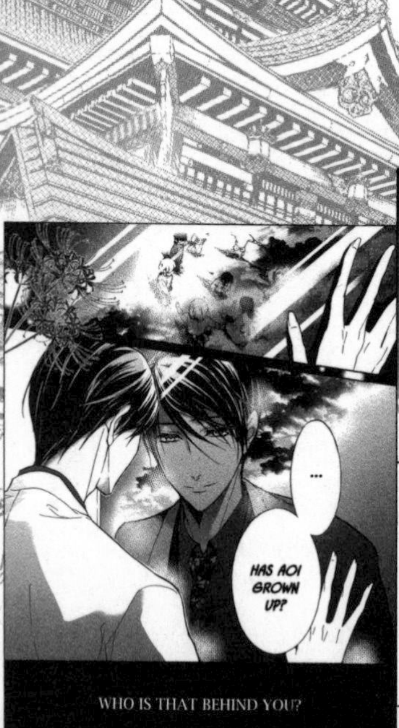
...
HAS AOI GROWN UP?
WHO IS THAT BEHIND YOU?

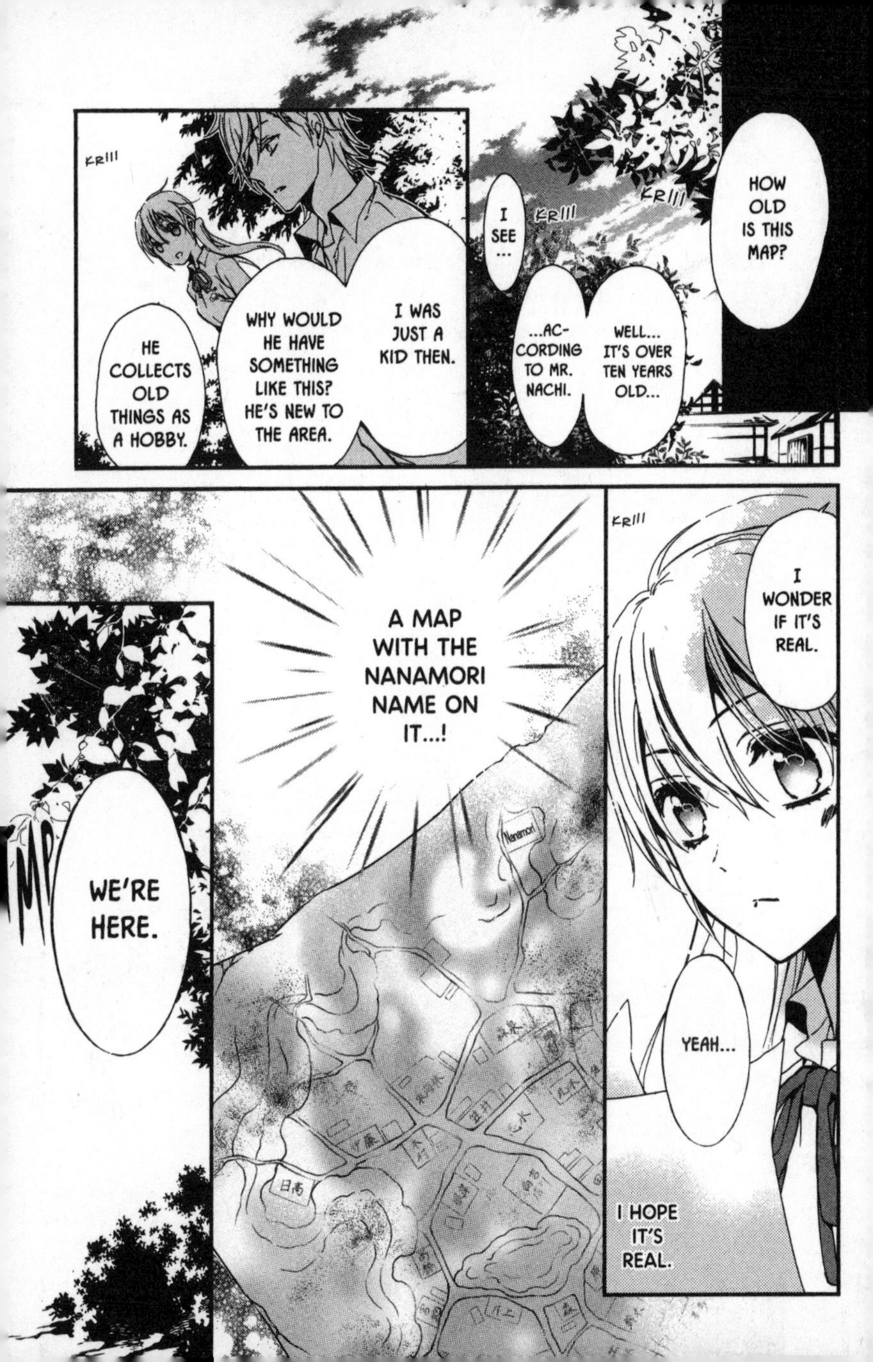
HOW OLD IS THIS MAP?
KRIII
KRIII
WELL... IT'S OVER TEN YEARS OLD...
...AC-CORDING TO MR. NACHI.
I SEE...
KRIII
I WAS JUST A KID THEN.
WHY WOULD HE HAVE SOMETHING LIKE THIS? HE'S NEW TO THE AREA.
HE COLLECTS OLD THINGS AS A HOBBY.
KRIII
I WONDER IF IT'S REAL.
YEAH...
I HOPE IT'S REAL.
A MAP WITH THE NANAMORI NAME ON IT...!
Nanamori
日高
WE'RE HERE.

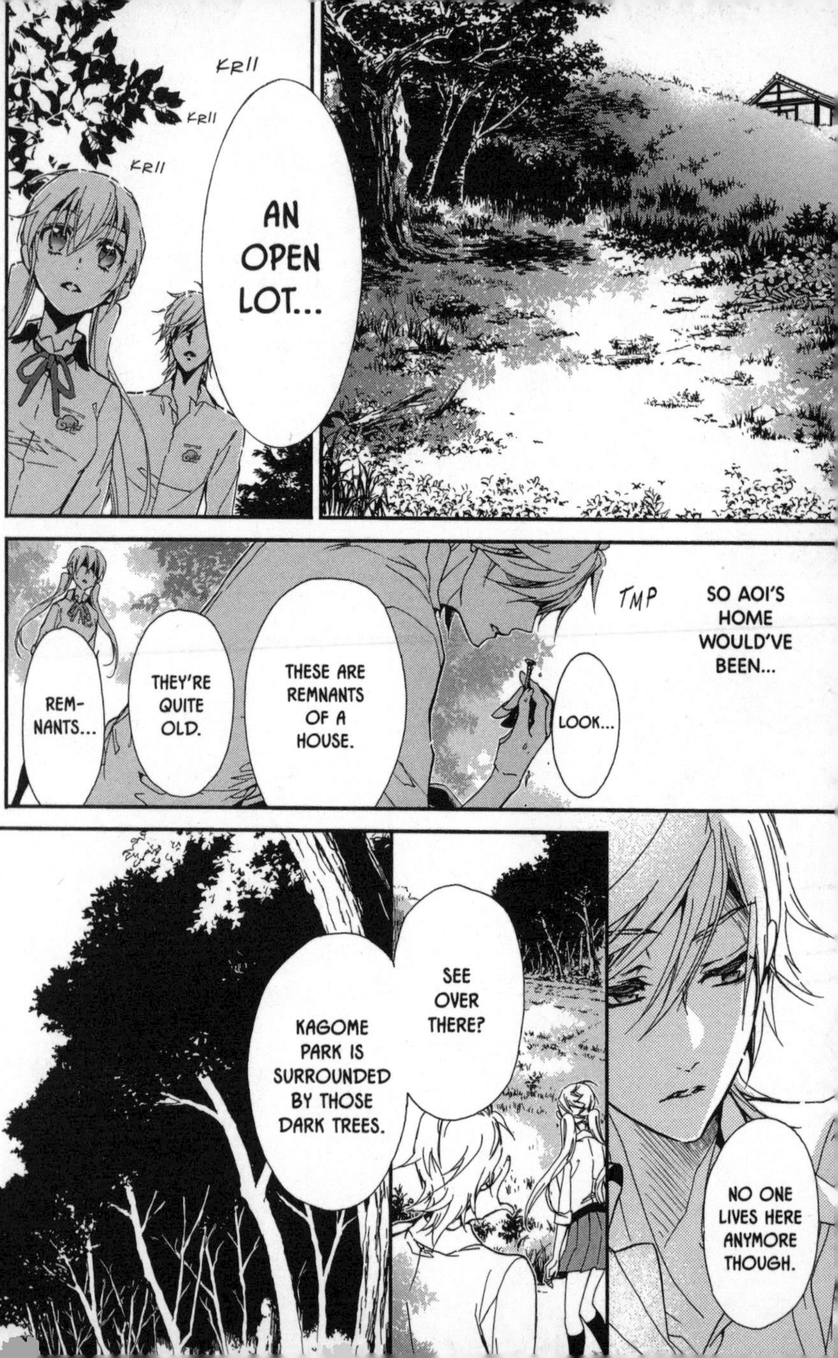
KRII
KRII
KRII
AN OPEN LOT...
SO AOI'S HOME WOULD'VE BEEN...
TMP
LOOK...
THESE ARE REMNANTS OF A HOUSE.
THEY'RE QUITE OLD.
REM-NANTS...
NO ONE LIVES HERE ANYMORE THOUGH.
SEE OVER THERE?
KAGOME PARK IS SURROUNDED BY THOSE DARK TREES.

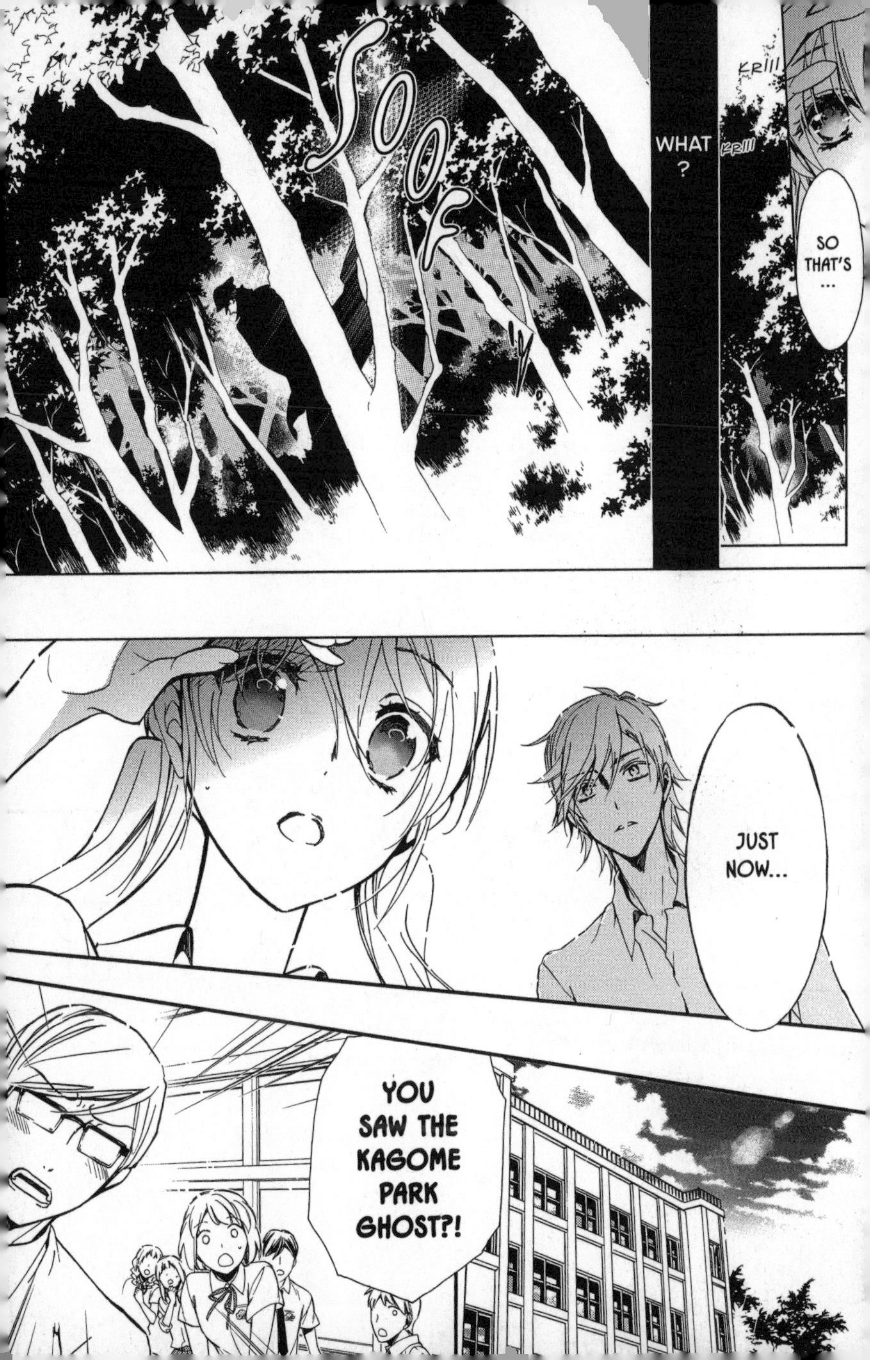
KRIII
SO THAT'S ...
KRIII
WHAT ?
JUST NOW...
YOU SAW THE KAGOME PARK GHOST?!

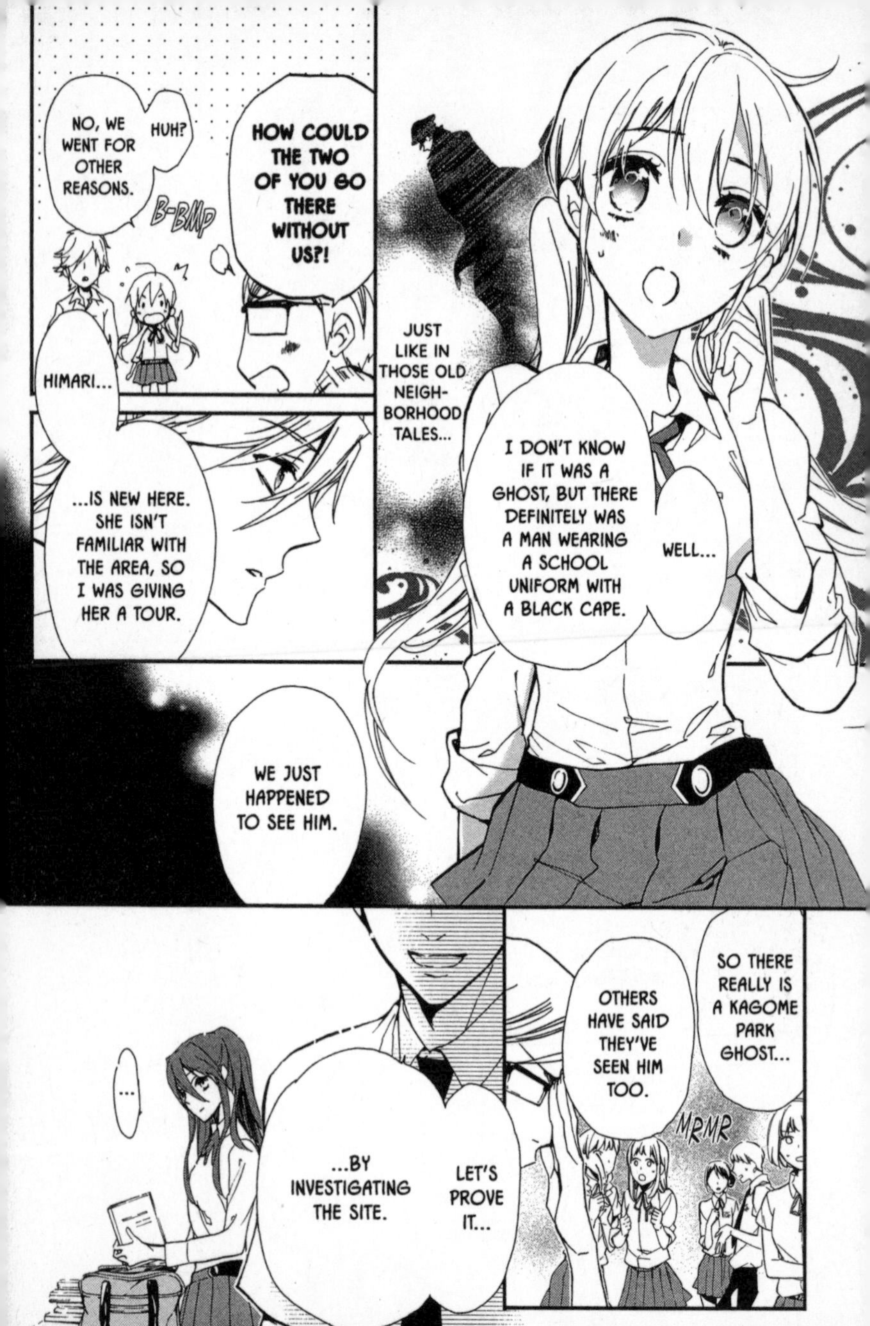
WELL...
I DON'T KNOW IF IT WAS A GHOST, BUT THERE DEFINITELY WAS A MAN WEARING A SCHOOL UNIFORM WITH A BLACK CAPE.
JUST LIKE IN THOSE OLD NEIGH-BORHOOD TALES...
HOW COULD THE TWO OF YOU GO THERE WITHOUT US?!
HUH?
B-BMP
NO, WE WENT FOR OTHER REASONS.
HIMARI...
...IS NEW HERE. SHE ISN'T FAMILIAR WITH THE AREA, SO I WAS GIVING HER A TOUR.
WE JUST HAPPENED TO SEE HIM.
SO THERE REALLY IS A KAGOME PARK GHOST...
OTHERS HAVE SAID THEY'VE SEEN HIM TOO.
MRMR
LET'S PROVE IT...
...BY INVESTIGATING THE SITE.
...

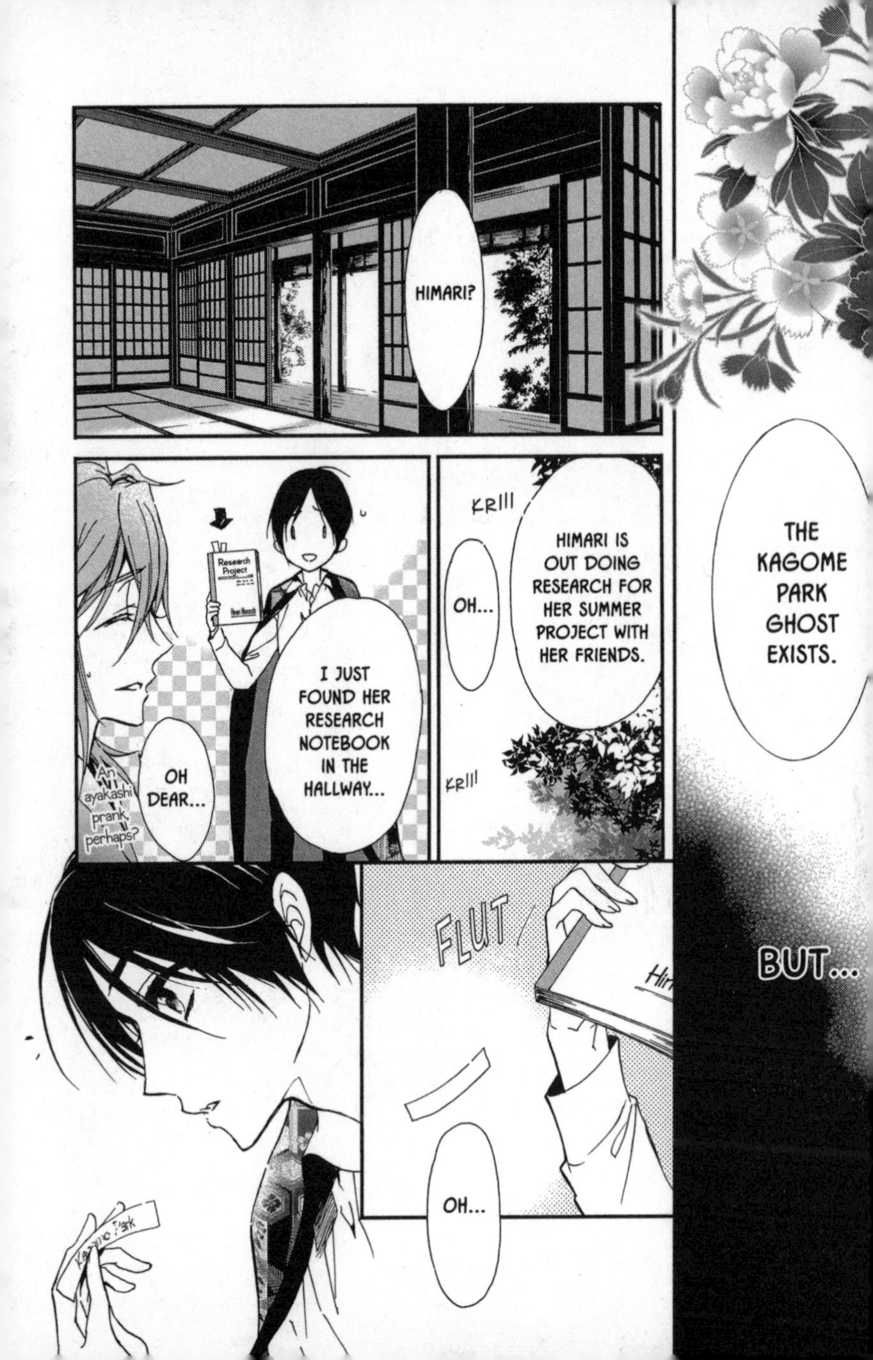
THE KAGOME PARK GHOST EXISTS.
BUT...
HIMARI?
KRIII
HIMARI IS OUT DOING RESEARCH FOR HER SUMMER PROJECT WITH HER FRIENDS.
OH...
KRIII
Research Project
I JUST FOUND HER RESEARCH NOTEBOOK IN THE HALLWAY...
OH DEAR...
An ayakashi prank, perhaps?
FLUT
OH...

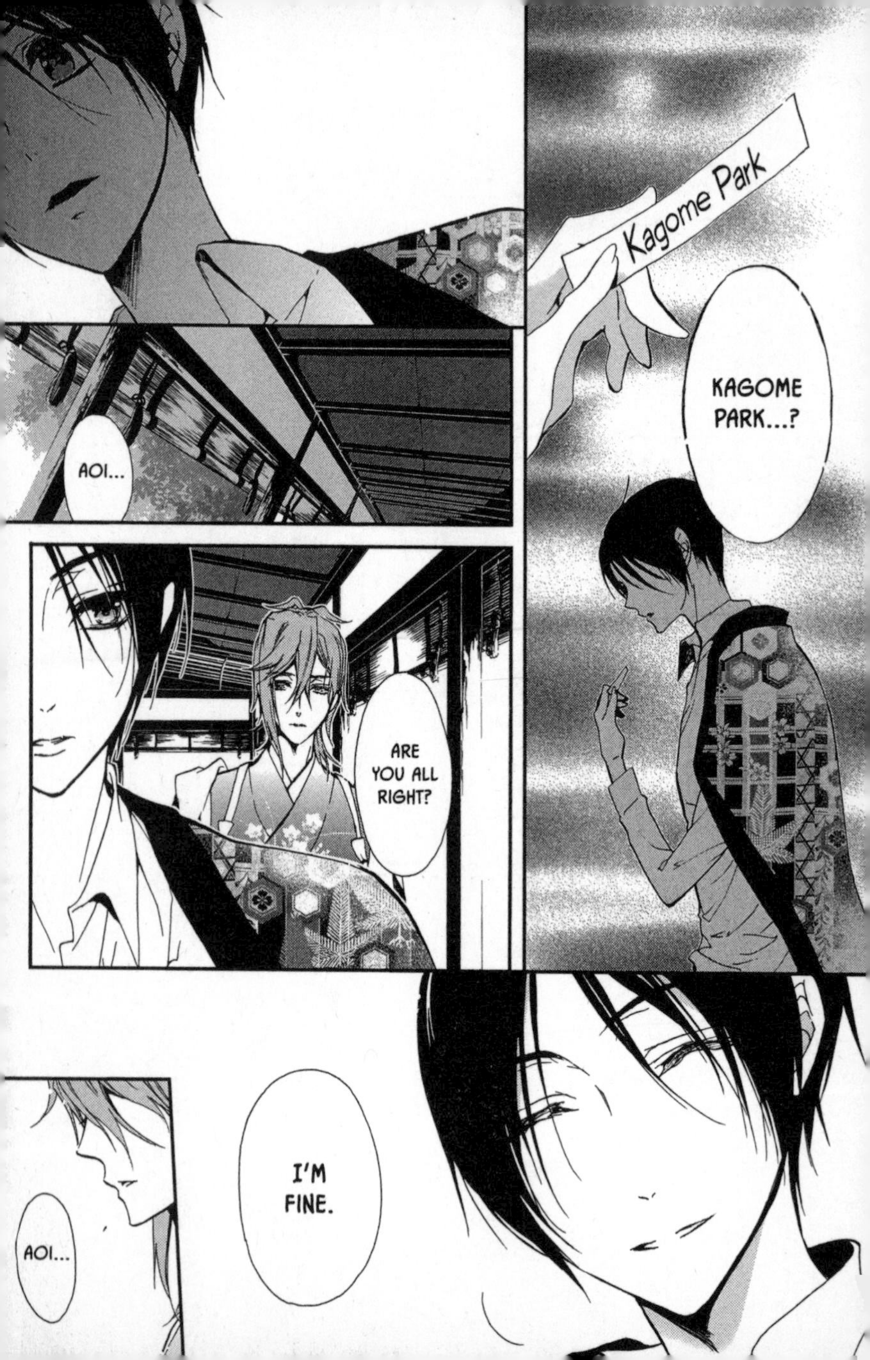
Kagome Park
KAGOME PARK...?
AOI...
ARE YOU ALL RIGHT?
I'M FINE.
AOI...

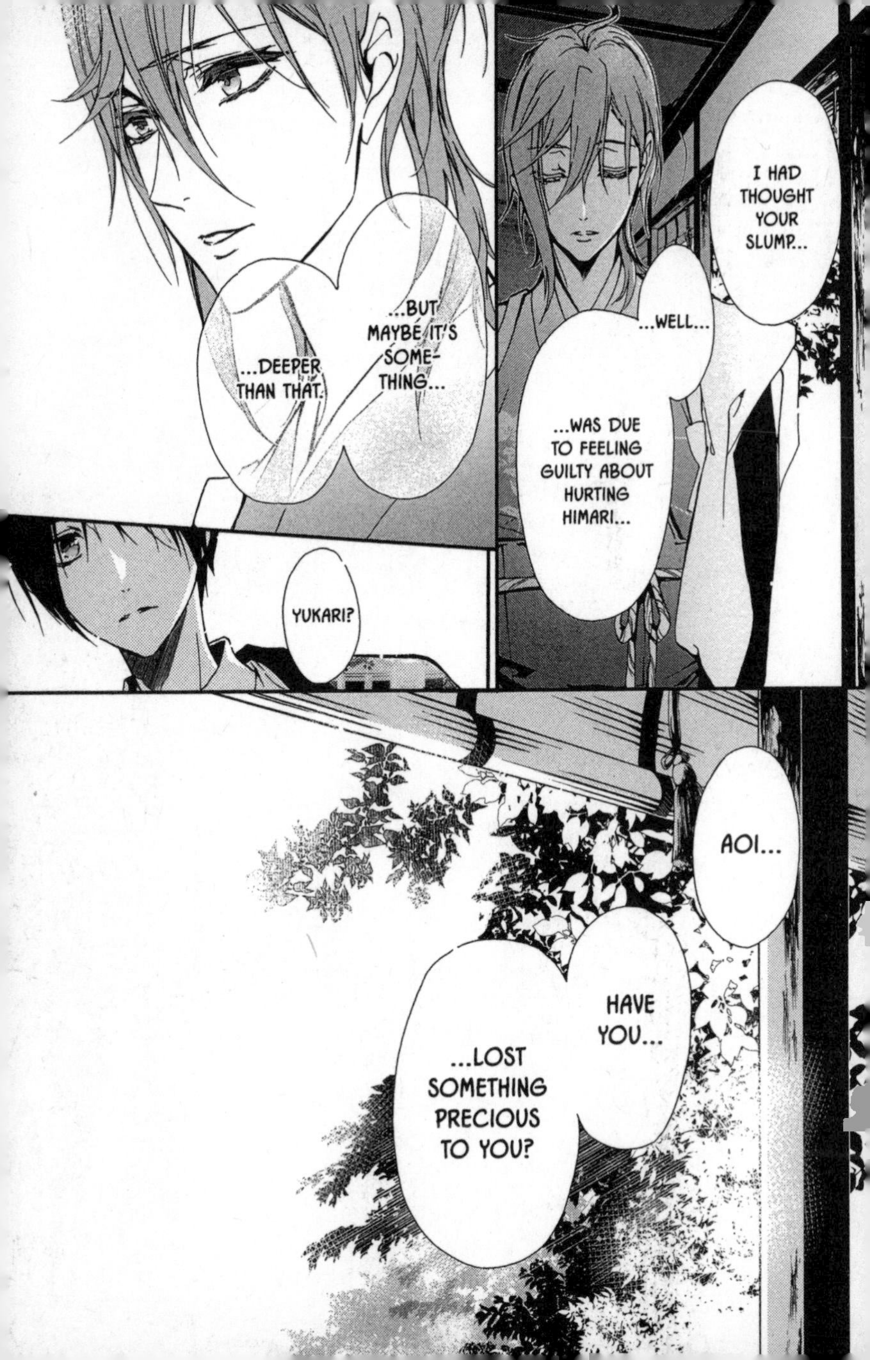
I HAD THOUGHT YOUR SLUMP...
...WELL...
...WAS DUE TO FEELING GUILTY ABOUT HURTING HIMARI...
...BUT MAYBE IT'S SOME-THING...
...DEEPER THAN THAT.
YUKARI?
AOI...
HAVE YOU...
...LOST SOMETHING PRECIOUS TO YOU?

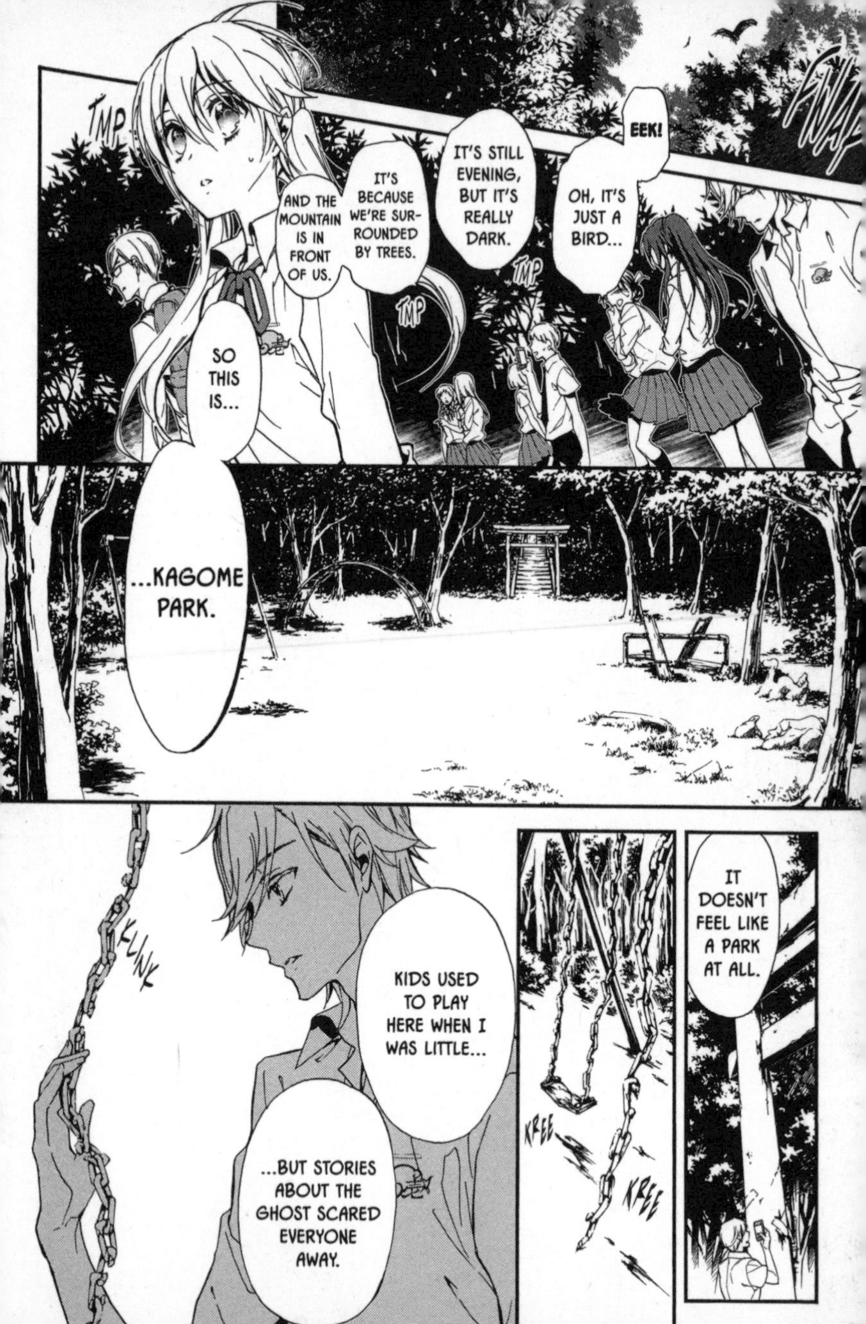
EEK!
OH, IT'S JUST A BIRD...
IT'S STILL EVENING, BUT IT'S REALLY DARK.
TMP
IT'S BECAUSE WE'RE SUR-ROUNDED BY TREES.
AND THE MOUNTAIN IS IN FRONT OF US.
TMP
TMP
SO THIS IS...
...KAGOME PARK.
IT DOESN'T FEEL LIKE A PARK AT ALL.
KREE
KREE
KIDS USED TO PLAY HERE WHEN I WAS LITTLE...
...BUT STORIES ABOUT THE GHOST SCARED EVERYONE AWAY.
KLINK

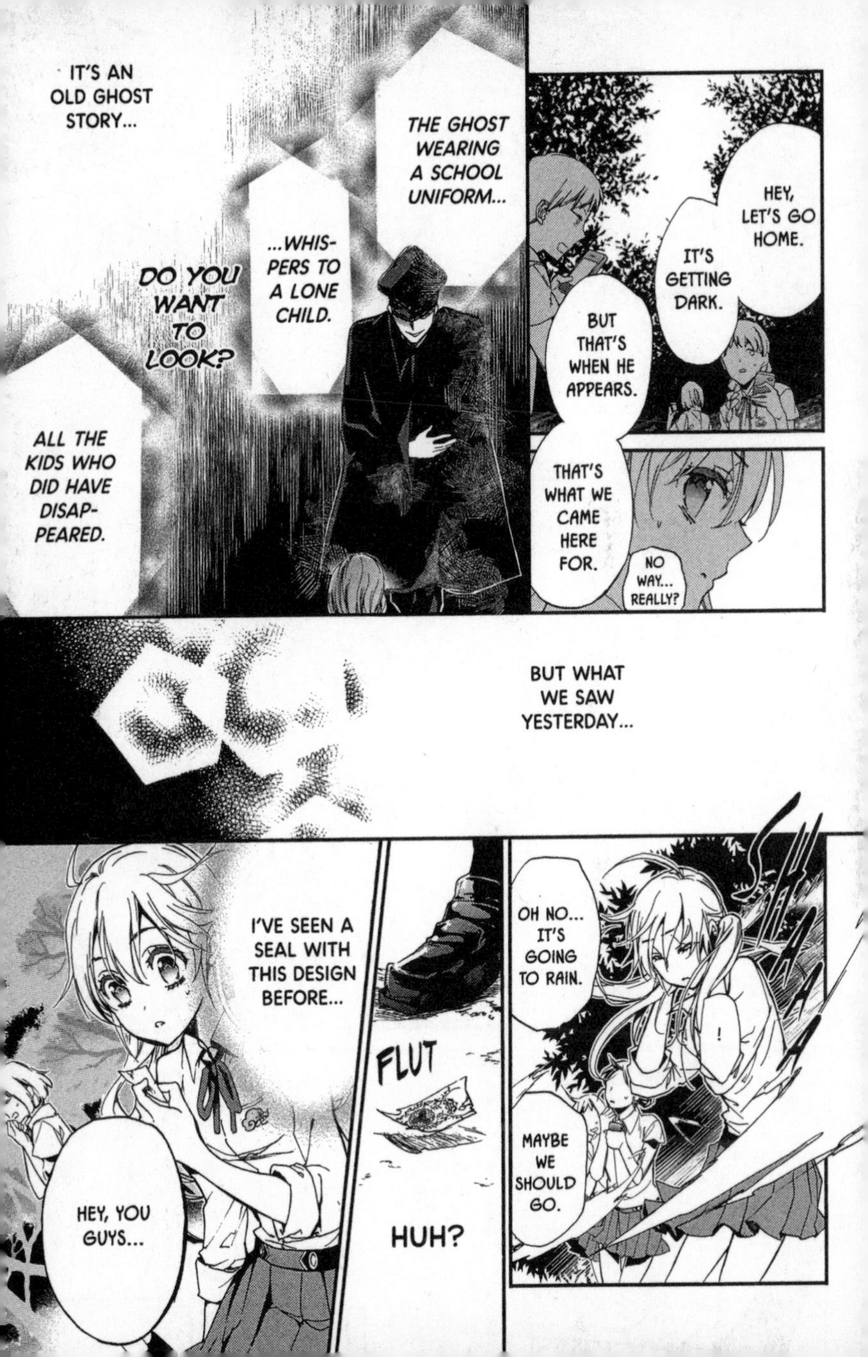
HEY, LET'S GO HOME.
IT'S GETTING DARK.
BUT THAT'S WHEN HE APPEARS.
THAT'S WHAT WE CAME HERE FOR.
NO WAY... REALLY?
IT'S AN OLD GHOST STORY...
THE GHOST WEARING A SCHOOL UNIFORM...
...WHISPERS TO A LONE CHILD.
DO YOU WANT TO LOOK?
ALL THE KIDS WHO DID HAVE DISAPPEARED.
BUT WHAT WE SAW YESTERDAY...
OH NO... IT'S GOING TO RAIN.
!
MAYBE WE SHOULD GO.
FLUT
HUH?
I'VE SEEN A SEAL WITH THIS DESIGN BEFORE...
HEY, YOU GUYS...

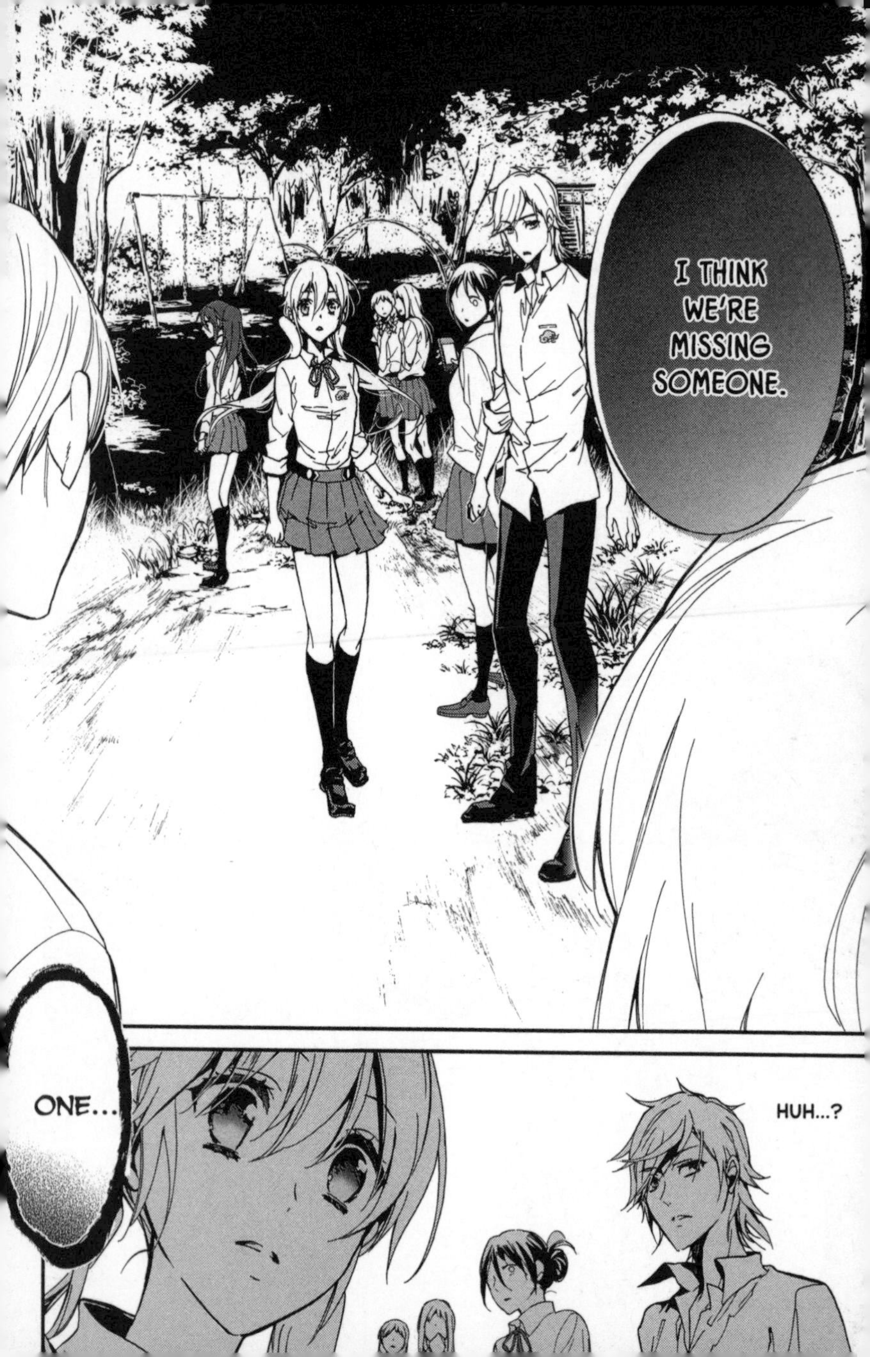
I THINK WE'RE MISSING SOMEONE.
HUH...?
ONE...

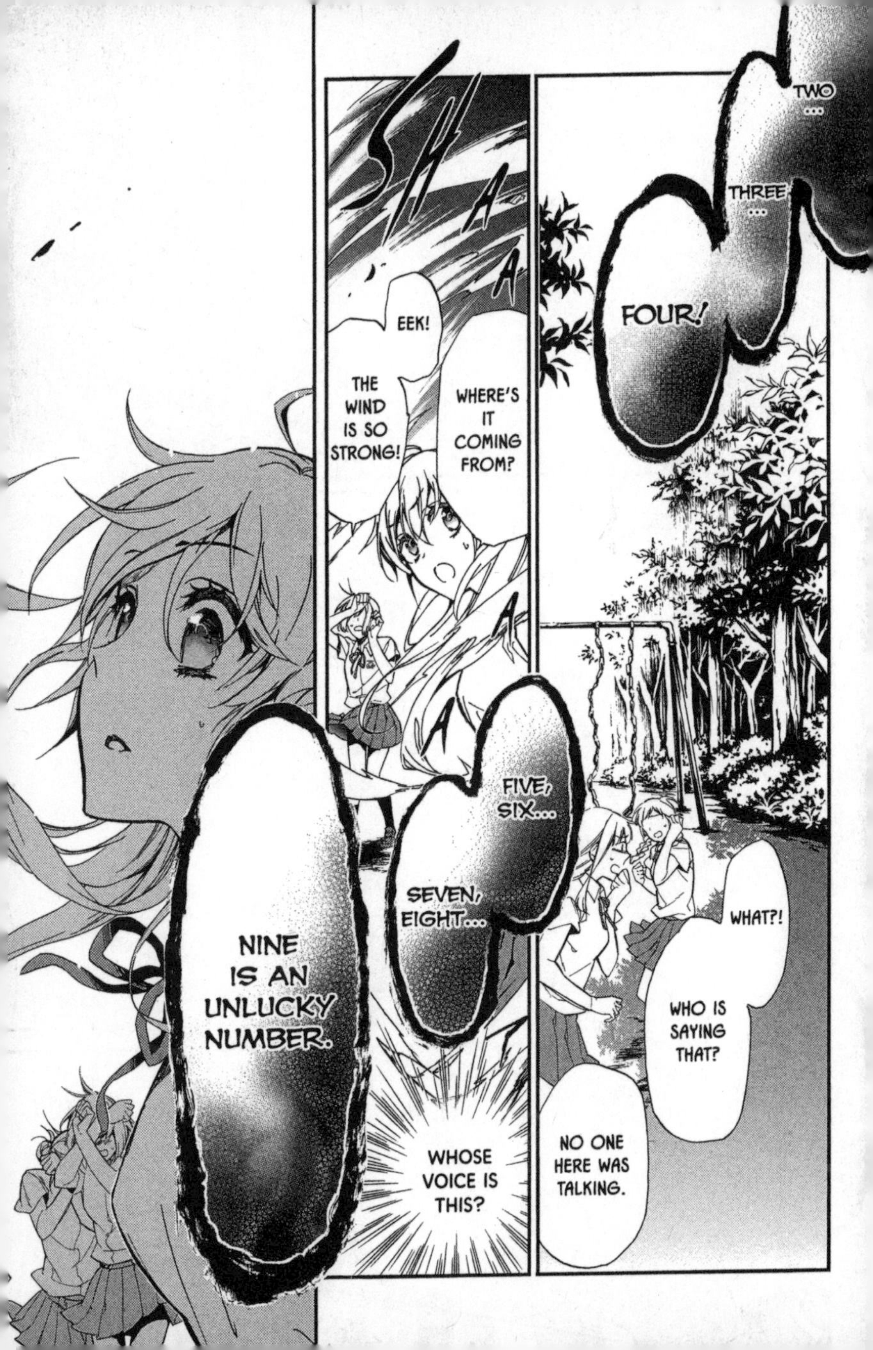
TWO...
THREE...
FOUR!
WHAT?!
WHO IS SAYING THAT?
NO ONE HERE WAS TALKING.
SHAAA
EEK!
WHERE'S IT COMING FROM?
THE WIND IS SO STRONG!
FIVE, SIX...
SEVEN, EIGHT...
WHOSE VOICE IS THIS?
NINE IS AN UNLUCKY NUMBER.

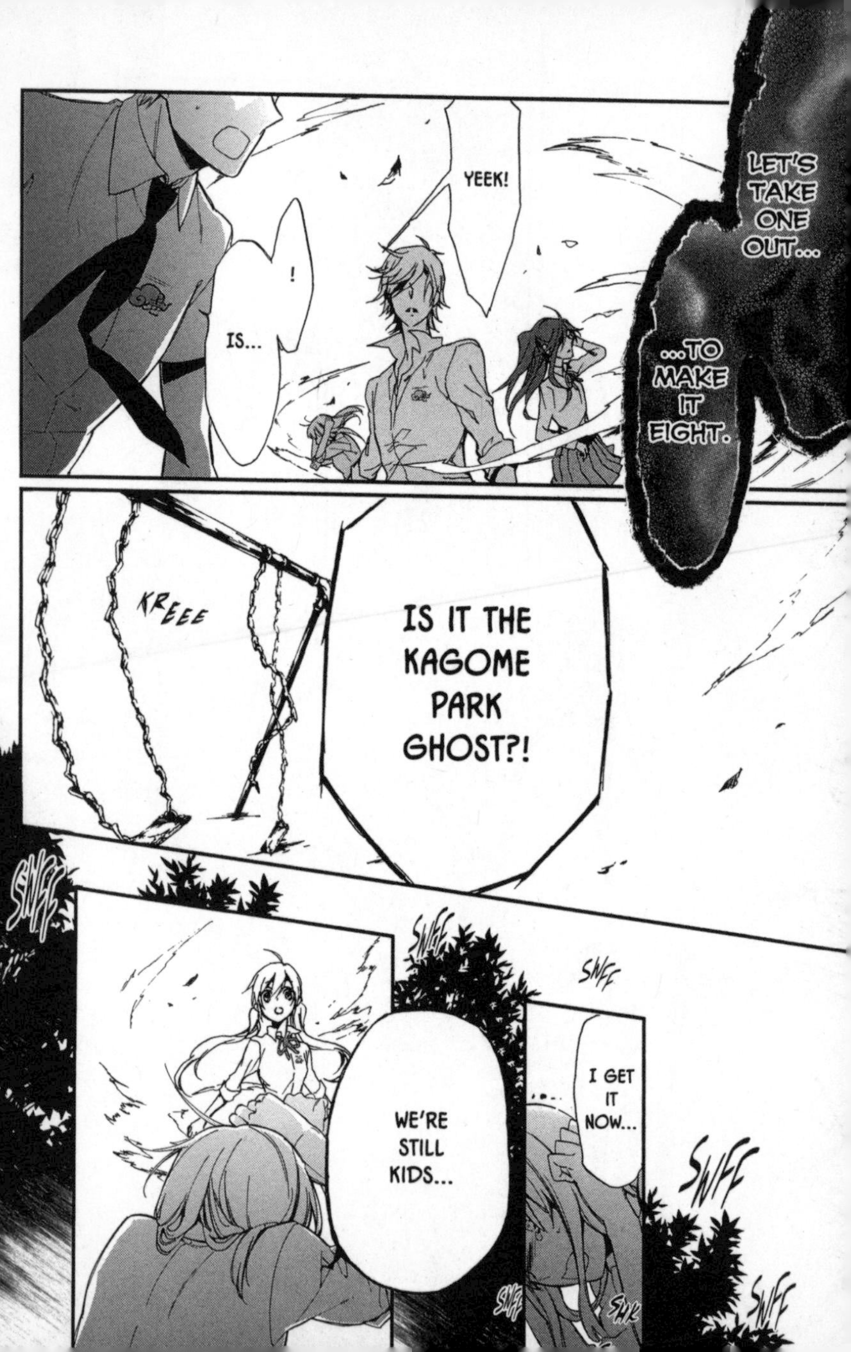
LET'S TAKE ONE OUT...
...TO MAKE IT EIGHT.
YEEK!
!
IS...
KREEE
IS IT THE KAGOME PARK GHOST?!
SWFF
SWFF
SWFF
I GET IT NOW...
SWFF
SHK
SWFF
WE'RE STILL KIDS...
SWFF

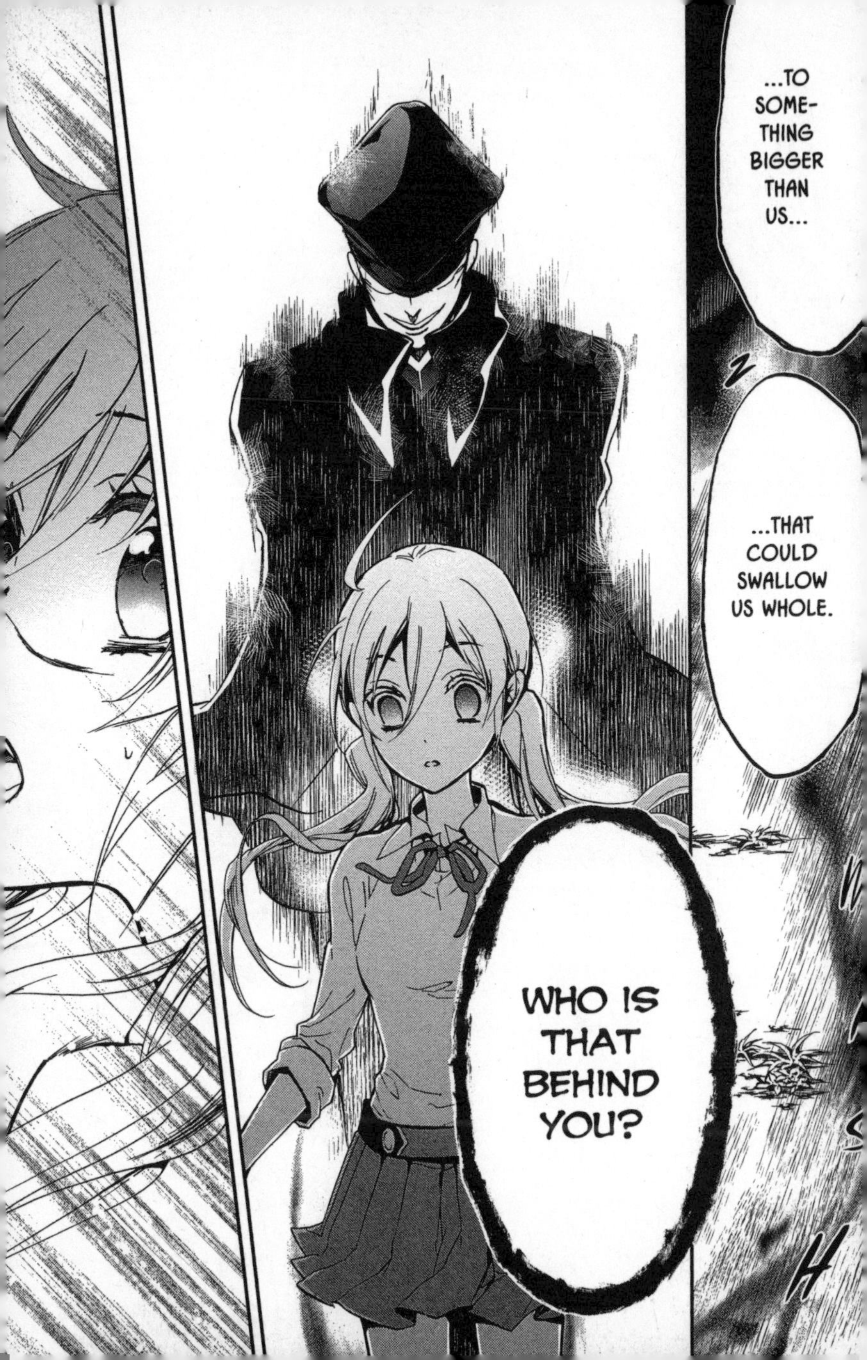
...TO SOME-THING BIGGER THAN US...
...THAT COULD SWALLOW US WHOLE.
WHO IS THAT BEHIND YOU?

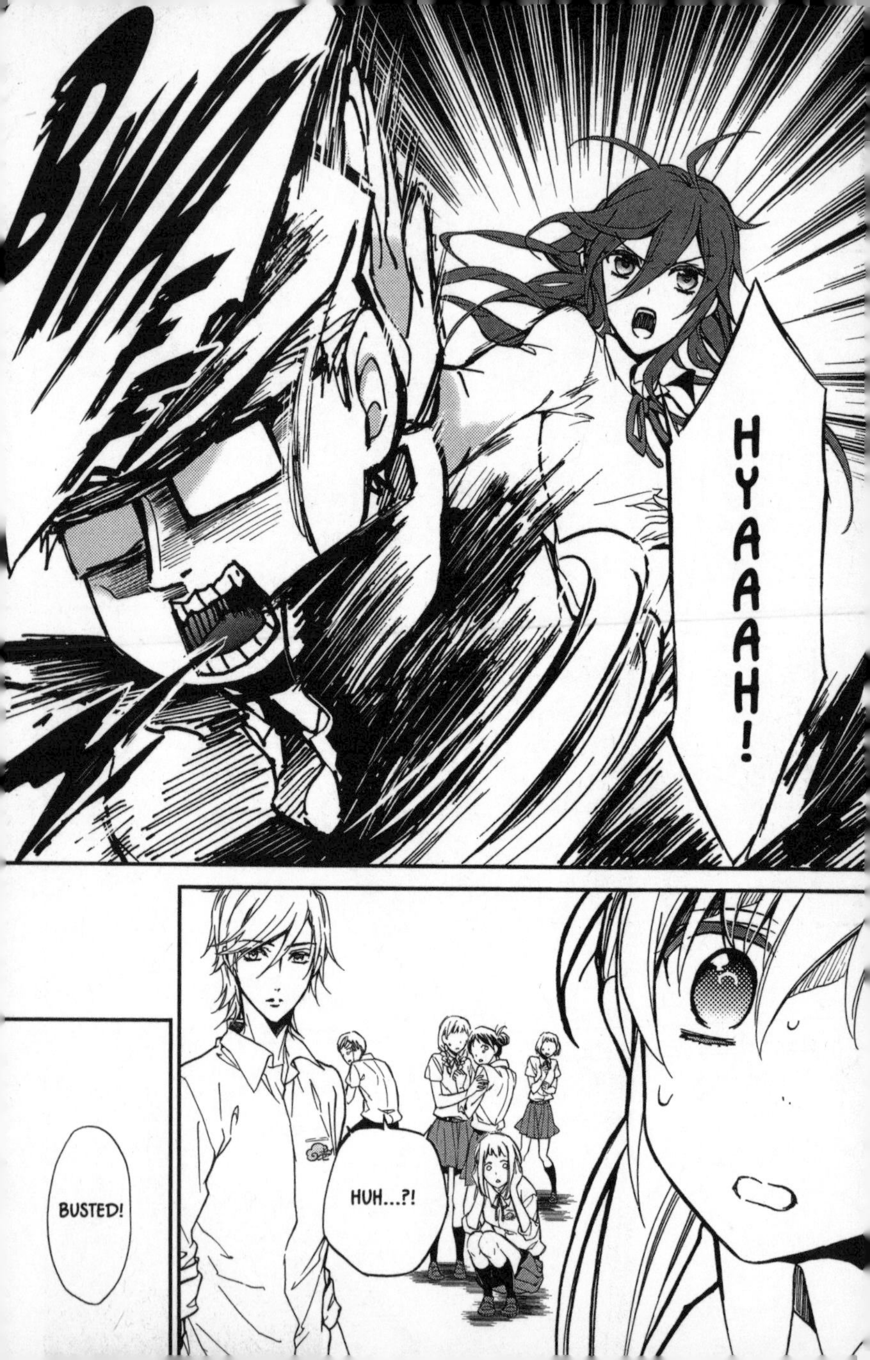
HYAAAAH!
HUH...?!
BUSTED!

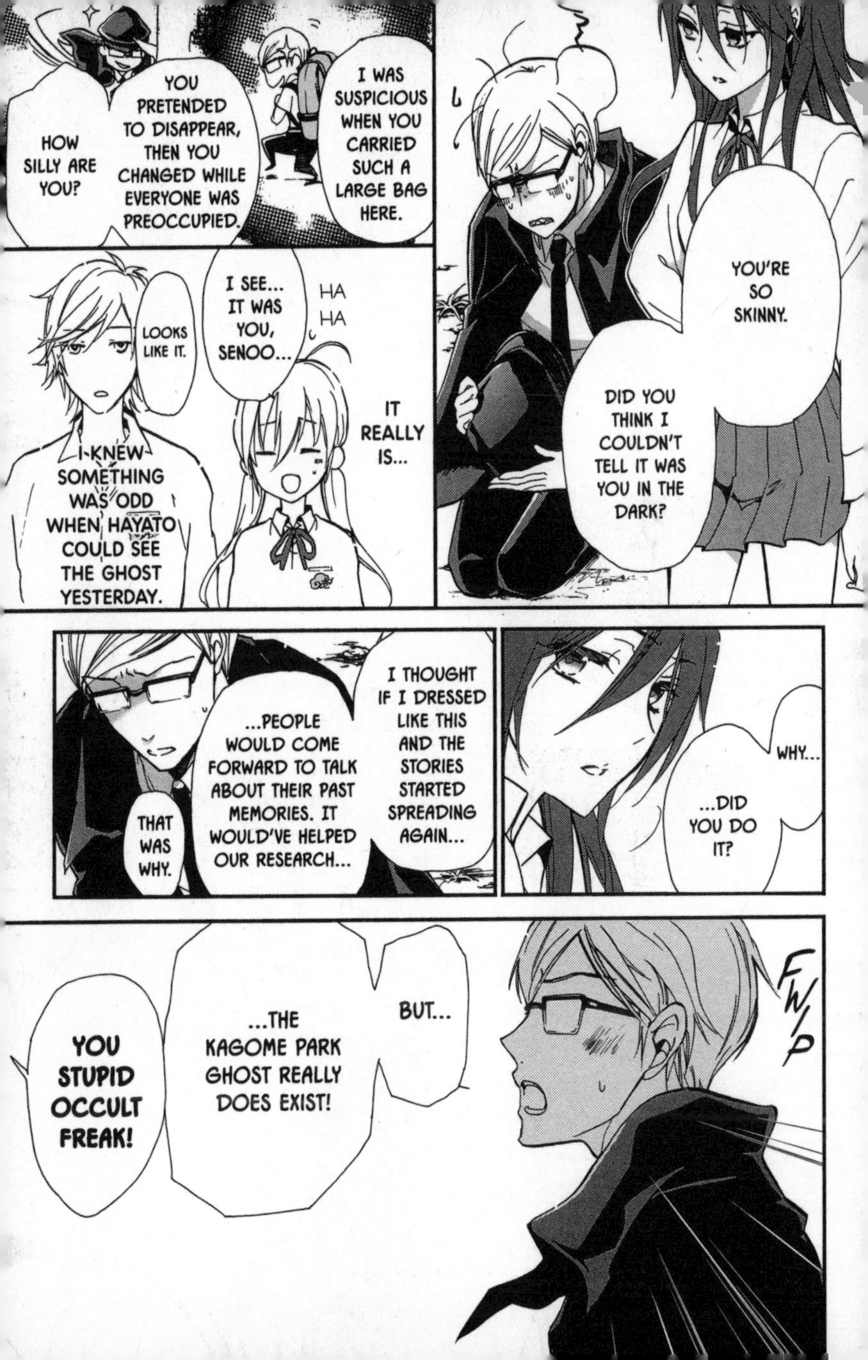
YOU'RE SO SKINNY.
DID YOU THINK I COULDN'T TELL IT WAS YOU IN THE DARK?
I WAS SUSPICIOUS WHEN YOU CARRIED SUCH A LARGE BAG HERE.
YOU PRETENDED TO DISAPPEAR, THEN YOU CHANGED WHILE EVERYONE WAS PREOCCUPIED.
HOW SILLY ARE YOU?
HA HA
I SEE... IT WAS YOU, SENOO...
IT REALLY IS...
LOOKS LIKE IT.
I KNEW SOMETHING WAS ODD WHEN HAYATO COULD SEE THE GHOST YESTERDAY.
WHY...
...DID YOU DO IT?
I THOUGHT IF I DRESSED LIKE THIS AND THE STORIES STARTED SPREADING AGAIN...
...PEOPLE WOULD COME FORWARD TO TALK ABOUT THEIR PAST MEMORIES. IT WOULD'VE HELPED OUR RESEARCH...
THAT WAS WHY.
FWIP
BUT...
...THE KAGOME PARK GHOST REALLY DOES EXIST!
YOU STUPID OCCULT FREAK!

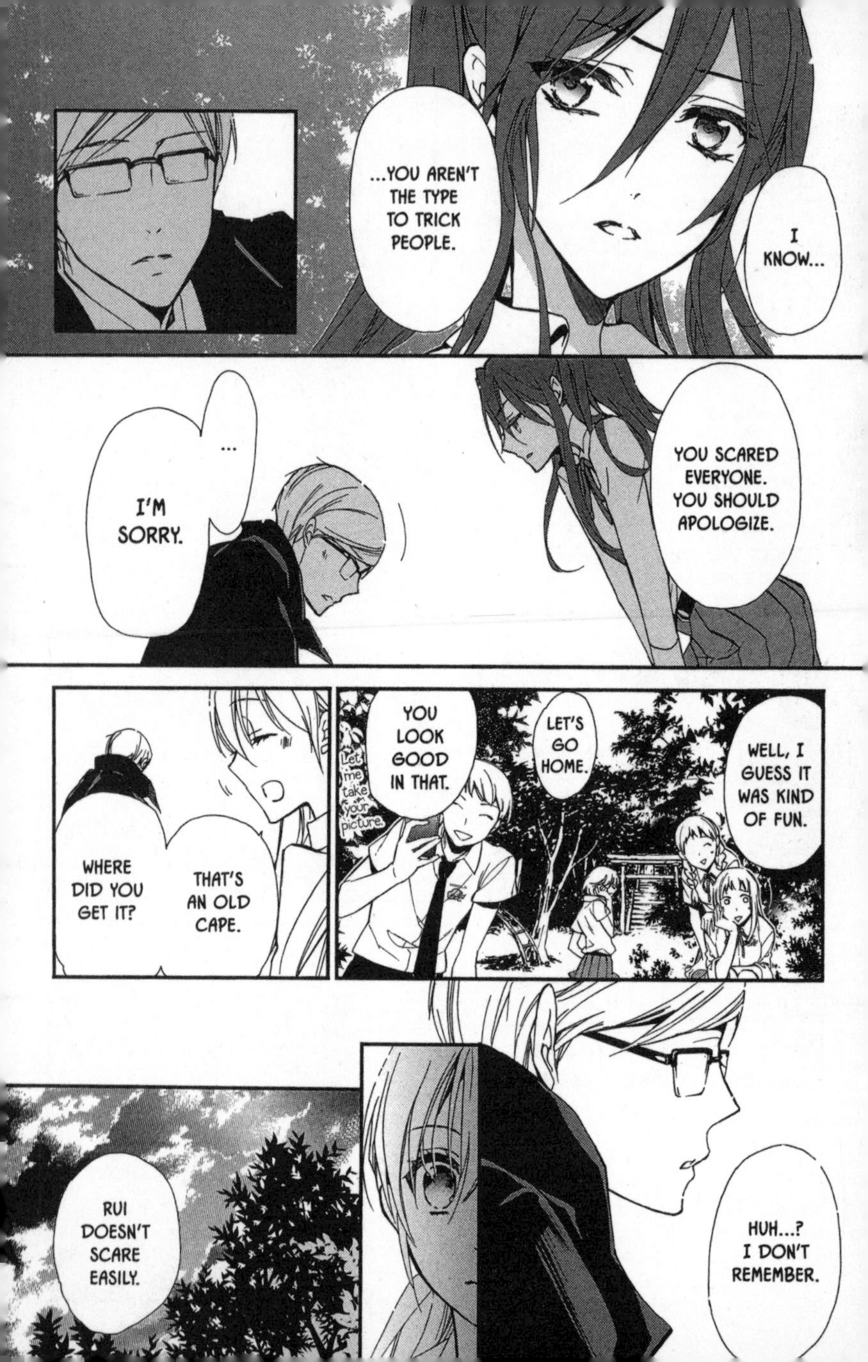
I KNOW...
...YOU AREN'T THE TYPE TO TRICK PEOPLE.
YOU SCARED EVERYONE. YOU SHOULD APOLOGIZE.
... I'M SORRY.
WELL, I GUESS IT WAS KIND OF FUN.
LET'S GO HOME.
YOU LOOK GOOD IN THAT.
Let me take your picture.
THAT'S AN OLD CAPE.
WHERE DID YOU GET IT?
HUH...? I DON'T REMEMBER.
RUI DOESN'T SCARE EASILY.

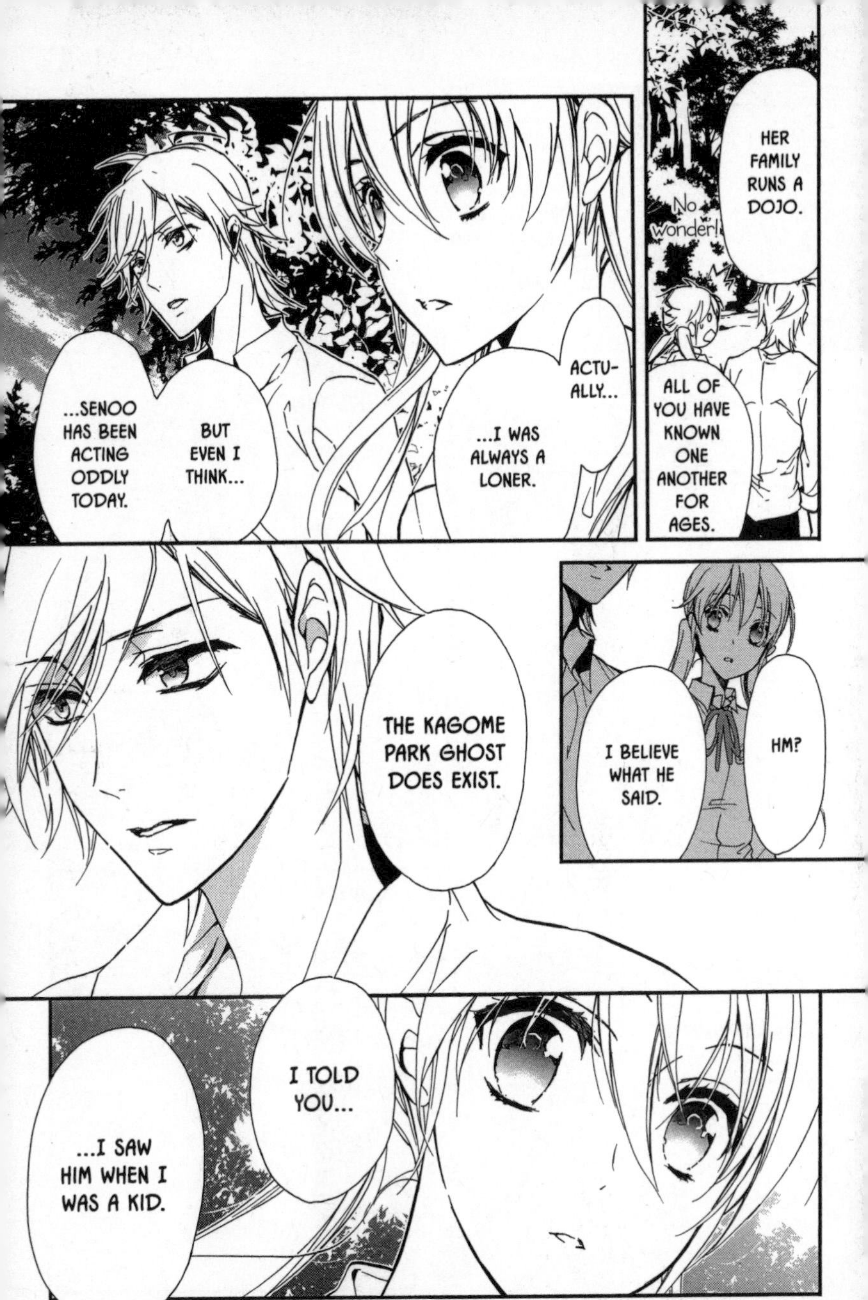
HER FAMILY RUNS A DOJO.
No wonder!
ALL OF YOU HAVE KNOWN ONE ANOTHER FOR AGES.
ACTU-ALLY...
...I WAS ALWAYS A LONER.
BUT EVEN I THINK...
...SENOO HAS BEEN ACTING ODDLY TODAY.
HM?
I BELIEVE WHAT HE SAID.
THE KAGOME PARK GHOST DOES EXIST.
I TOLD YOU...
...I SAW HIM WHEN I WAS A KID.

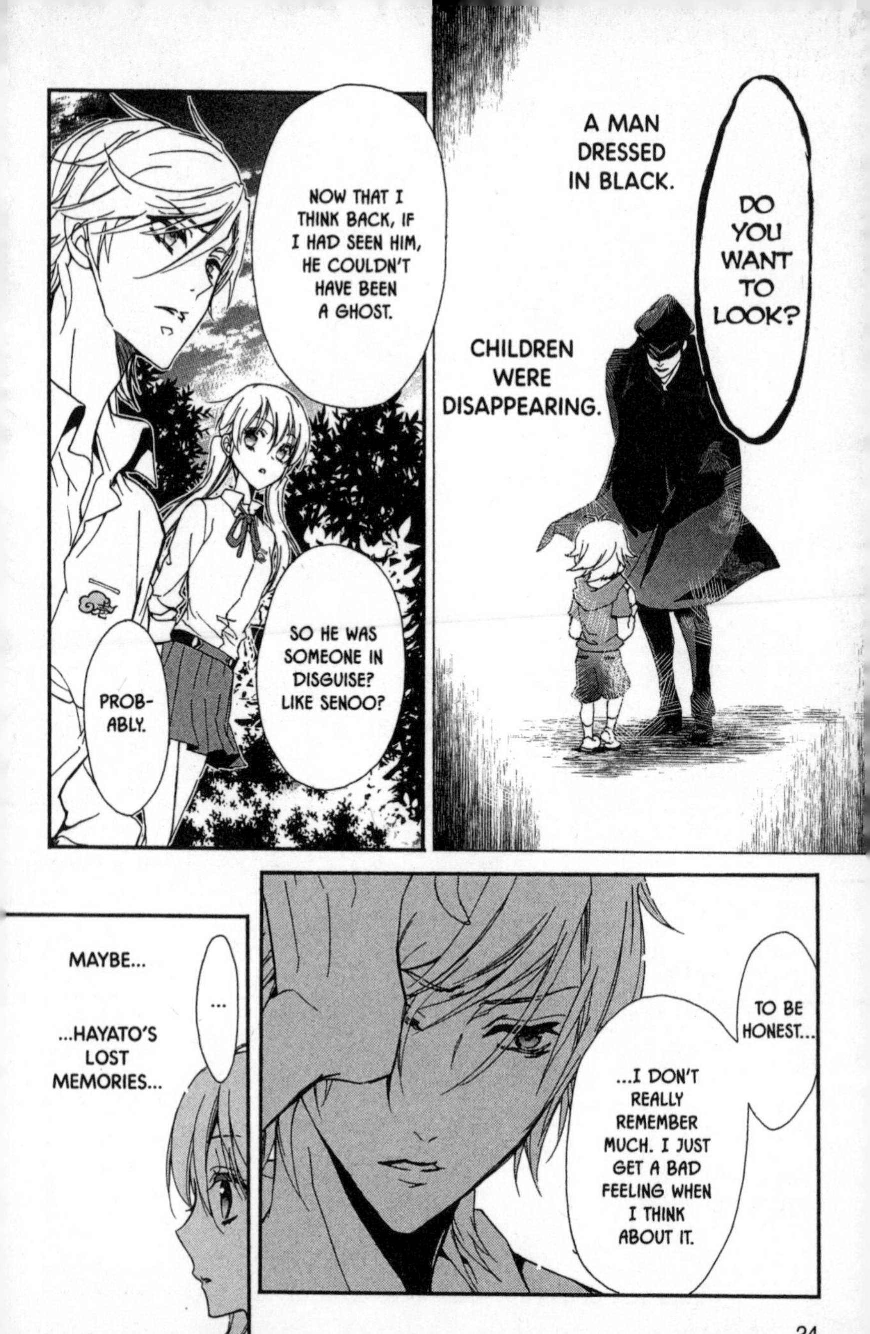
DO YOU WANT TO LOOK?
A MAN DRESSED IN BLACK.
CHILDREN WERE DISAPPEARING.
NOW THAT I THINK BACK, IF I HAD SEEN HIM, HE COULDN'T HAVE BEEN A GHOST.
SO HE WAS SOMEONE IN DISGUISE? LIKE SENOO?
PROB-ABLY.
TO BE HONEST...
...I DON'T REALLY REMEMBER MUCH. I JUST GET A BAD FEELING WHEN I THINK ABOUT IT.
...
MAYBE...
...HAYATO'S LOST MEMORIES...

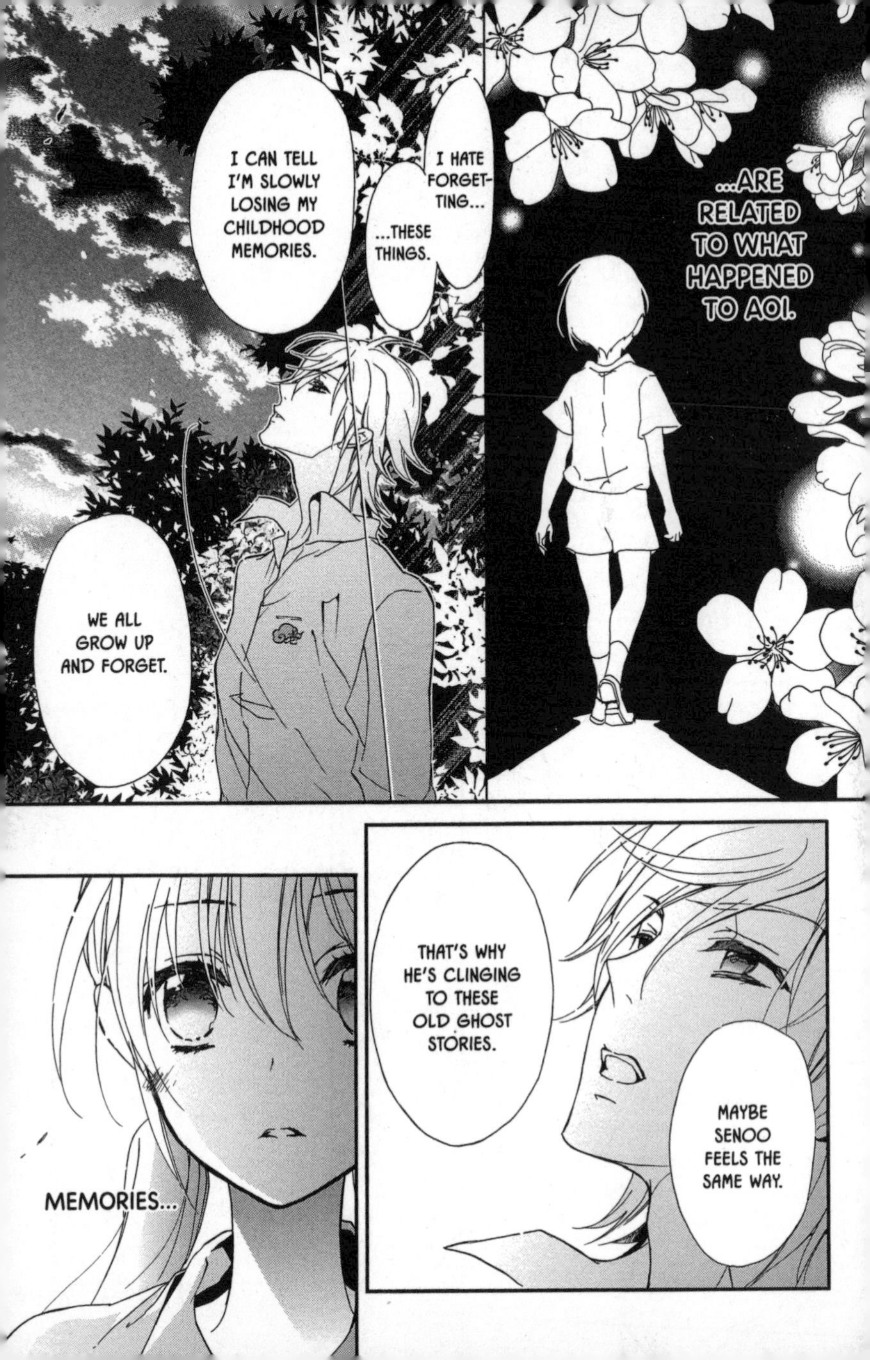
...ARE RELATED TO WHAT HAPPENED TO AOI.
I HATE FORGET-TING...
...THESE THINGS.
I CAN TELL I'M SLOWLY LOSING MY CHILDHOOD MEMORIES.
WE ALL GROW UP AND FORGET.
MAYBE SENOO FEELS THE SAME WAY.
THAT'S WHY HE'S CLINGING TO THESE OLD GHOST STORIES.
MEMORIES...

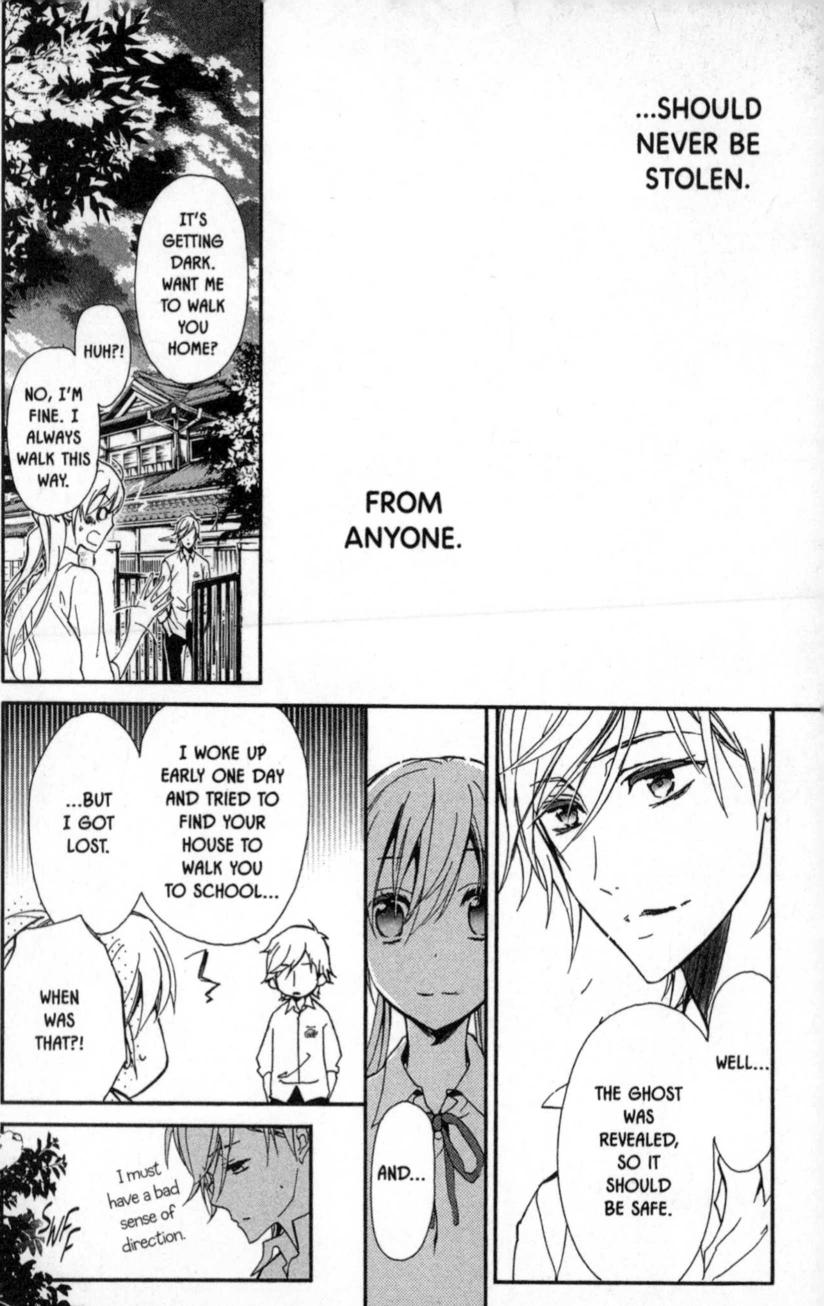
...SHOULD NEVER BE STOLEN.
FROM ANYONE.
IT'S GETTING DARK. WANT ME TO WALK YOU HOME?
HUH?!
NO, I'M FINE. I ALWAYS WALK THIS WAY.
WELL...
THE GHOST WAS REVEALED, SO IT SHOULD BE SAFE.
AND...
I WOKE UP EARLY ONE DAY AND TRIED TO FIND YOUR HOUSE TO WALK YOU TO SCHOOL...
...BUT I GOT LOST.
WHEN WAS THAT?!
I must have a bad sense of direction.

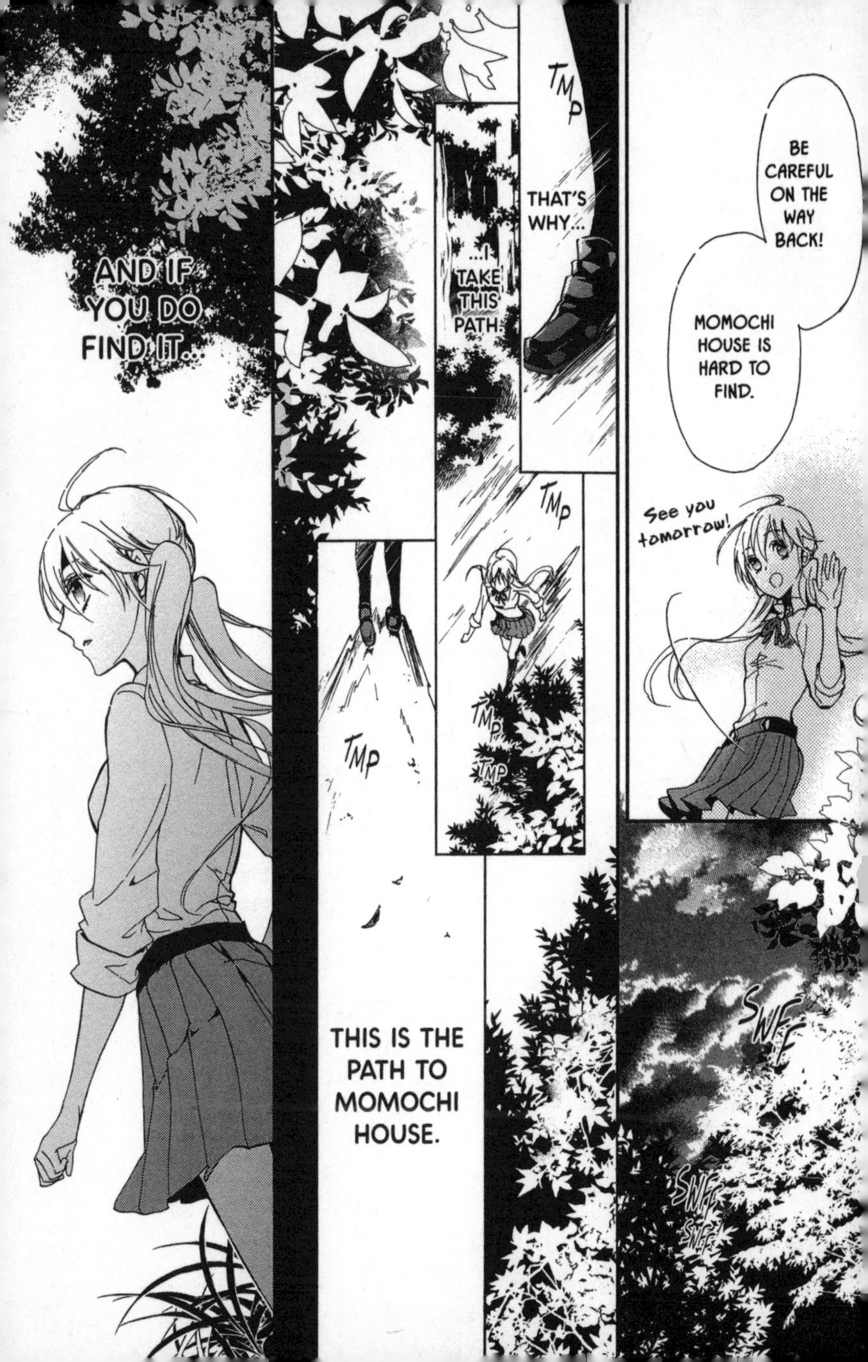
BE CAREFUL ON THE WAY BACK!
MOMOCHI HOUSE IS HARD TO FIND.
See you tomorrow!
TMP
THAT'S WHY...
...I TAKE THIS PATH.
TMP
TMP
TMP
TMP
SWFF
SWFF
SWFF
THIS IS THE PATH TO MOMOCHI HOUSE.
AND IF YOU DO FIND IT...

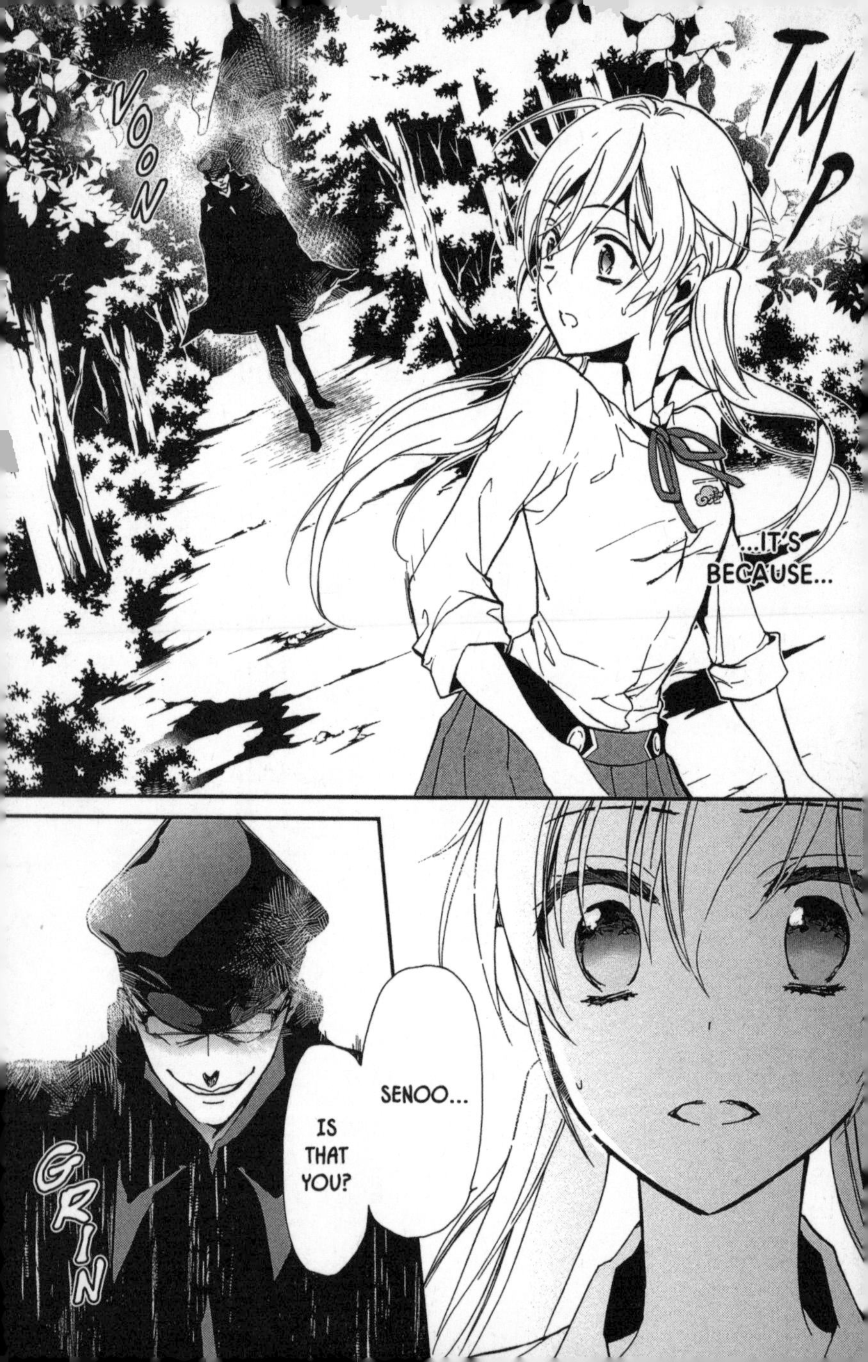
TMP
VOON
...IT'S BECAUSE...
SENOO... IS THAT YOU?
GRIN

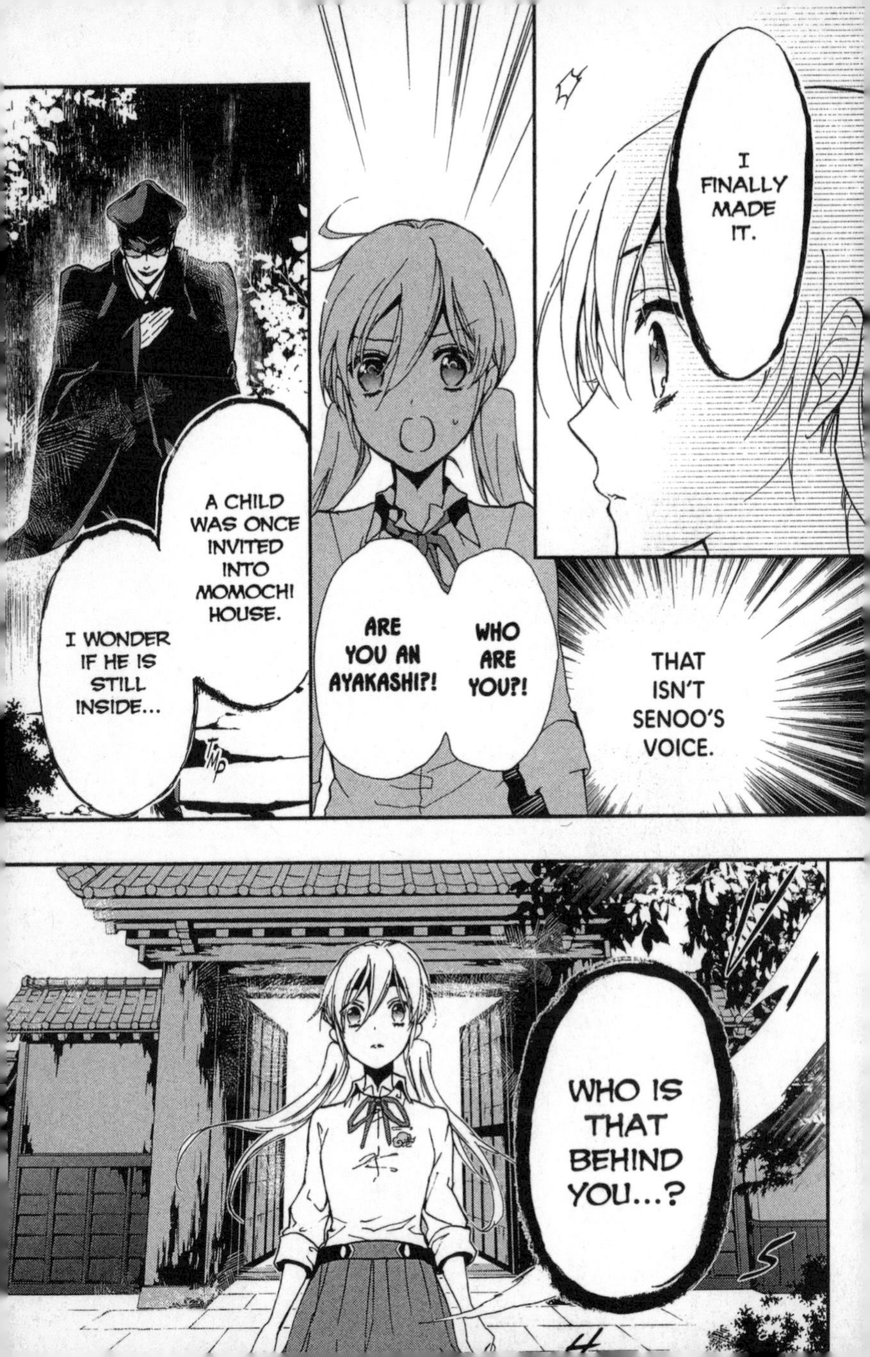
I FINALLY MADE IT.
THAT ISN'T SENOO'S VOICE.
WHO ARE YOU?!
ARE YOU AN AYAKASHI?!
A CHILD WAS ONCE INVITED INTO MOMOCHI HOUSE.
I WONDER IF HE IS STILL INSIDE...
TMP
WHO IS THAT BEHIND YOU...?

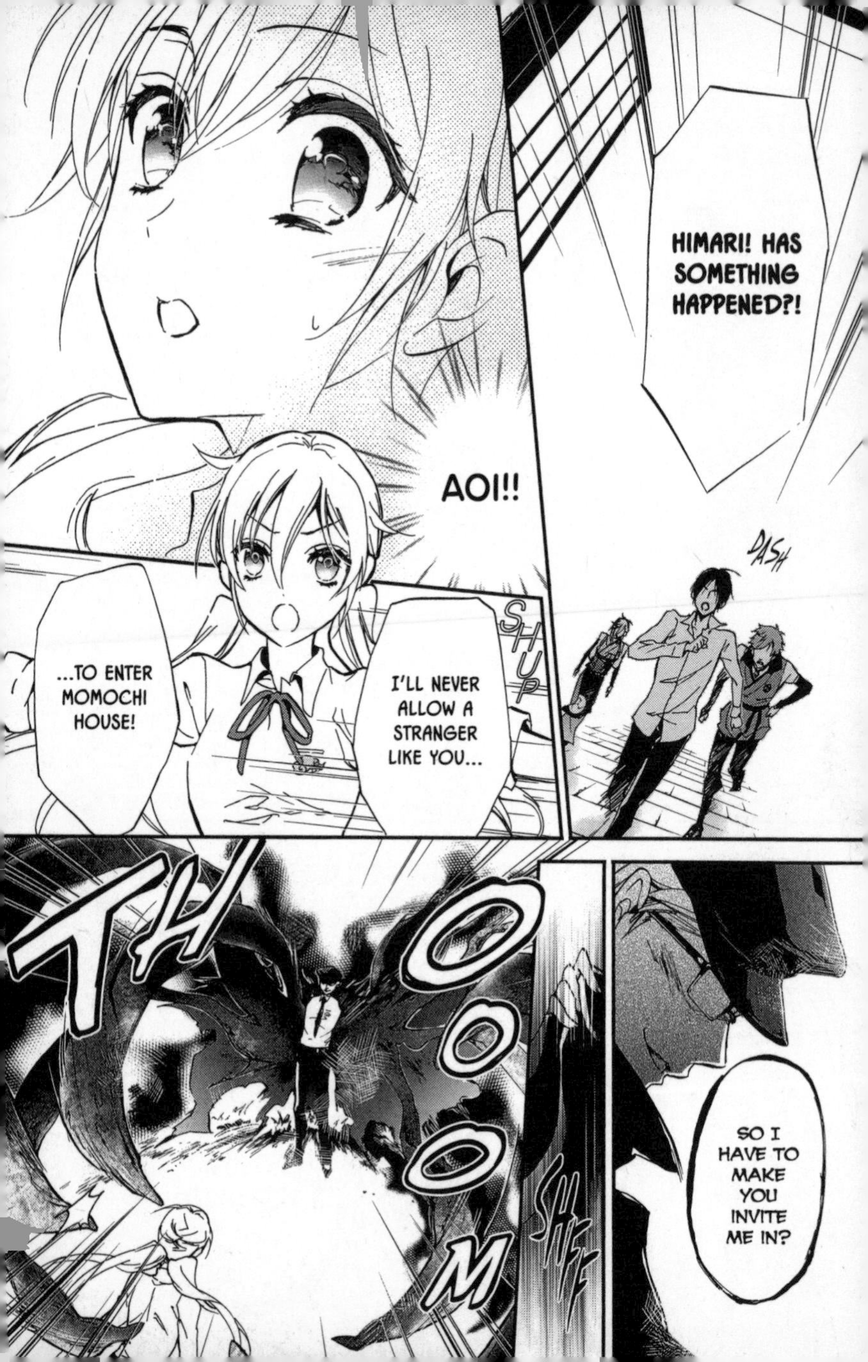
HIMARI! HAS SOMETHING HAPPENED?!
DASH
AOI!!
SHUP
I'LL NEVER ALLOW A STRANGER LIKE YOU...
...TO ENTER MOMOCHI HOUSE!
SO I HAVE TO MAKE YOU INVITE ME IN?
SHFF
WHOOOOM

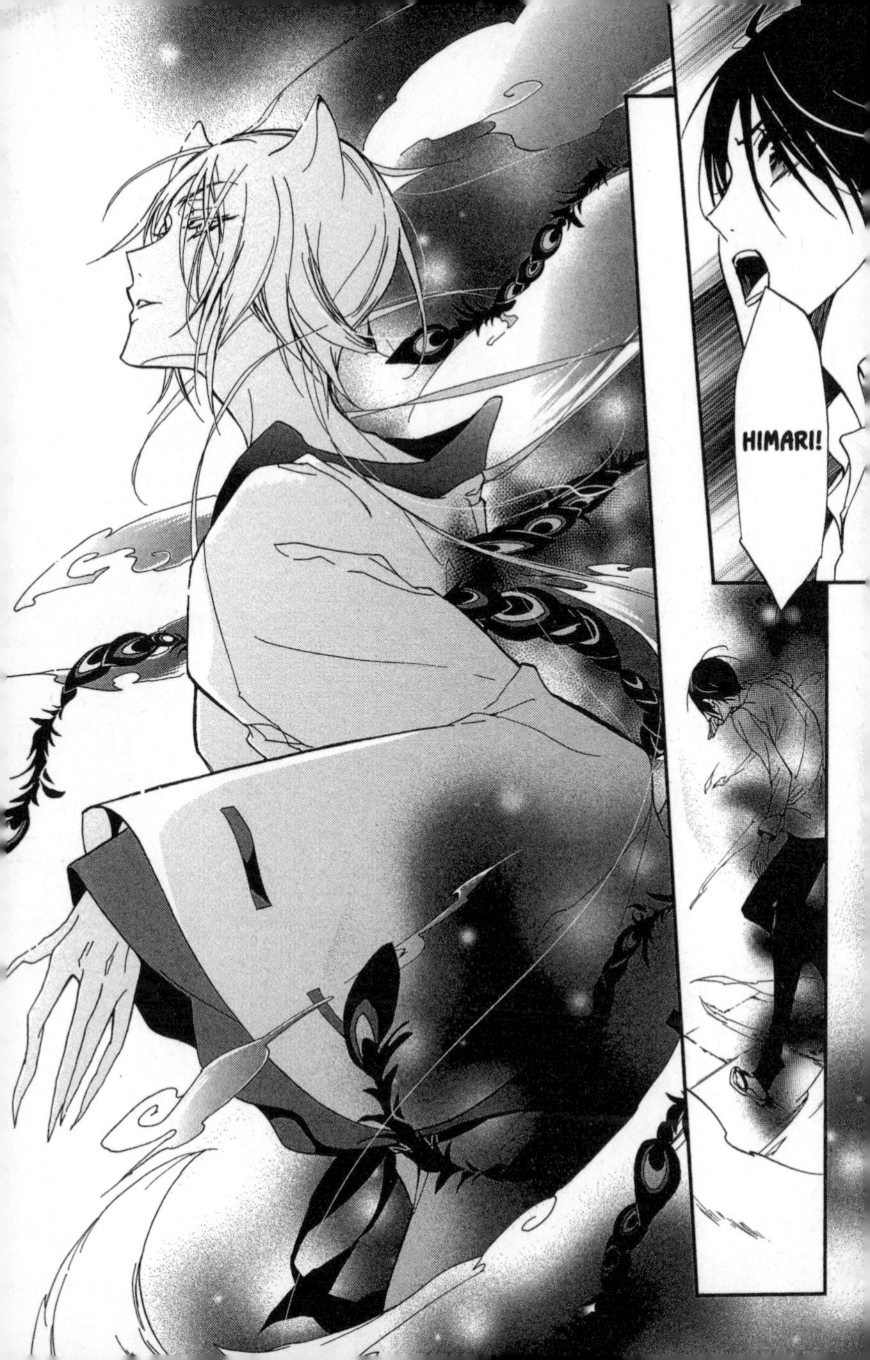
HIMARI!

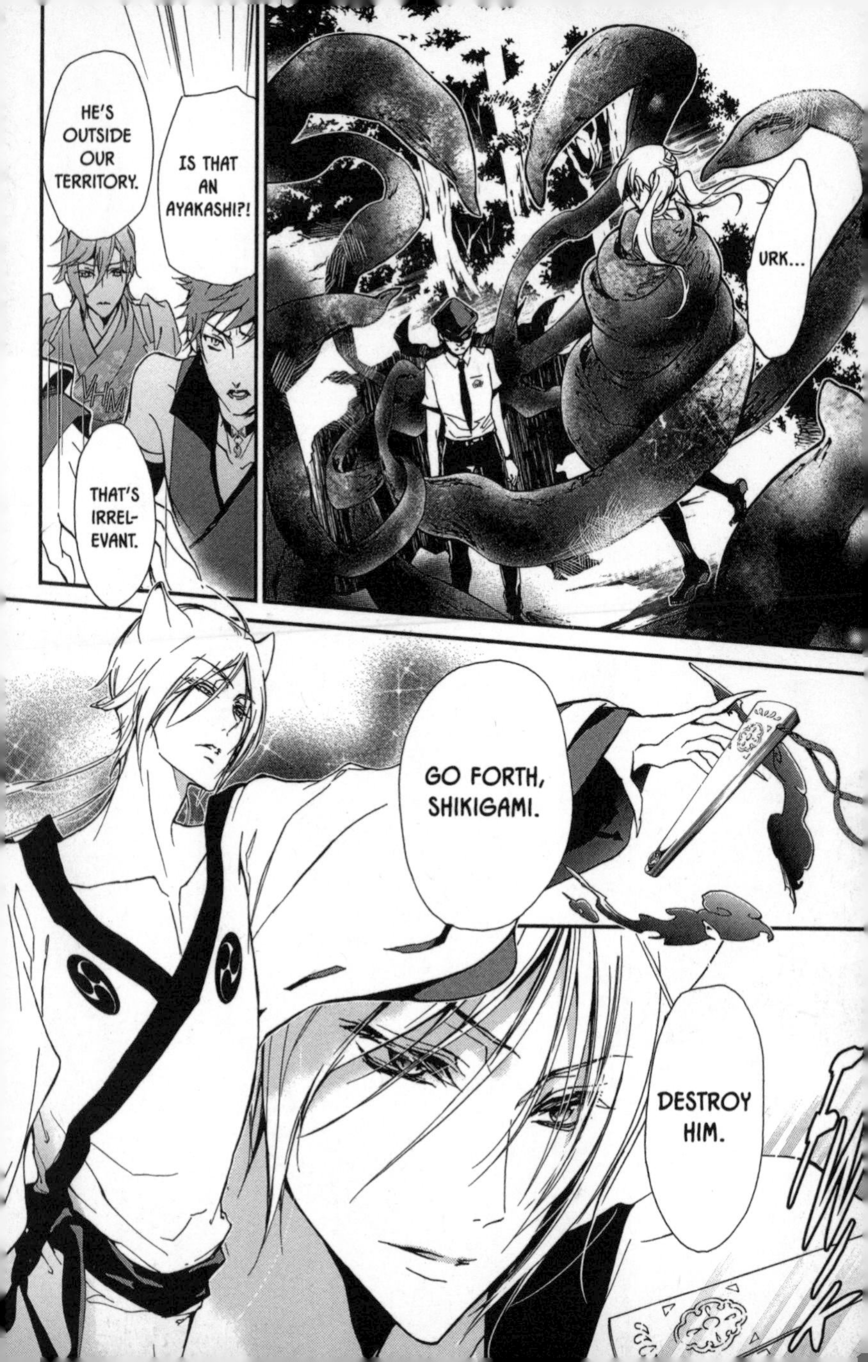
URK...
IS THAT AN AYAKASHI?!
HE'S OUTSIDE OUR TERRITORY.
THAT'S IRREL-EVANT.
GO FORTH, SHIKIGAMI.
DESTROY HIM.

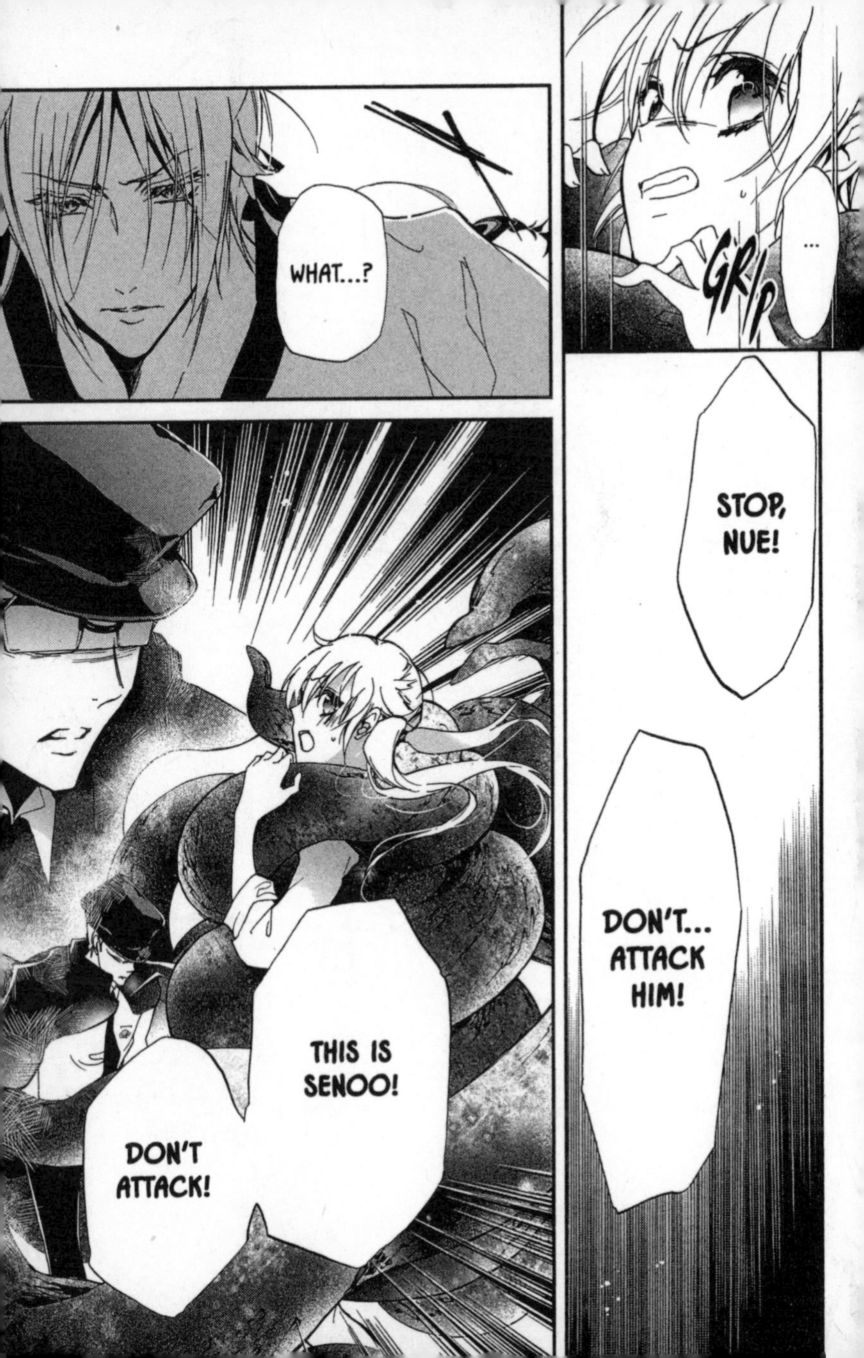
GRIP
...
WHAT...?
STOP, NUE!
DON'T... ATTACK HIM!
THIS IS SENOO!
DON'T ATTACK!

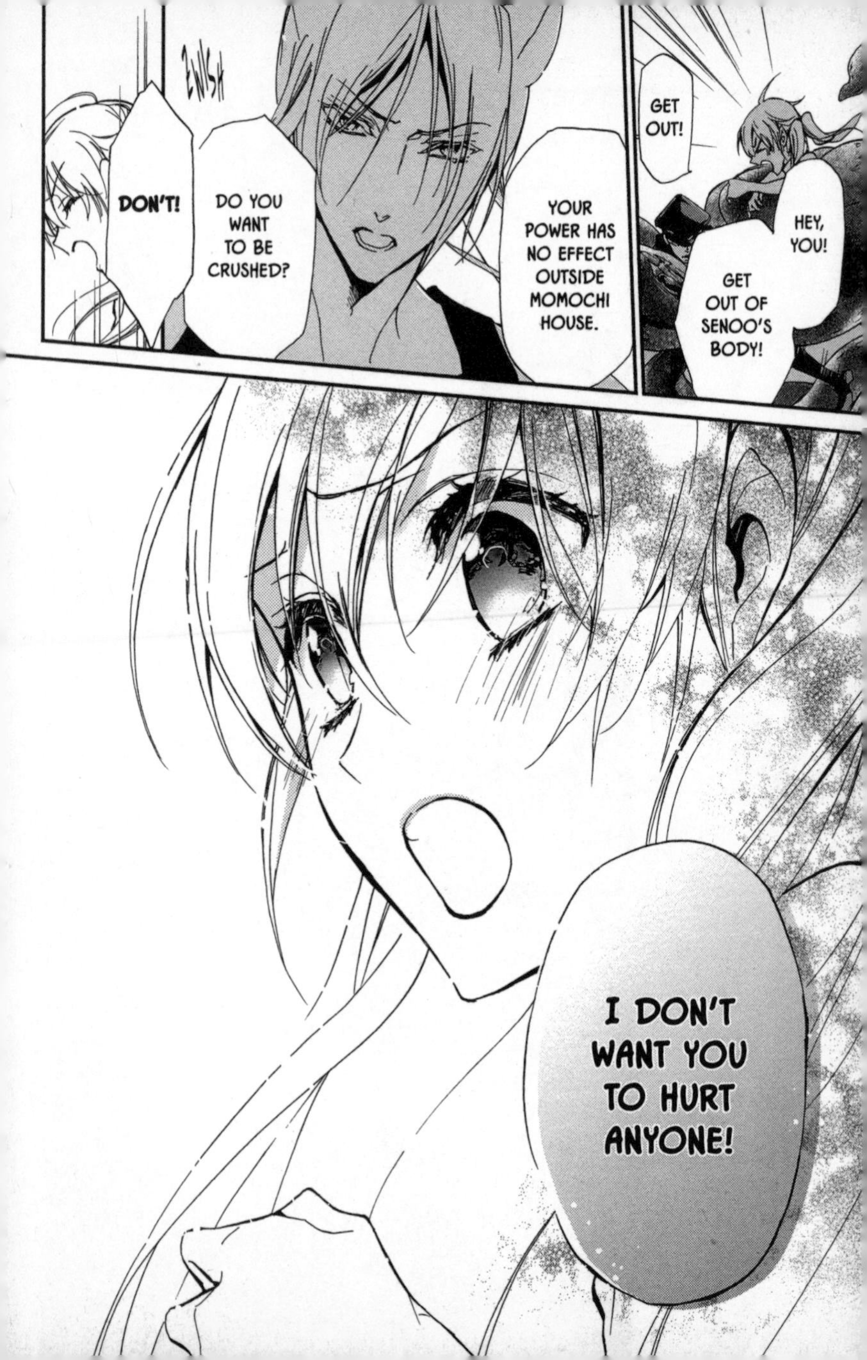
GET OUT!
HEY, YOU!
GET OUT OF SENOO'S BODY!
YOUR POWER HAS NO EFFECT OUTSIDE MOMOCHI HOUSE.
DO YOU WANT TO BE CRUSHED?
ZWISH
DON'T!
I DON'T WANT YOU TO HURT ANYONE!

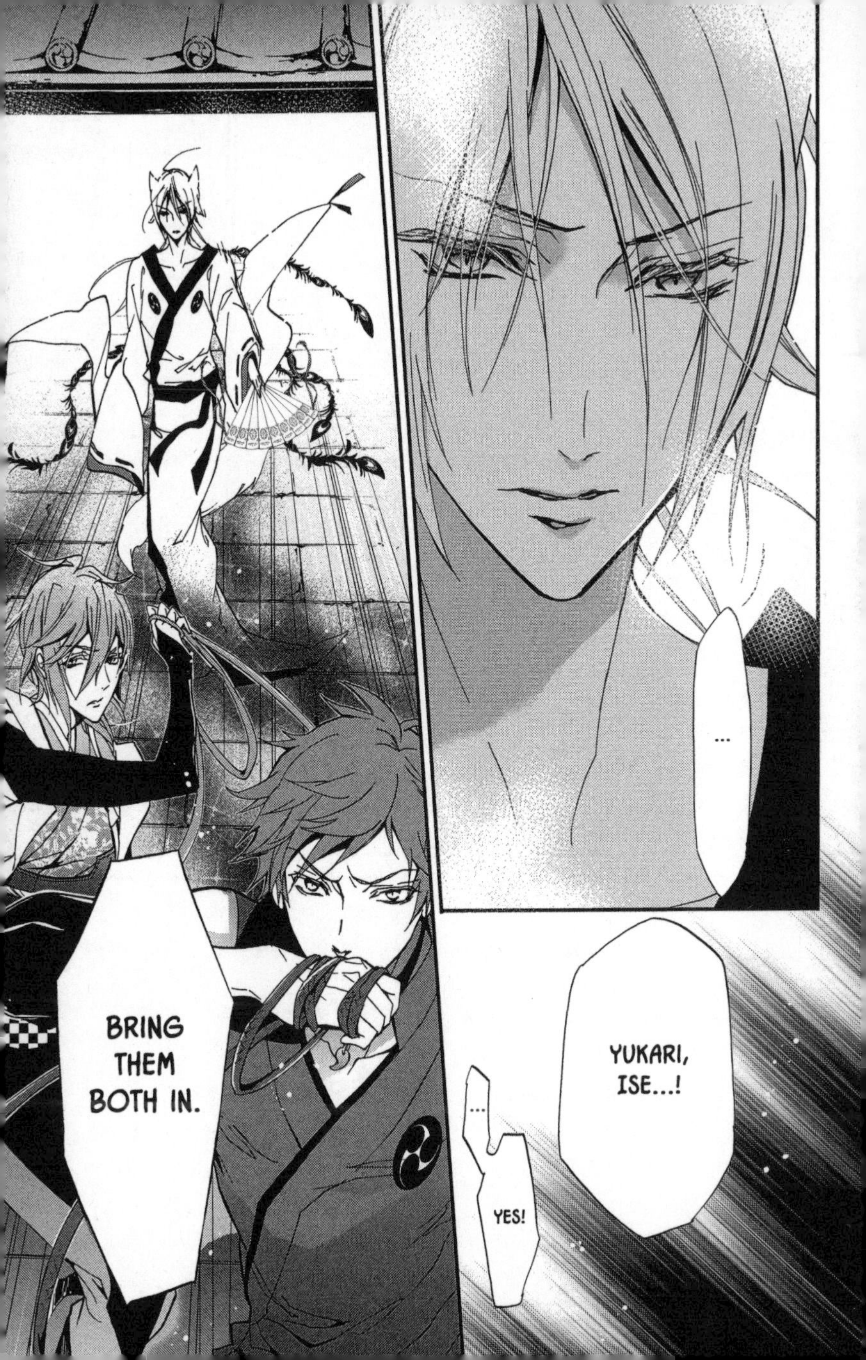
...
YUKARI, ISE...!
...
YES!
BRING THEM BOTH IN.

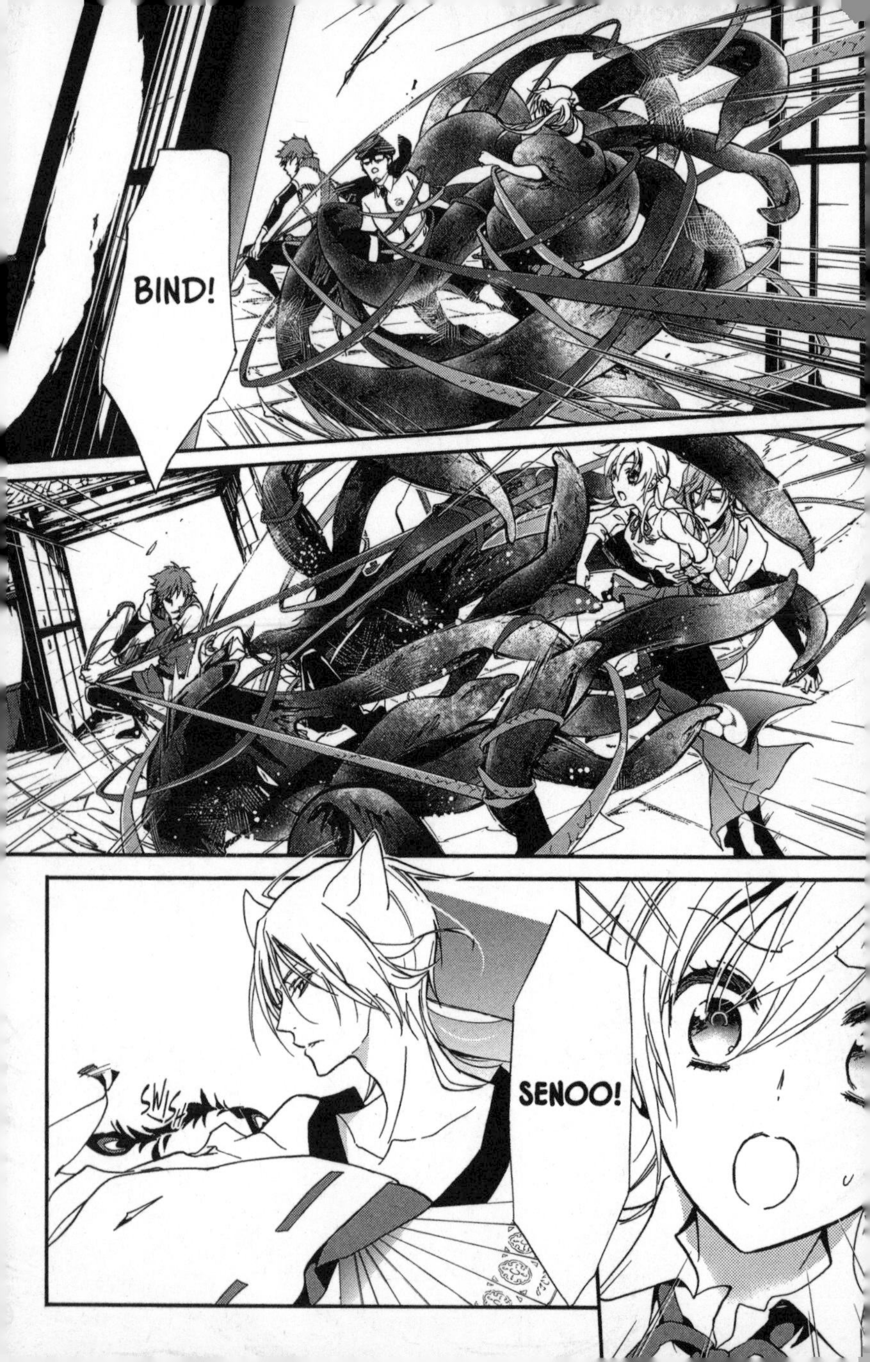
BIND!
SENOO!
SWISH

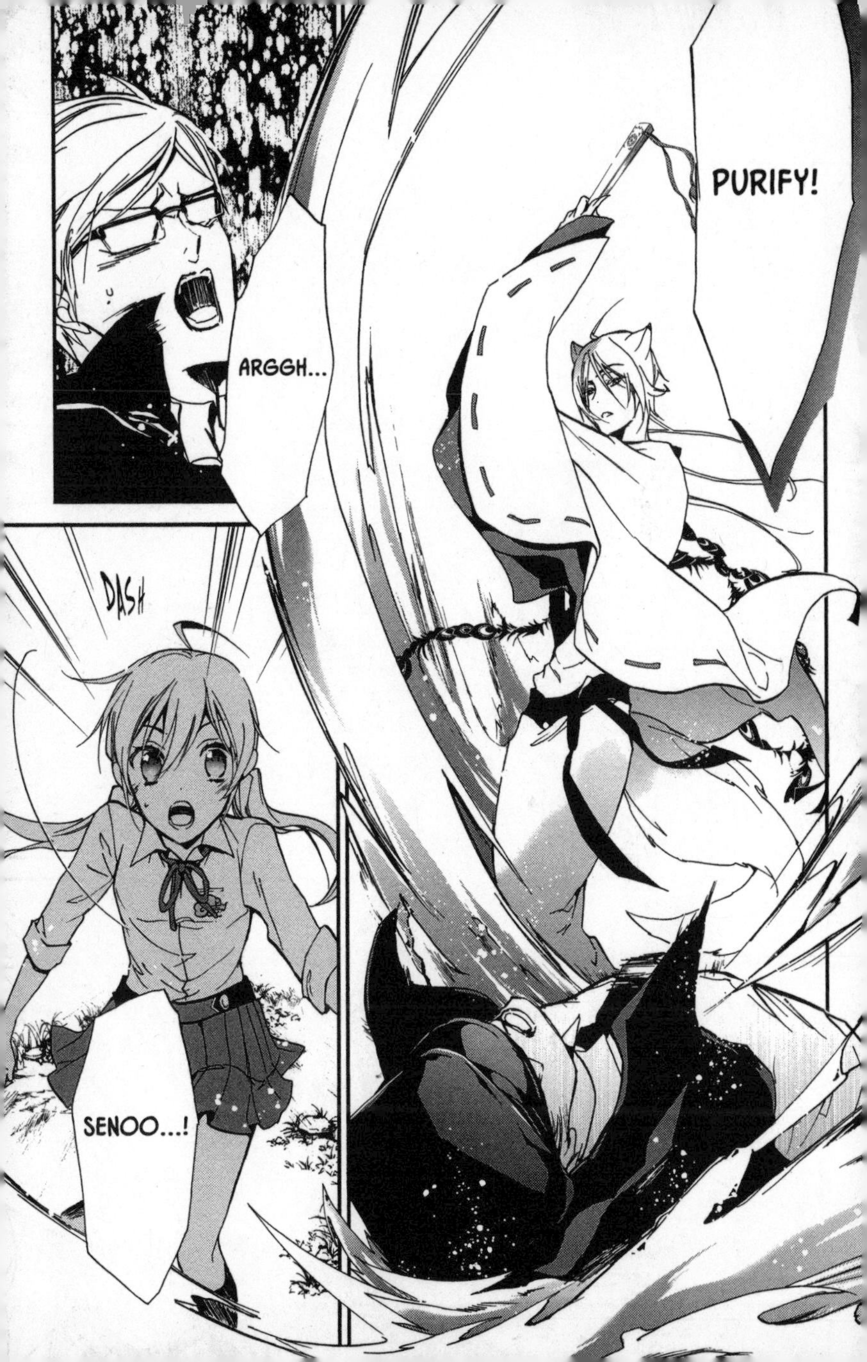
PURIFY!
ARGGH...
DASH
SENOO...!

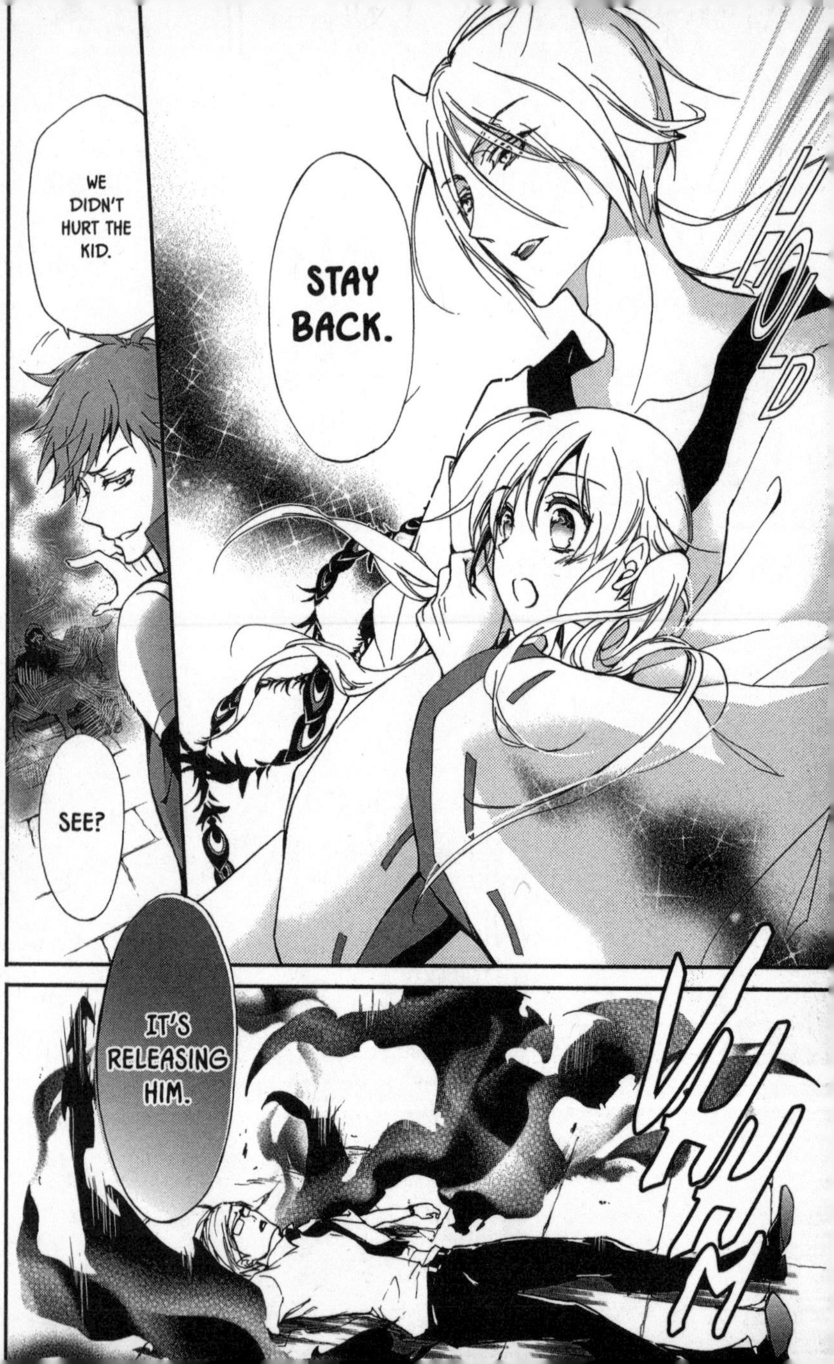
HOLD
STAY BACK.
WE DIDN'T HURT THE KID.
SEE?
IT'S RELEASING HIM.

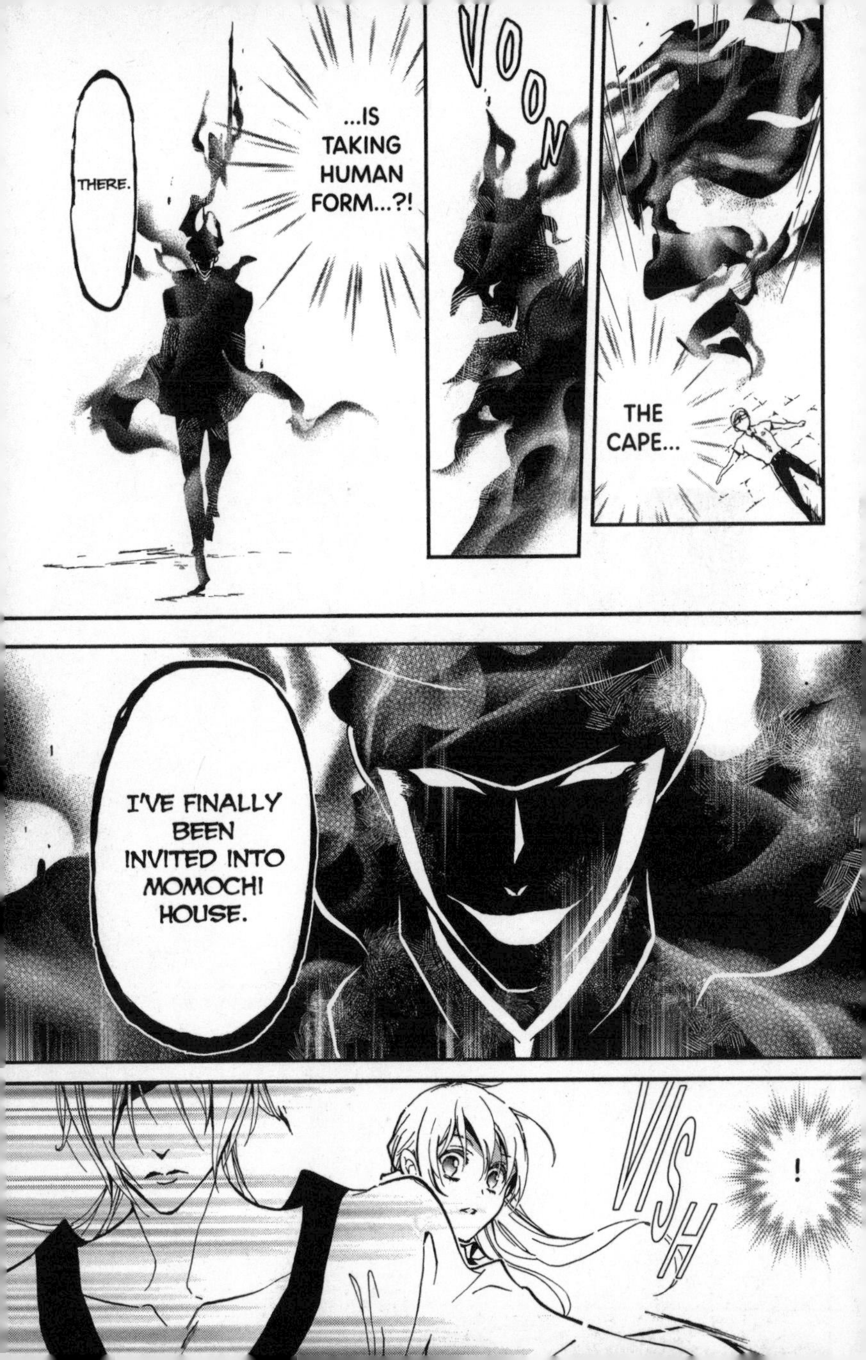
THE CAPE...
VOON
...IS TAKING HUMAN FORM...?!
THERE.
I'VE FINALLY BEEN INVITED INTO MOMOCHI HOUSE.
!
VISH

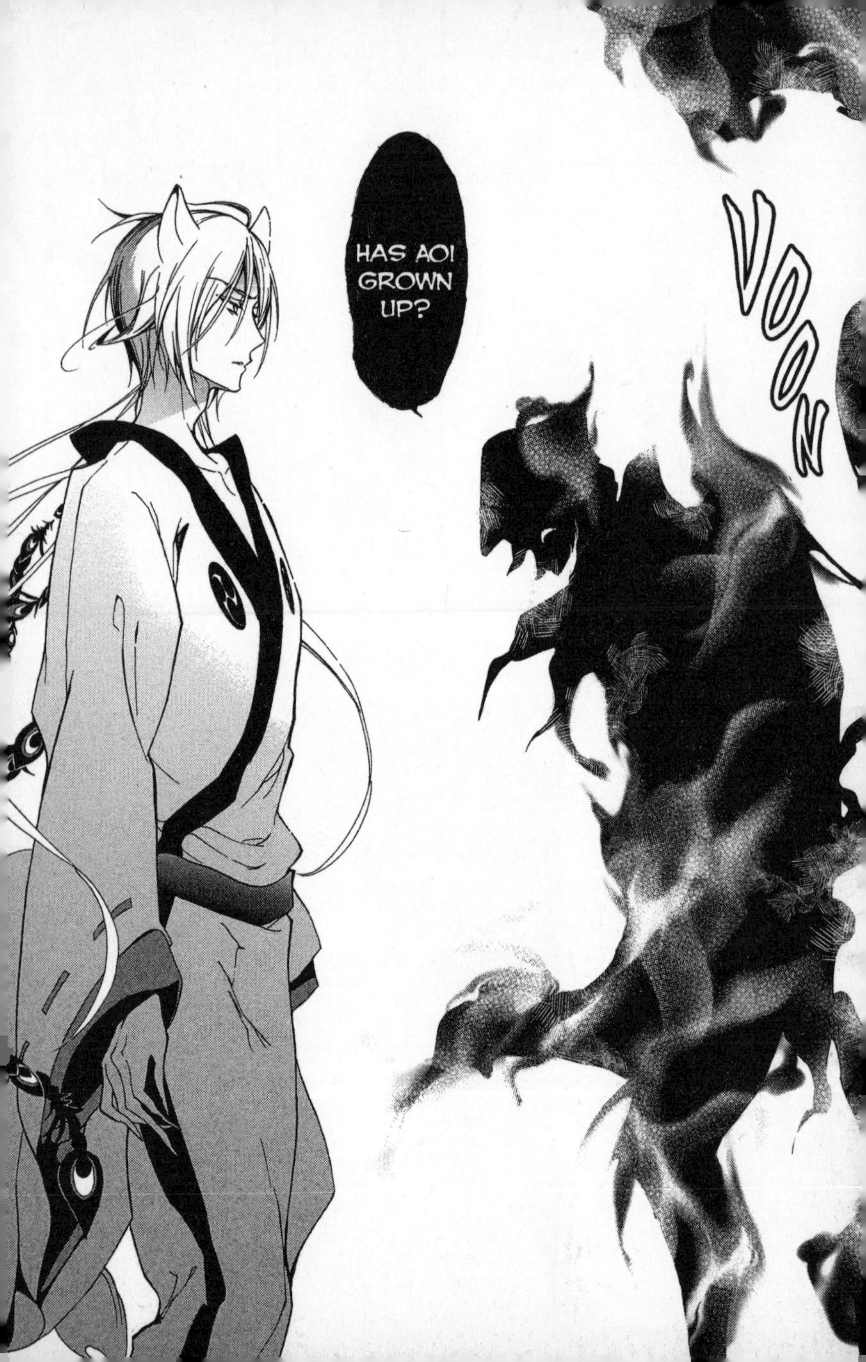
VOOON
HAS AOI GROWN UP?

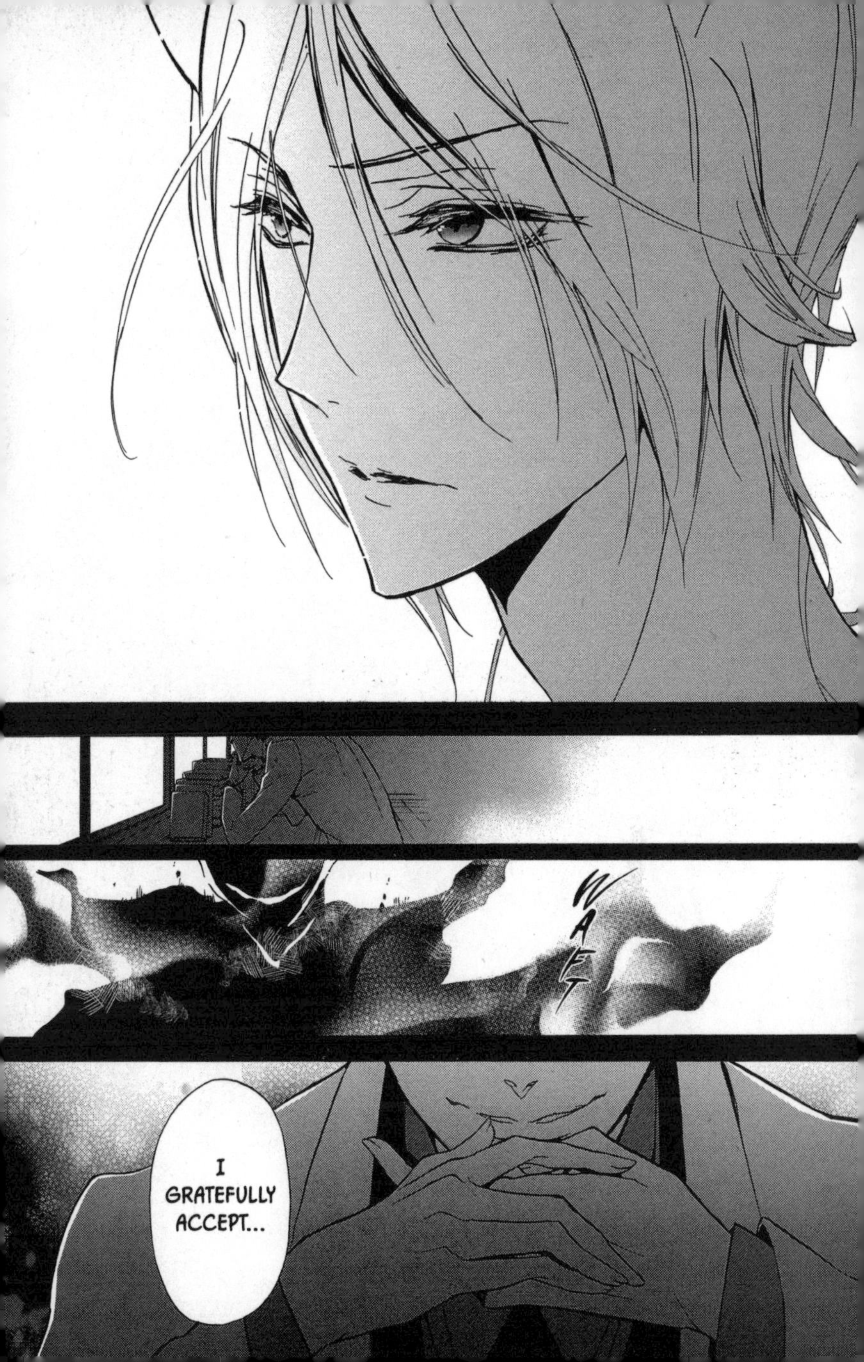
WAFT
I GRATEFULLY ACCEPT...

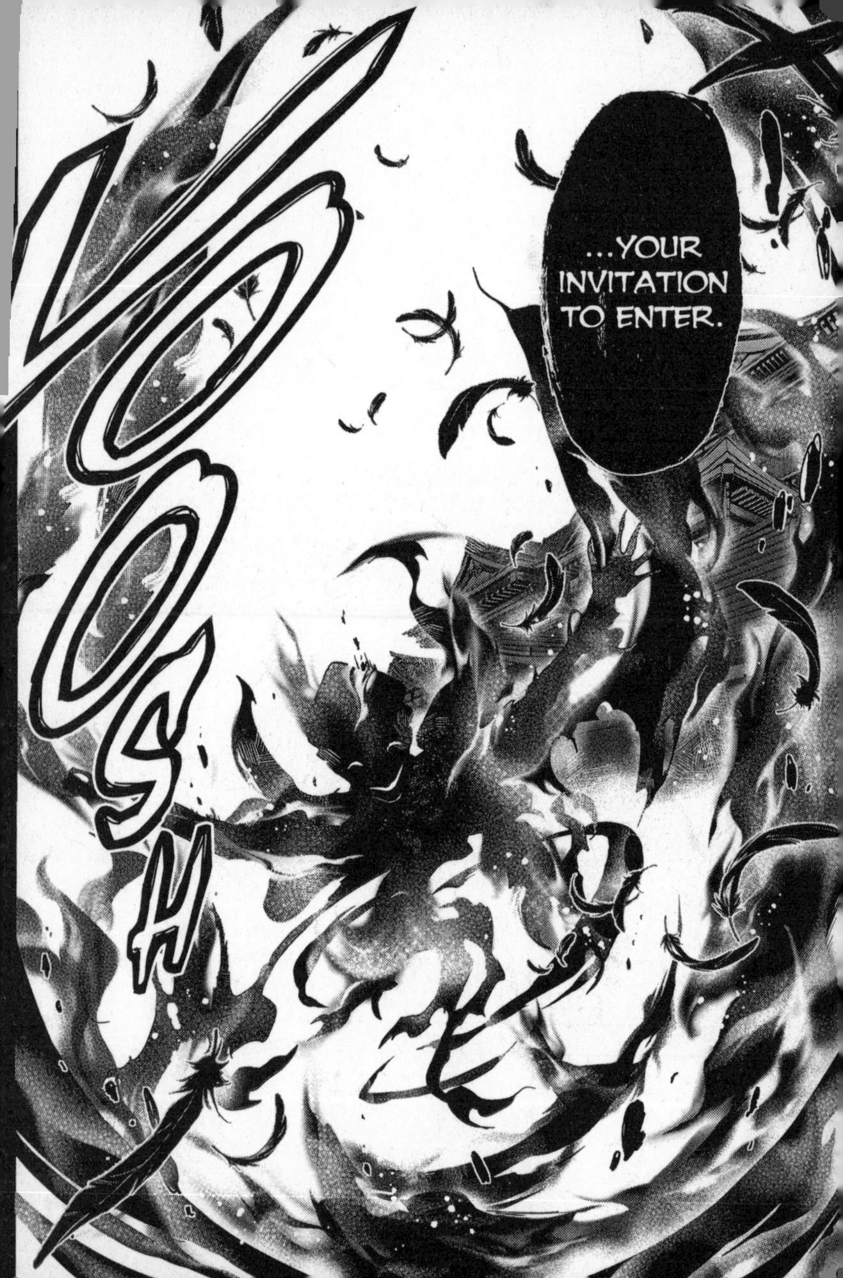
...YOUR INVITATION TO ENTER.
WOOOSH

The
DEMON
PRINCE
of MOMOCHI
HOUSE

The
DEMON
PRINCE
of MOMOCHI
HOUSE

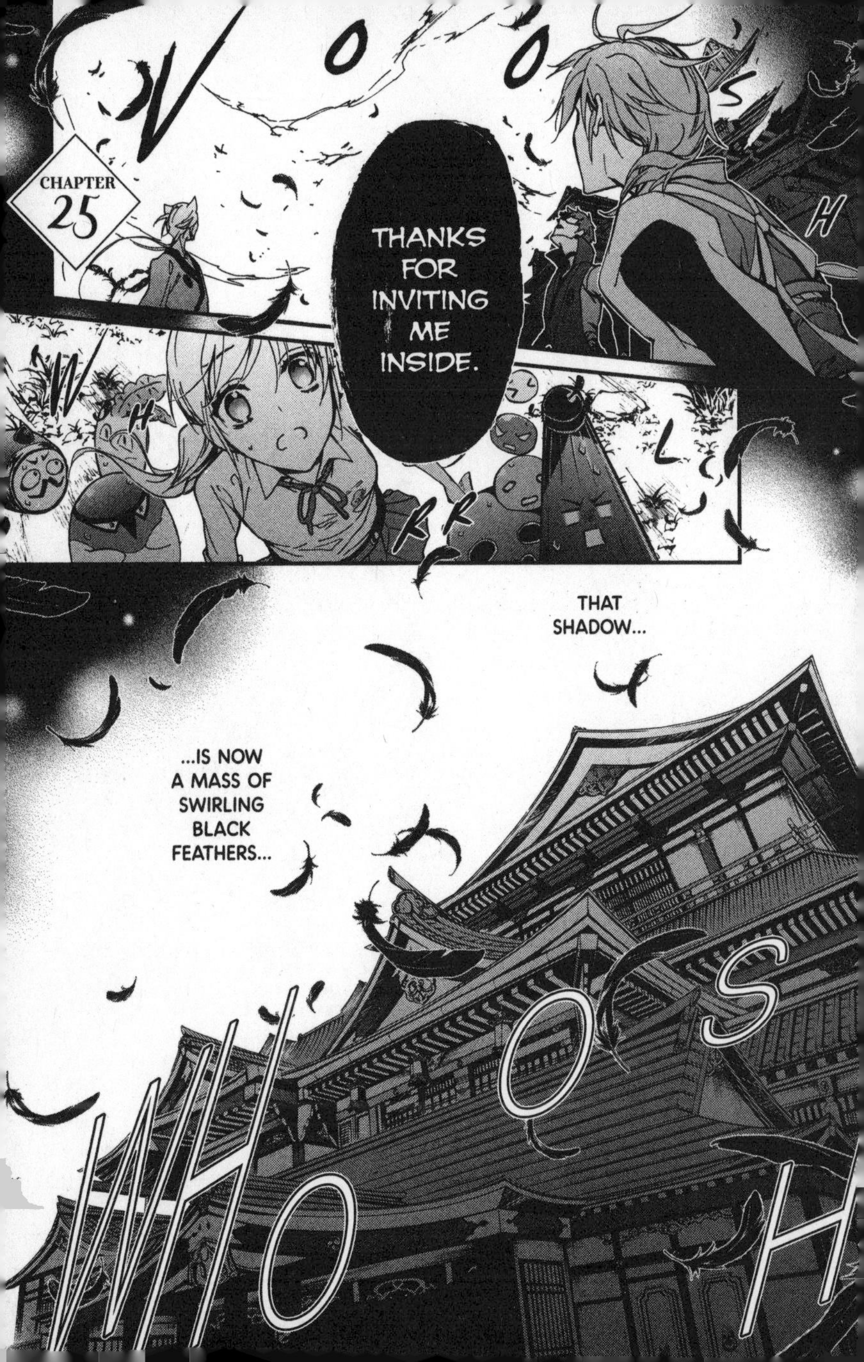
VOOSH
CHAPTER 25
THANKS FOR INVITING ME INSIDE.
THAT SHADOW...
...IS NOW A MASS OF SWIRLING BLACK FEATHERS...
WHOOSH

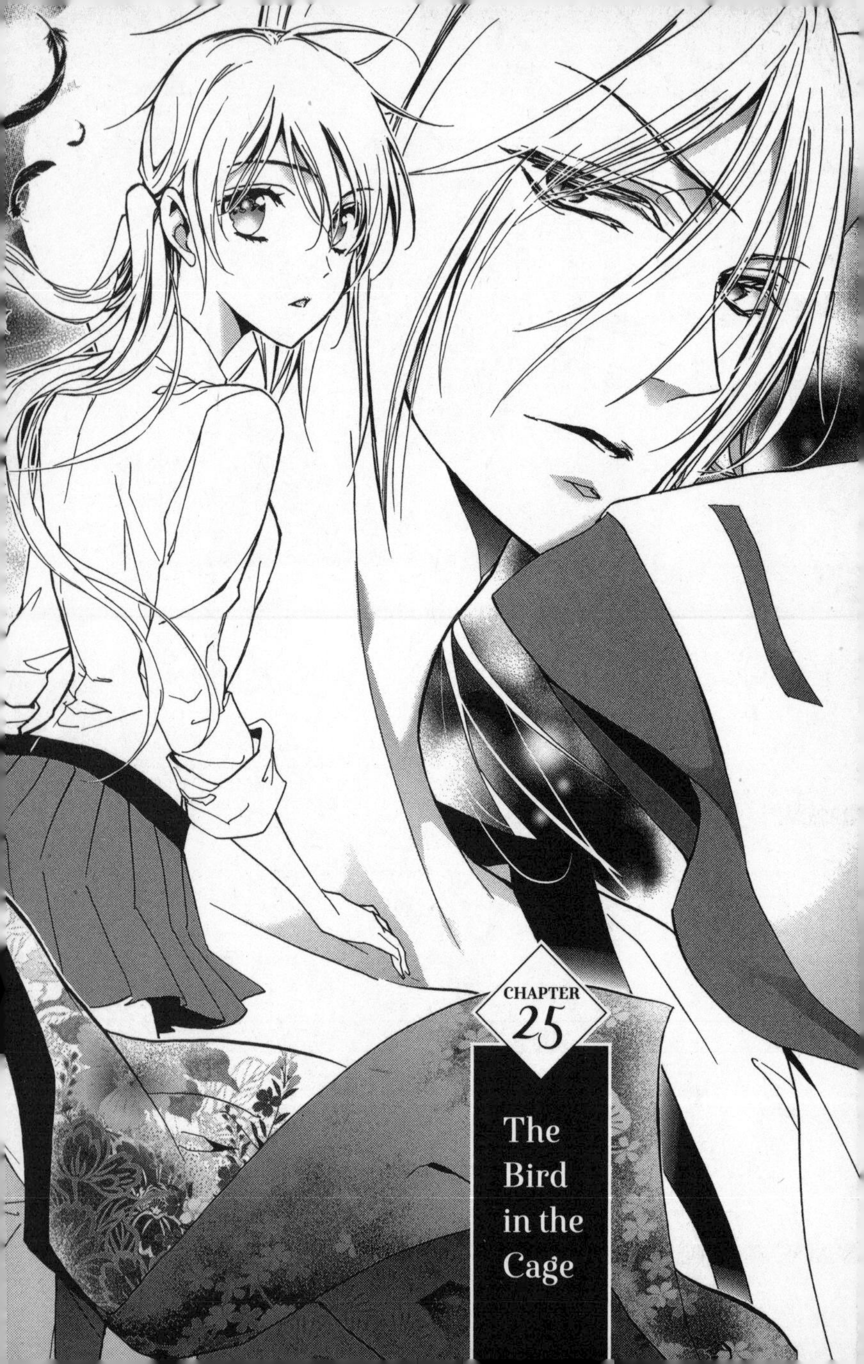
CHAPTER
25
The Bird in the Cage

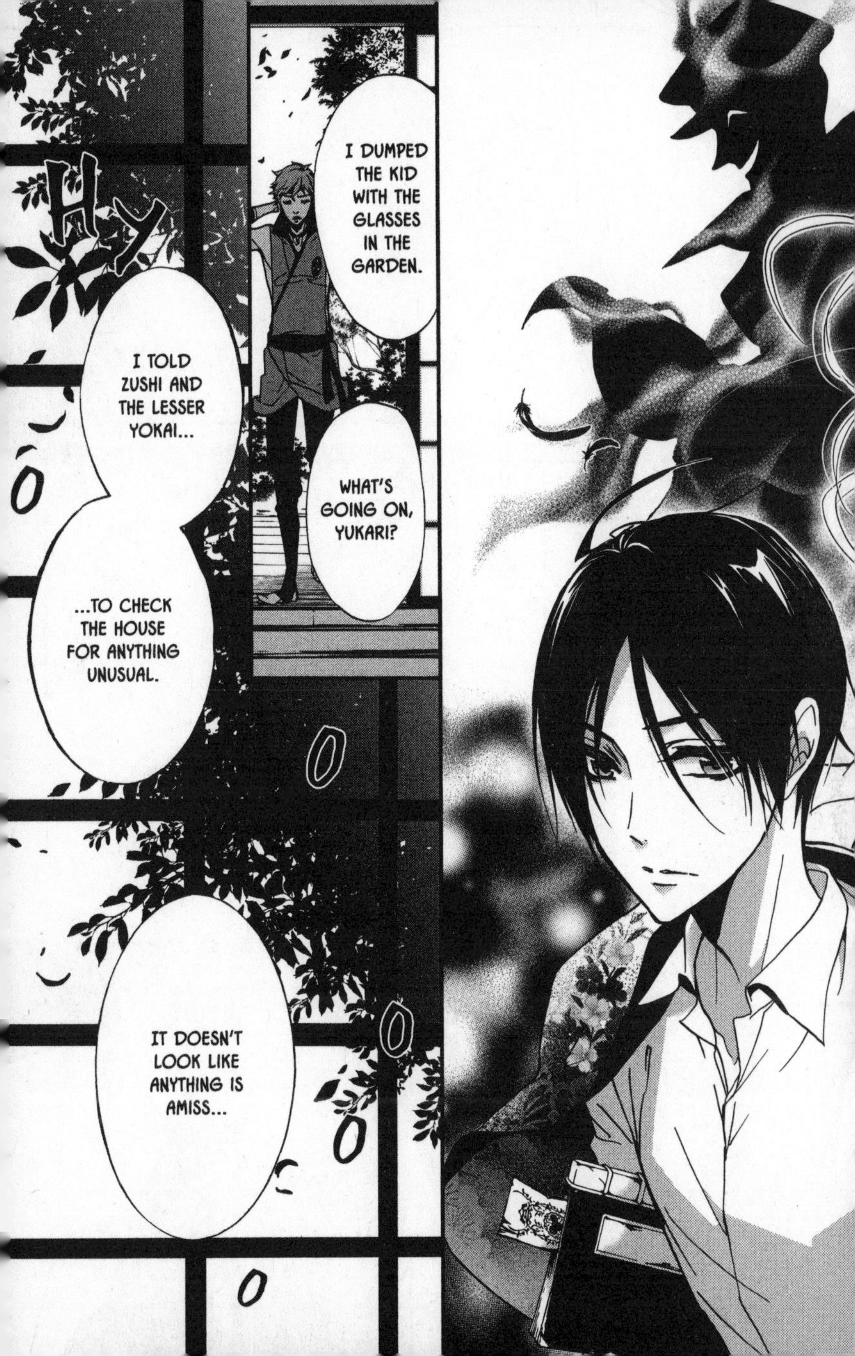
I DUMPED THE KID WITH THE GLASSES IN THE GARDEN.
WHAT'S GOING ON, YUKARI?
I TOLD ZUSHI AND THE LESSER YOKAI...
...TO CHECK THE HOUSE FOR ANYTHING UNUSUAL.
HYOOOOO
IT DOESN'T LOOK LIKE ANYTHING IS AMISS...

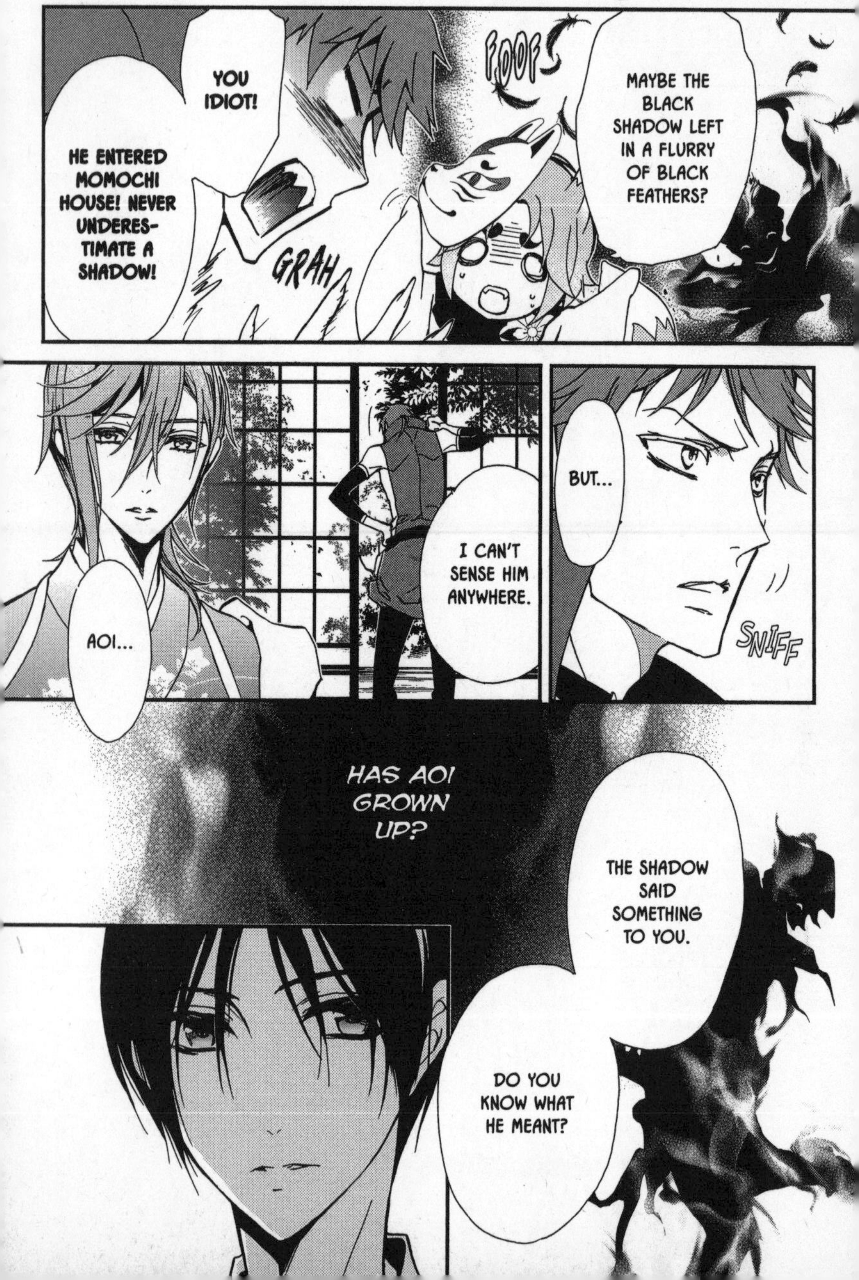
FOOF
MAYBE THE BLACK SHADOW LEFT IN A FLURRY OF BLACK FEATHERS?
YOU IDIOT!
HE ENTERED MOMOCHI HOUSE! NEVER UNDERES-TIMATE A SHADOW!
GRAH
BUT...
SNIFF
I CAN'T SENSE HIM ANYWHERE.
AOI...
HAS AOI GROWN UP?
THE SHADOW SAID SOMETHING TO YOU.
DO YOU KNOW WHAT HE MEANT?

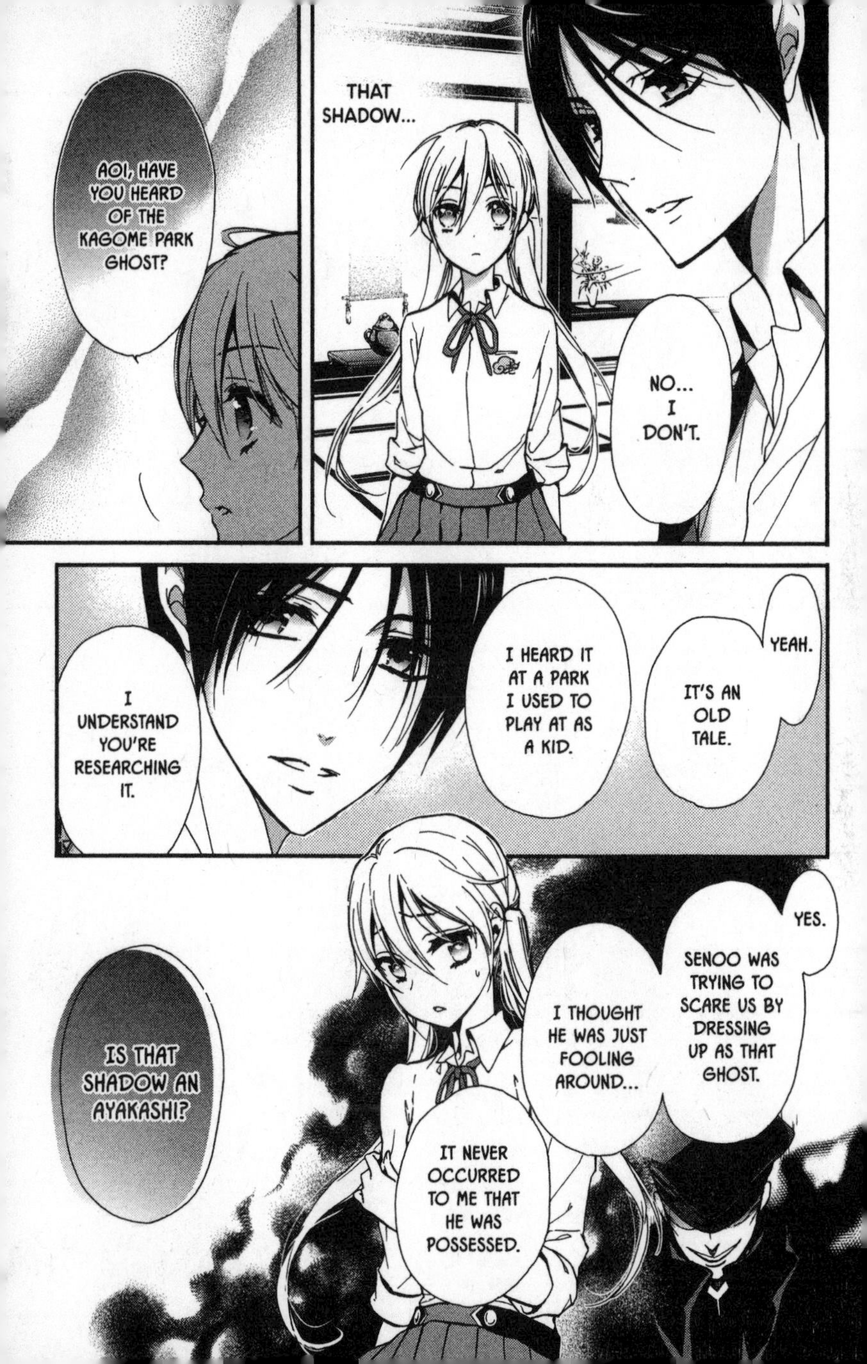
THAT SHADOW...
NO... I DON'T.
AOI, HAVE YOU HEARD OF THE KAGOME PARK GHOST?
YEAH.
IT'S AN OLD TALE.
I HEARD IT AT A PARK I USED TO PLAY AT AS A KID.
I UNDERSTAND YOU'RE RESEARCHING IT.
YES.
SENOO WAS TRYING TO SCARE US BY DRESSING UP AS THAT GHOST.
I THOUGHT HE WAS JUST FOOLING AROUND...
IT NEVER OCCURRED TO ME THAT HE WAS POSSESSED.
IS THAT SHADOW AN AYAKASHI?

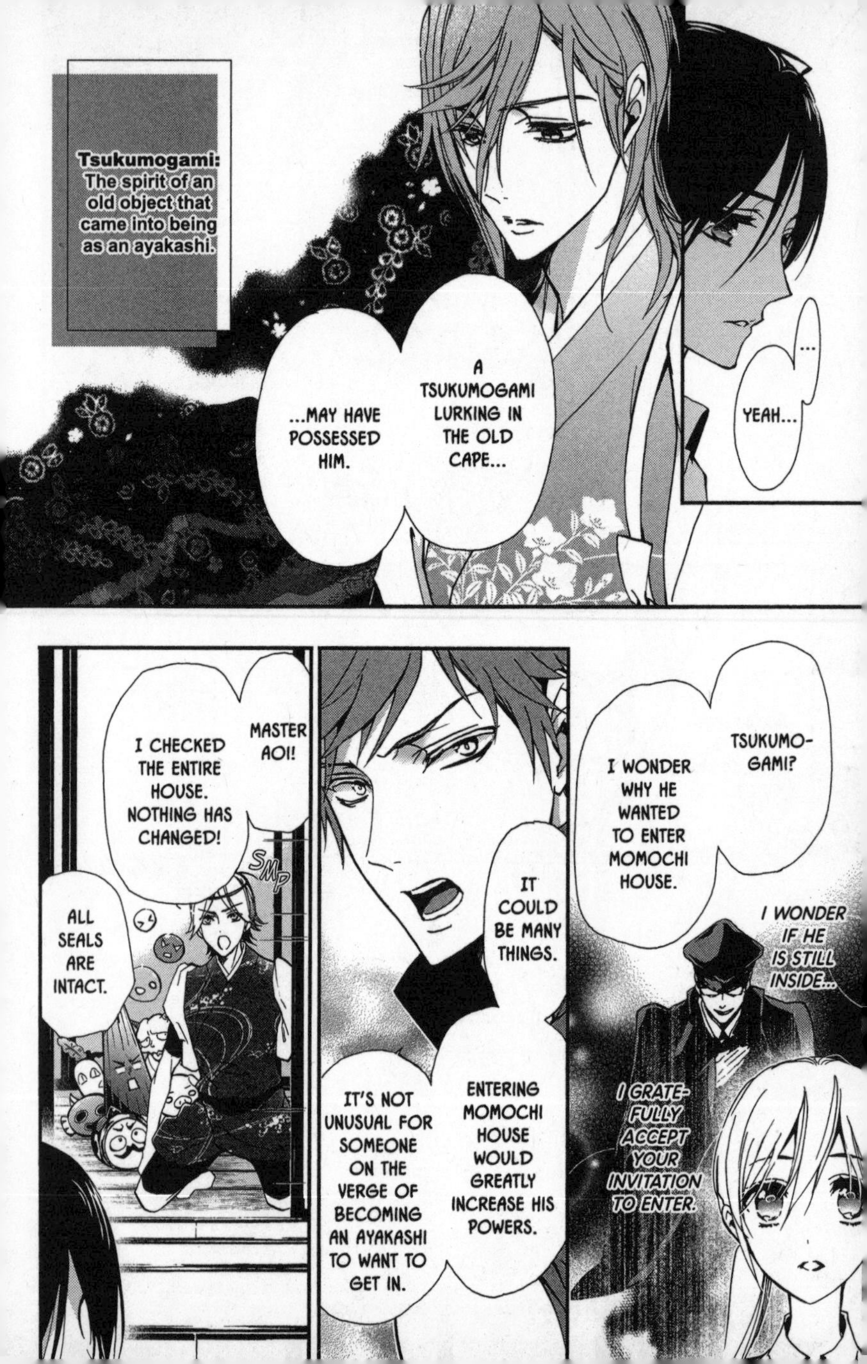
...
YEAH...
A TSUKUMOGAMI LURKING IN THE OLD CAPE...
...MAY HAVE POSSESSED HIM.
Tsukumogami: The spirit of an old object that came into being as an ayakashi.
TSUKUMO-GAMI?
I WONDER WHY HE WANTED TO ENTER MOMOCHI HOUSE.
I WONDER IF HE IS STILL INSIDE...
I GRATE-FULLY ACCEPT YOUR INVITATION TO ENTER.
IT COULD BE MANY THINGS.
ENTERING MOMOCHI HOUSE WOULD GREATLY INCREASE HIS POWERS.
IT'S NOT UNUSUAL FOR SOMEONE ON THE VERGE OF BECOMING AN AYAKASHI TO WANT TO GET IN.
MASTER AOI!
I CHECKED THE ENTIRE HOUSE. NOTHING HAS CHANGED!
SMP
ALL SEALS ARE INTACT.

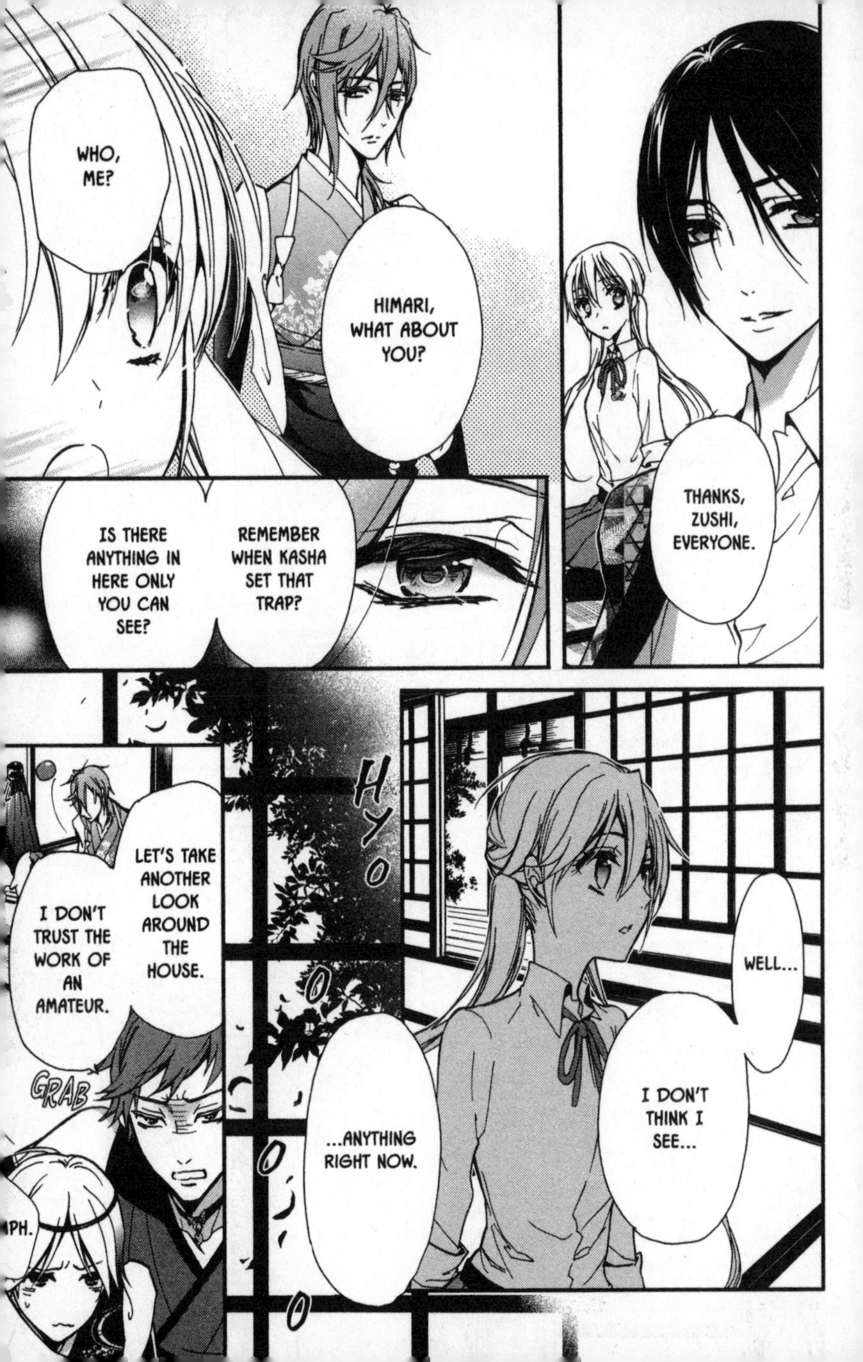
THANKS, ZUSHI, EVERYONE.
HIMARI, WHAT ABOUT YOU?
WHO, ME?
REMEMBER WHEN KASHA SET THAT TRAP?
IS THERE ANYTHING IN HERE ONLY YOU CAN SEE?
WELL...
I DON'T THINK I SEE...
...ANYTHING RIGHT NOW.
HYOOOO
LET'S TAKE ANOTHER LOOK AROUND THE HOUSE.
I DON'T TRUST THE WORK OF AN AMATEUR.
GRAB
PH.

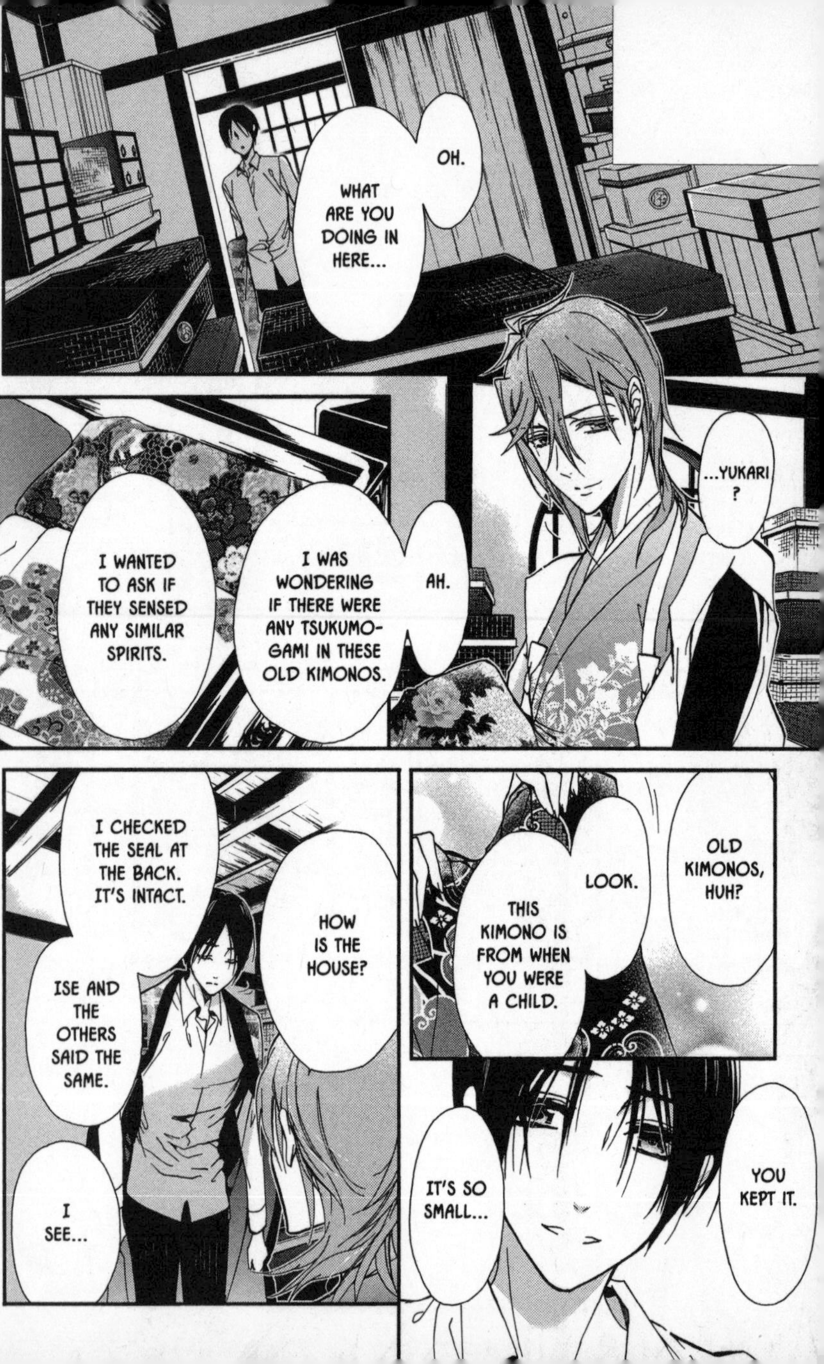
OH.
WHAT ARE YOU DOING IN HERE...
...YUKARI?
AH.
I WAS WONDERING IF THERE WERE ANY TSUKUMO-GAMI IN THESE OLD KIMONOS.
I WANTED TO ASK IF THEY SENSED ANY SIMILAR SPIRITS.
OLD KIMONOS, HUH?
LOOK.
THIS KIMONO IS FROM WHEN YOU WERE A CHILD.
YOU KEPT IT.
IT'S SO SMALL...
HOW IS THE HOUSE?
I CHECKED THE SEAL AT THE BACK. IT'S INTACT.
ISE AND THE OTHERS SAID THE SAME.
I SEE...

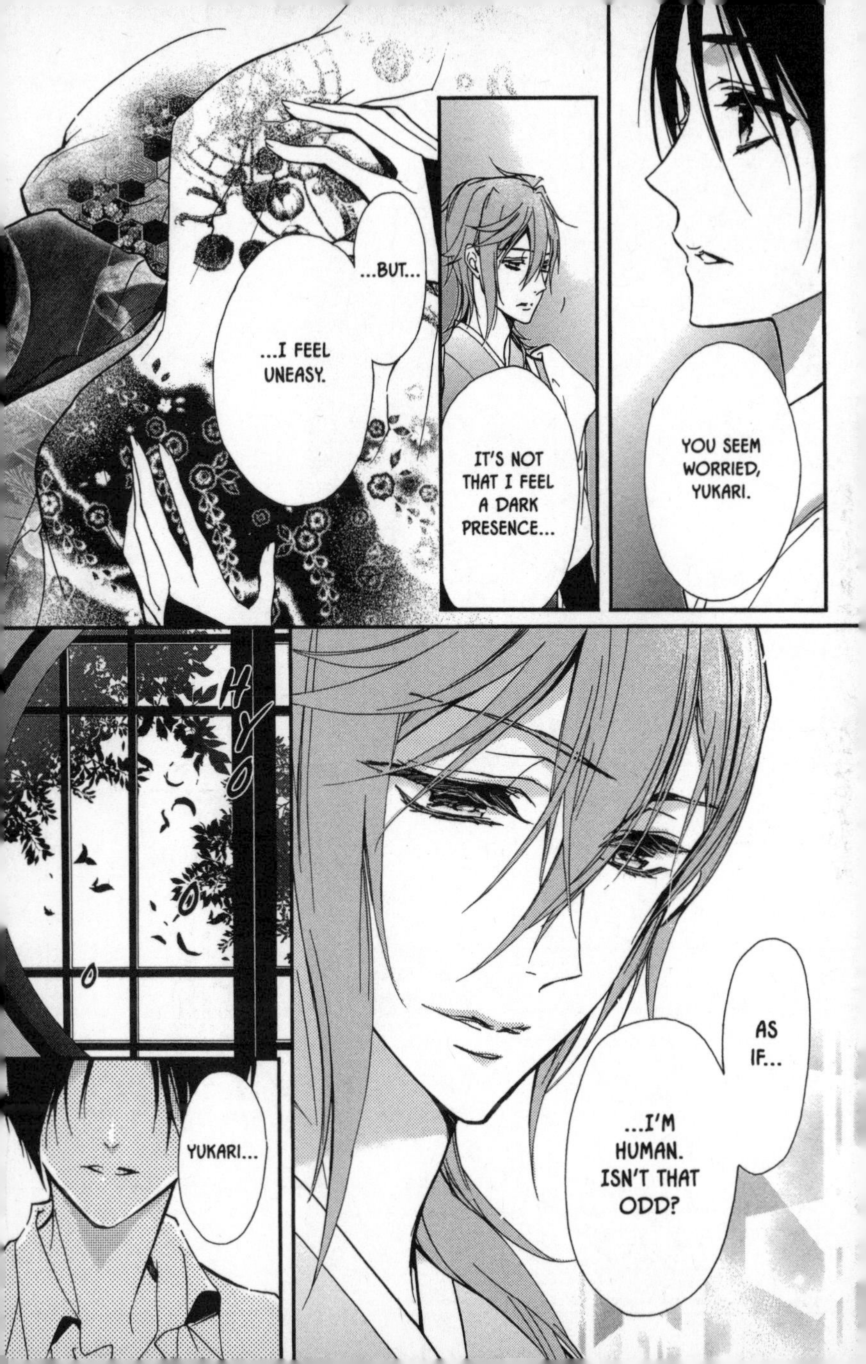
YOU SEEM WORRIED, YUKARI.
IT'S NOT THAT I FEEL A DARK PRESENCE...
...BUT...
...I FEEL UNEASY.
AS IF...
...I'M HUMAN. ISN'T THAT ODD?
YUKARI...

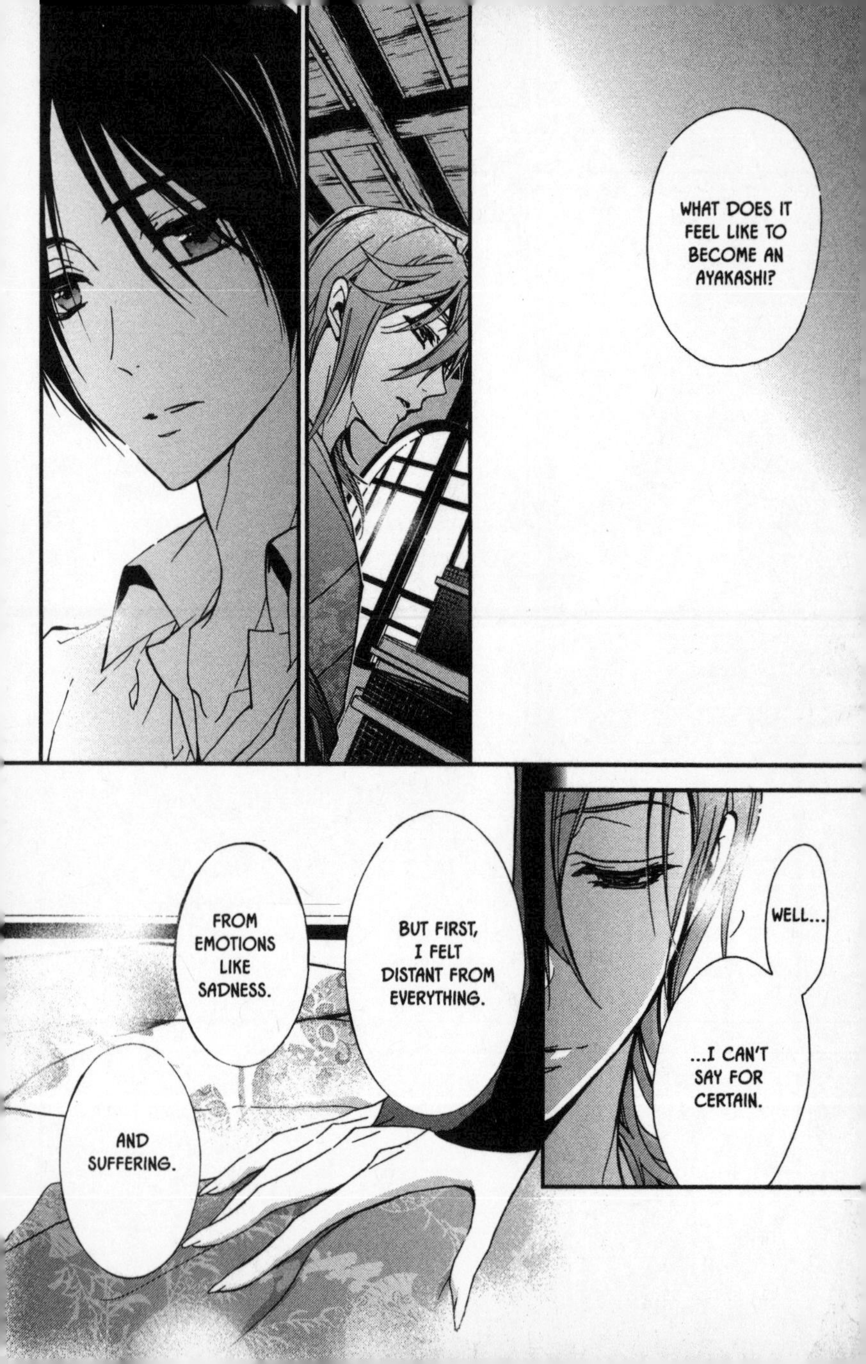
WHAT DOES IT FEEL LIKE TO BECOME AN AYAKASHI?
WELL...
...I CAN'T SAY FOR CERTAIN.
BUT FIRST, I FELT DISTANT FROM EVERYTHING.
FROM EMOTIONS LIKE SADNESS.
AND SUFFERING.

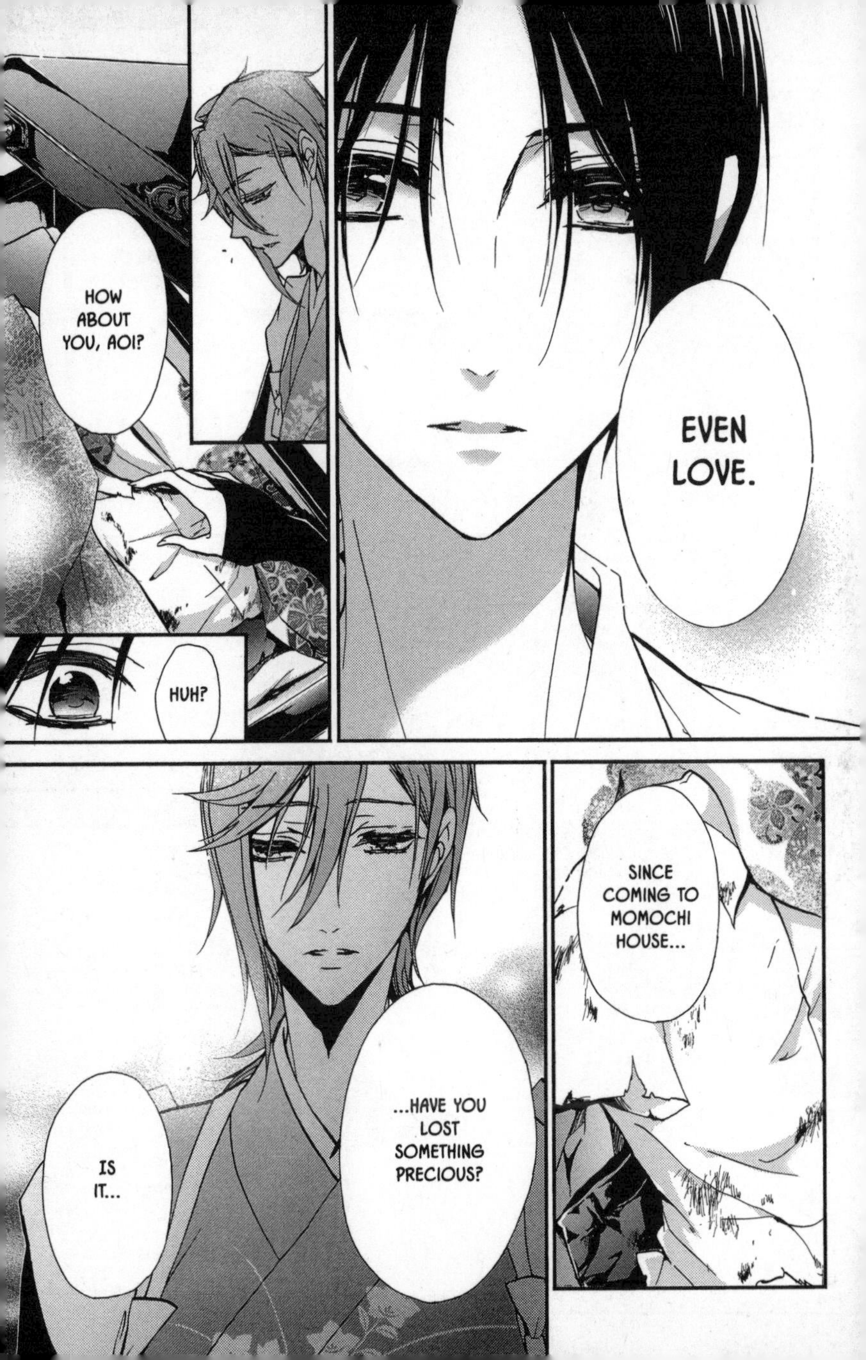
EVEN LOVE.
HOW ABOUT YOU, AOI?
HUH?
SINCE COMING TO MOMOCHI HOUSE...
...HAVE YOU LOST SOMETHING PRECIOUS?
IS IT...

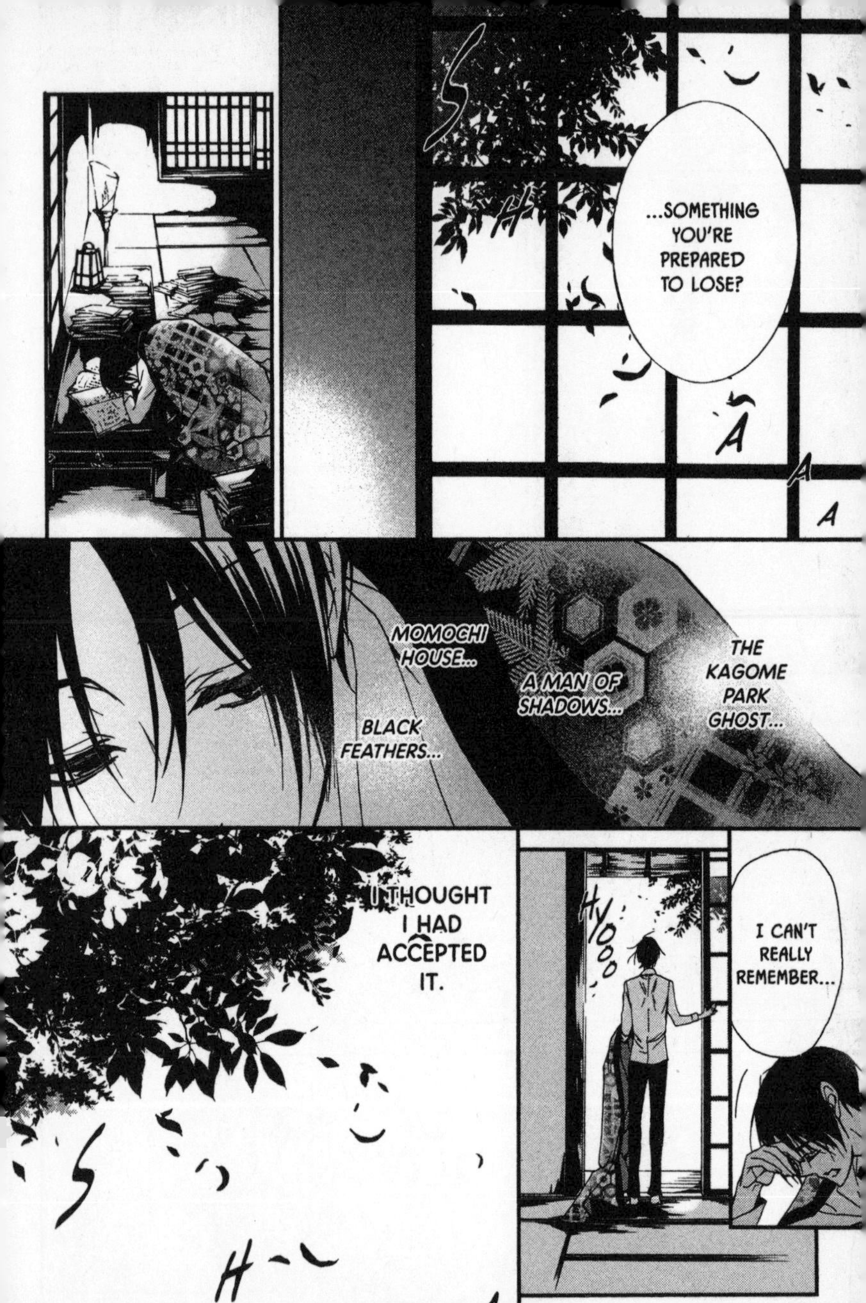
SHHAAA
...SOMETHING YOU'RE PREPARED TO LOSE?
THE KAGOME PARK GHOST...
A MAN OF SHADOWS...
MOMOCHI HOUSE...
BLACK FEATHERS...
I CAN'T REALLY REMEMBER...
HYOOO
I THOUGHT I HAD ACCEPTED IT.
SHHAAA

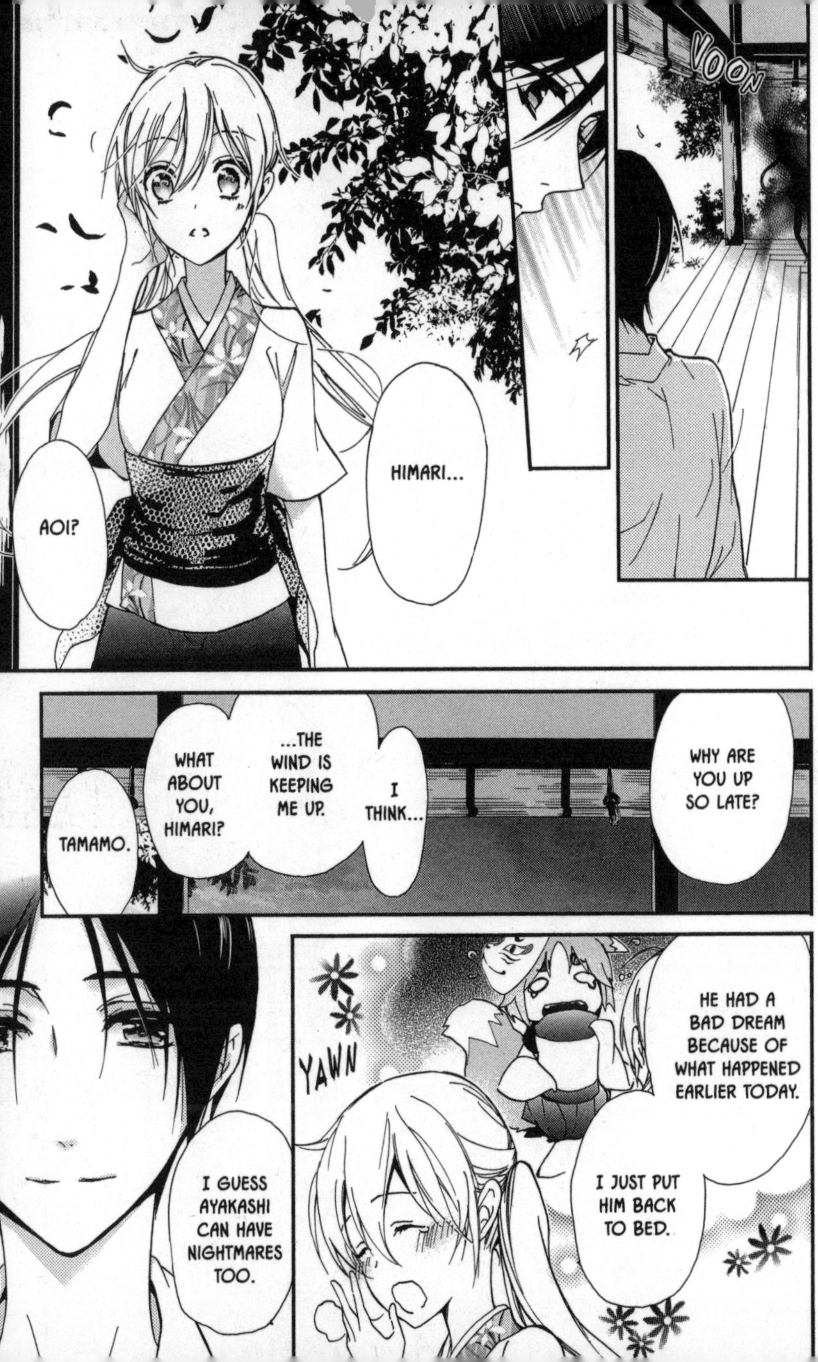
VOON
HIMARI...
AOI?
WHY ARE YOU UP SO LATE?
I THINK...
...THE WIND IS KEEPING ME UP.
WHAT ABOUT YOU, HIMARI?
TAMAMO.
HE HAD A BAD DREAM BECAUSE OF WHAT HAPPENED EARLIER TODAY.
YAWN
I JUST PUT HIM BACK TO BED.
I GUESS AYAKASHI CAN HAVE NIGHTMARES TOO.

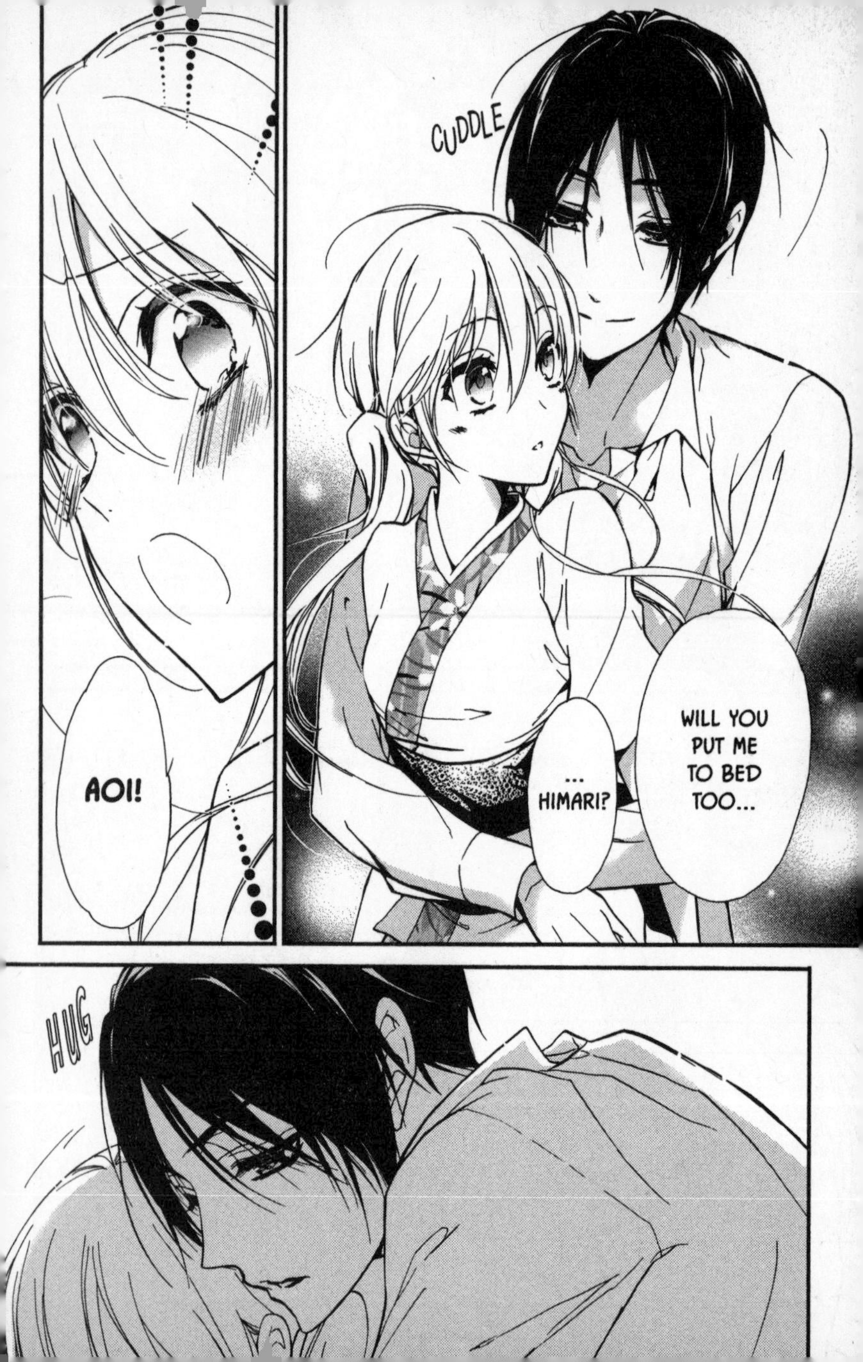
CUDDLE
WILL YOU PUT ME TO BED TOO...
... HIMARI?
AOI!
HUG

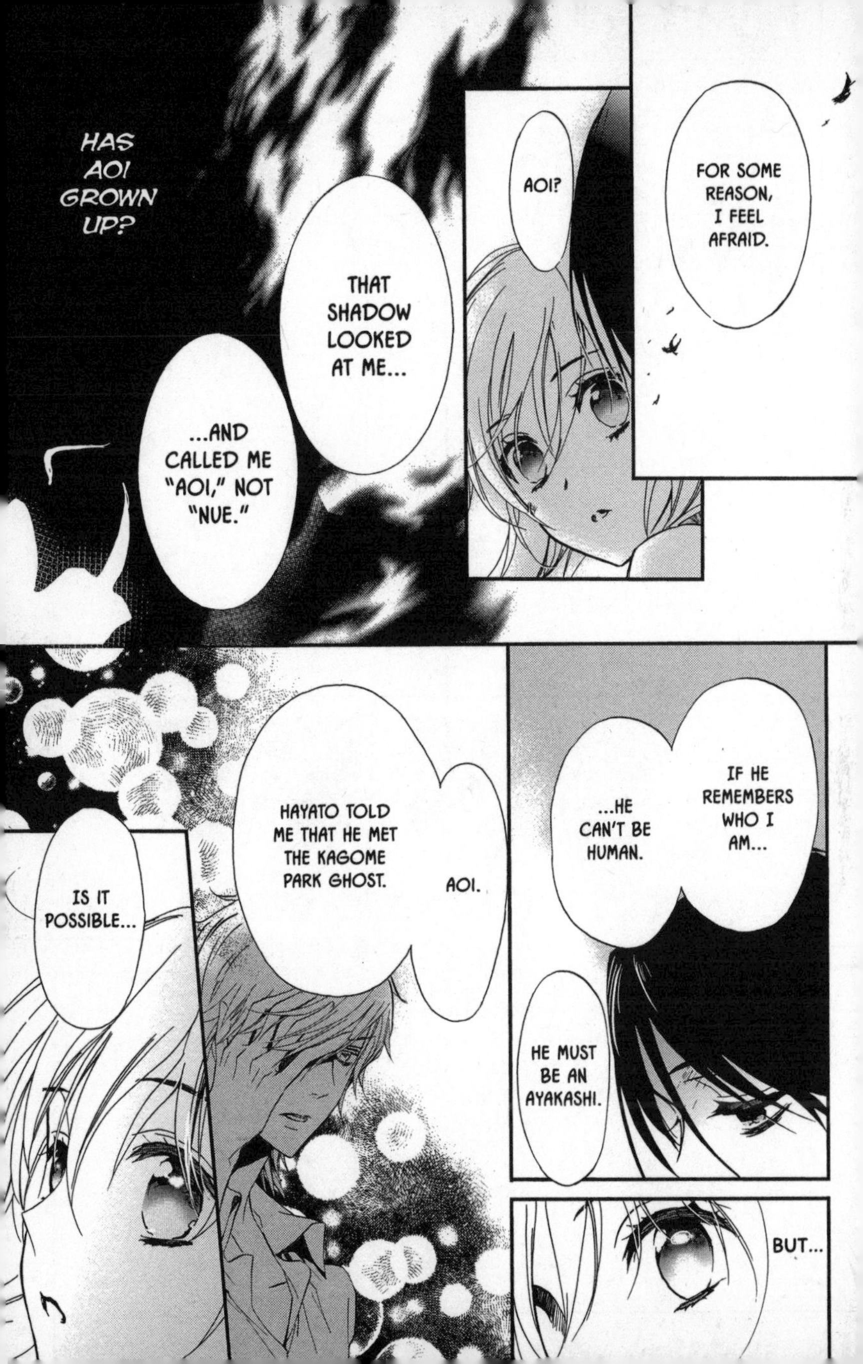
FOR SOME REASON, I FEEL AFRAID.
AOI?
THAT SHADOW LOOKED AT ME...
...AND CALLED ME "AOI," NOT "NUE."
HAS AOI GROWN UP?
IF HE REMEMBERS WHO I AM...
...HE CAN'T BE HUMAN.
HE MUST BE AN AYAKASHI.
BUT...
AOI.
HAYATO TOLD ME THAT HE MET THE KAGOME PARK GHOST.
IS IT POSSIBLE...

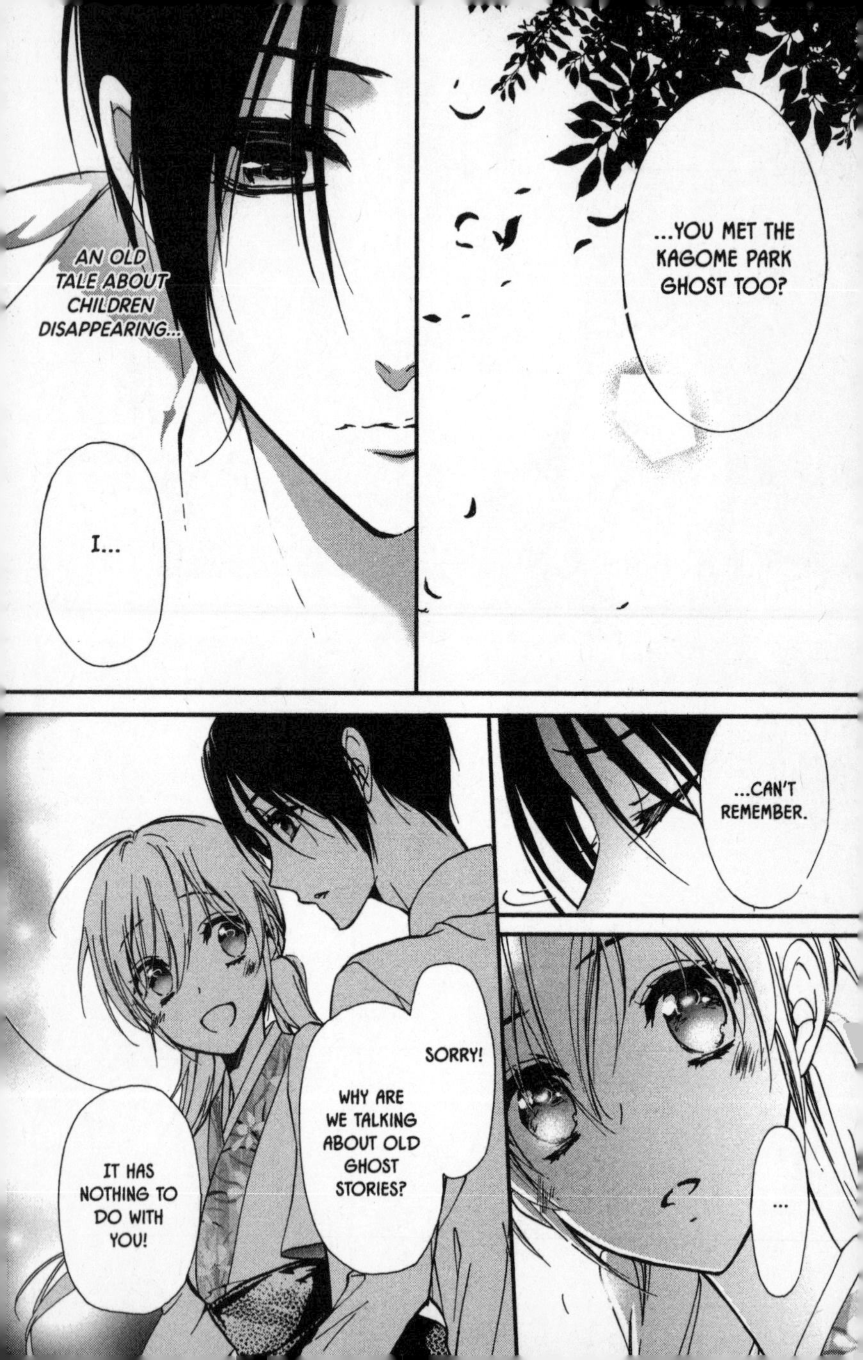
...YOU MET THE KAGOME PARK GHOST TOO?
AN OLD TALE ABOUT CHILDREN DISAPPEARING...
I...
...CAN'T REMEMBER.
...
SORRY!
WHY ARE WE TALKING ABOUT OLD GHOST STORIES?
IT HAS NOTHING TO DO WITH YOU!

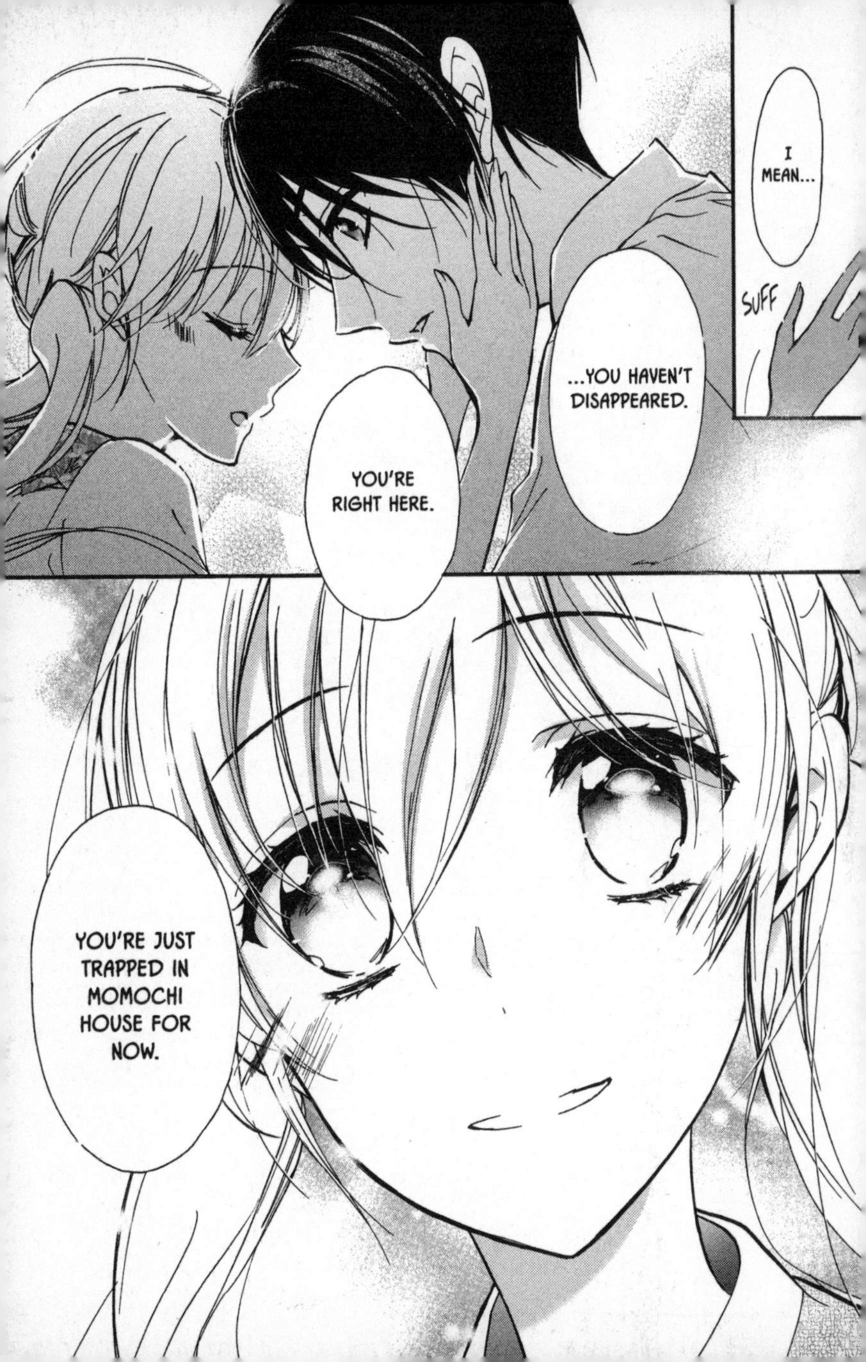
I MEAN...
SUFF
...YOU HAVEN'T DISAPPEARED.
YOU'RE RIGHT HERE.
YOU'RE JUST TRAPPED IN MOMOCHI HOUSE FOR NOW.

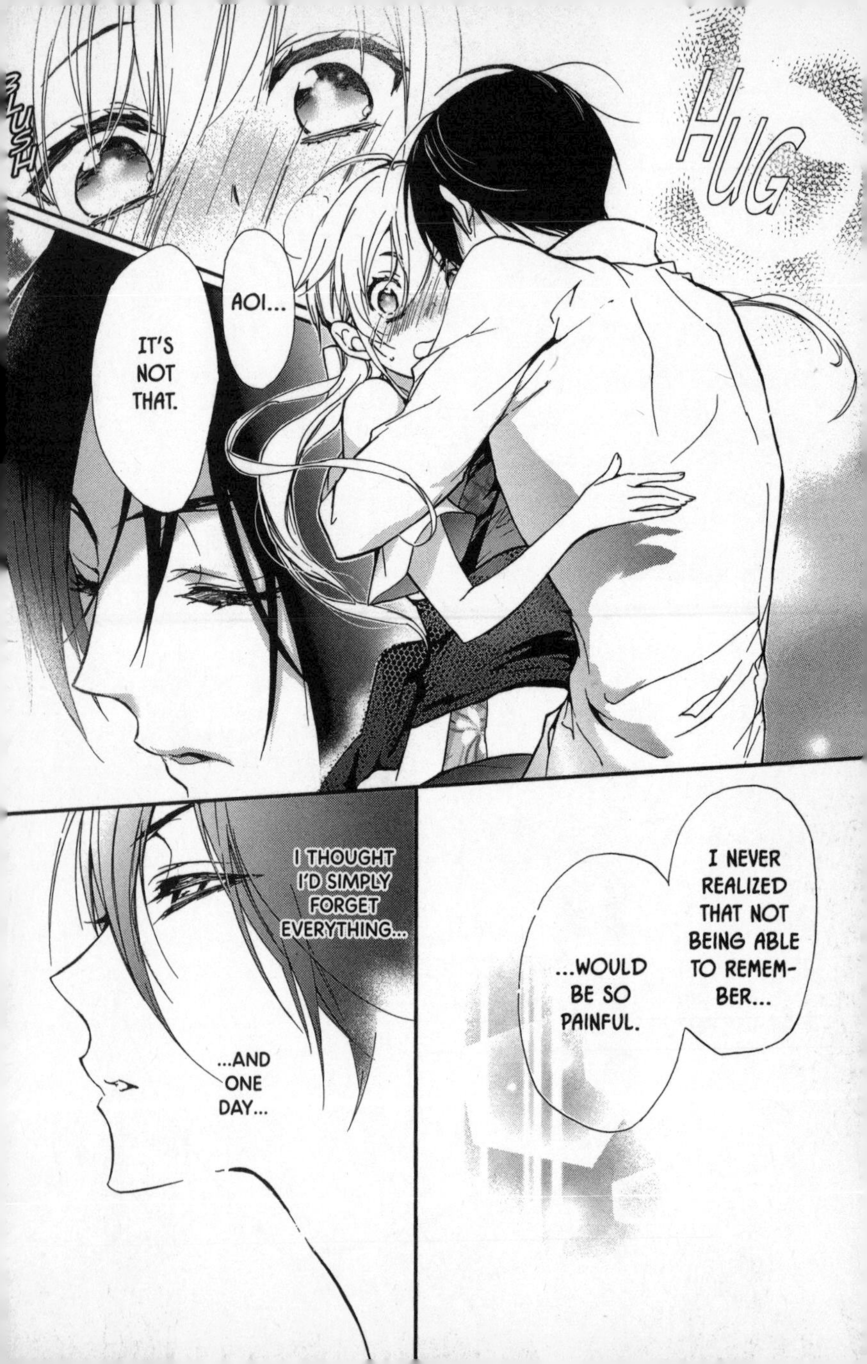
HUG
BLUSH
AOI...
IT'S NOT THAT.
I NEVER REALIZED THAT NOT BEING ABLE TO REMEMBER...
...WOULD BE SO PAINFUL.
I THOUGHT I'D SIMPLY FORGET EVERYTHING...
...AND ONE DAY...

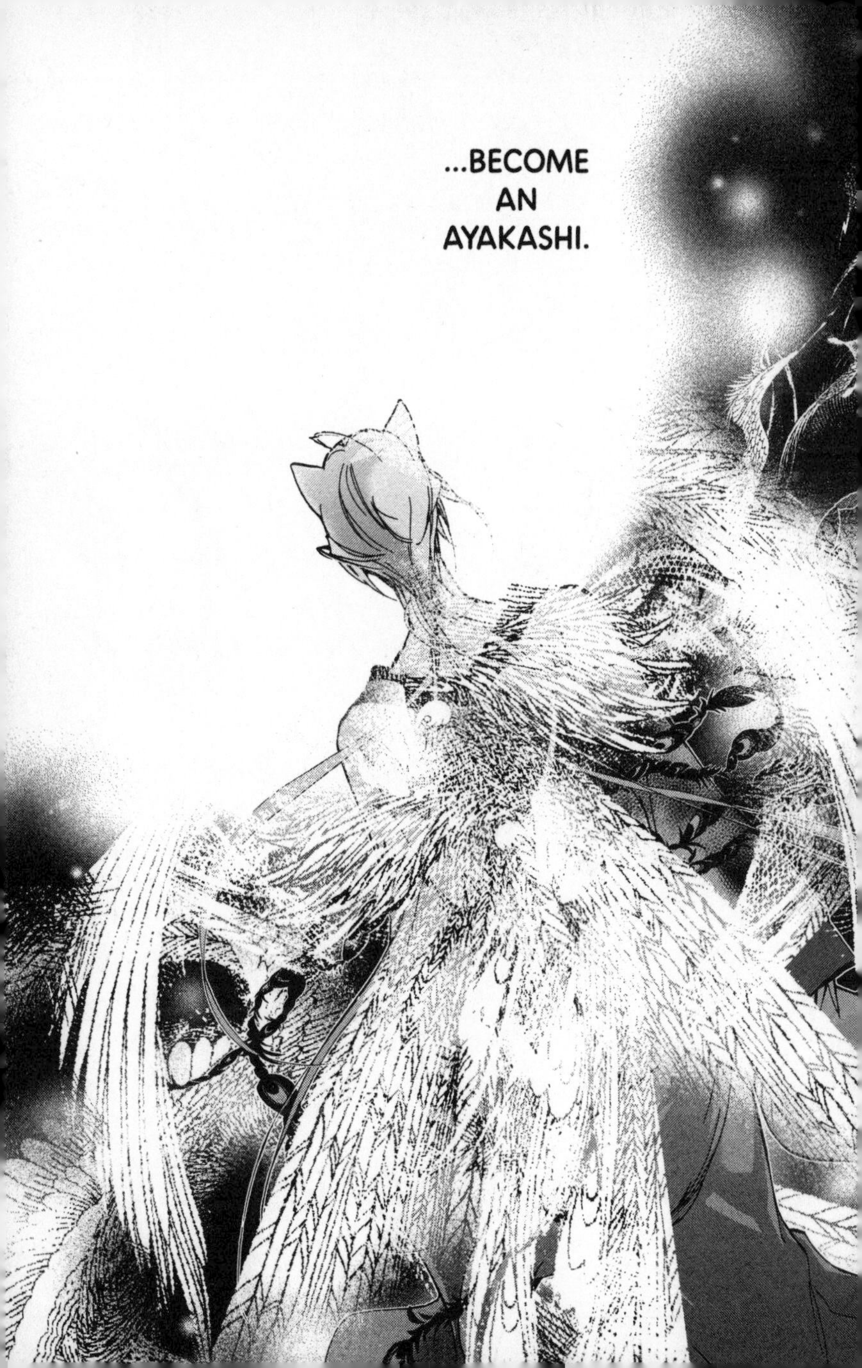
...BECOME AN AYAKASHI.

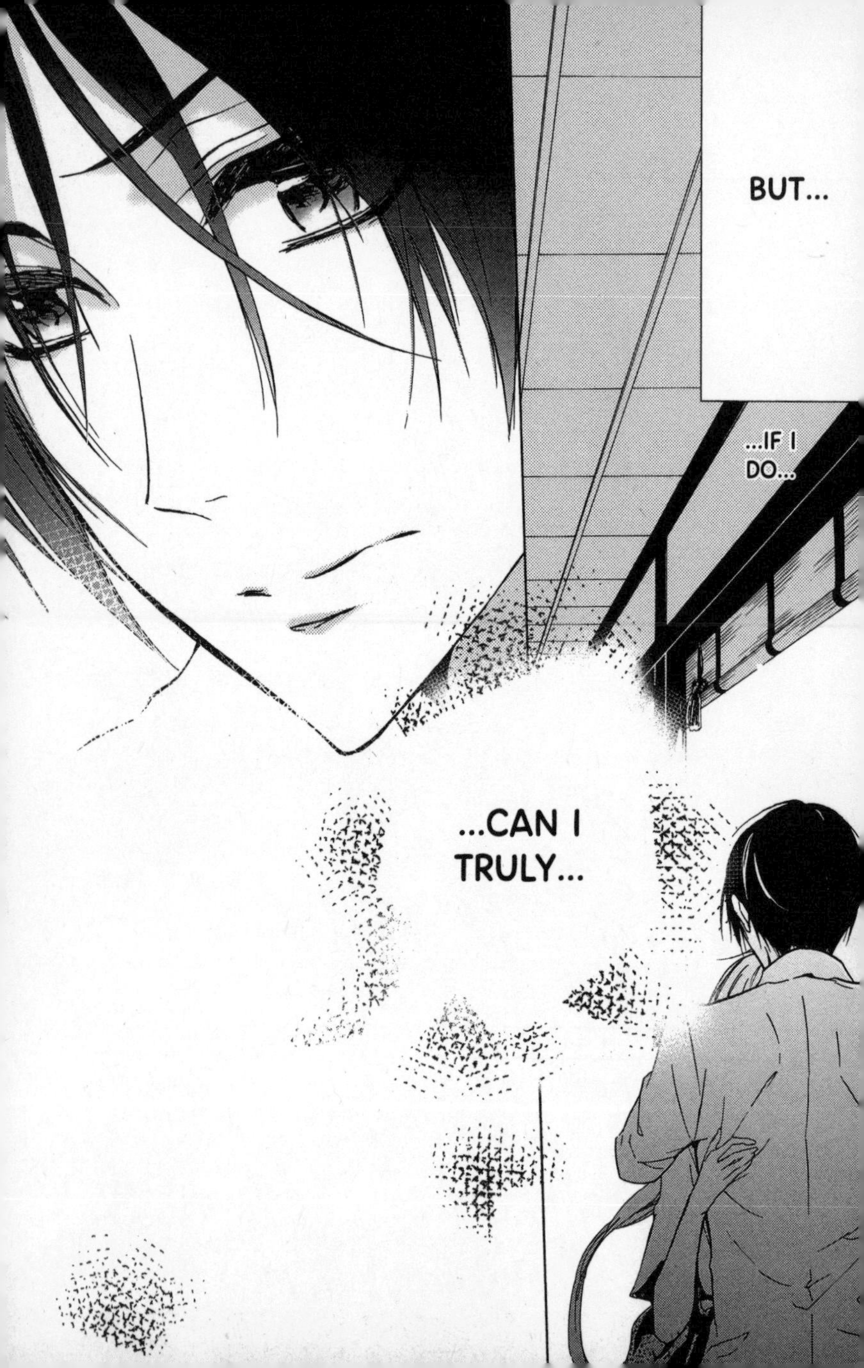
BUT...
...IF I DO...
...CAN I TRULY...

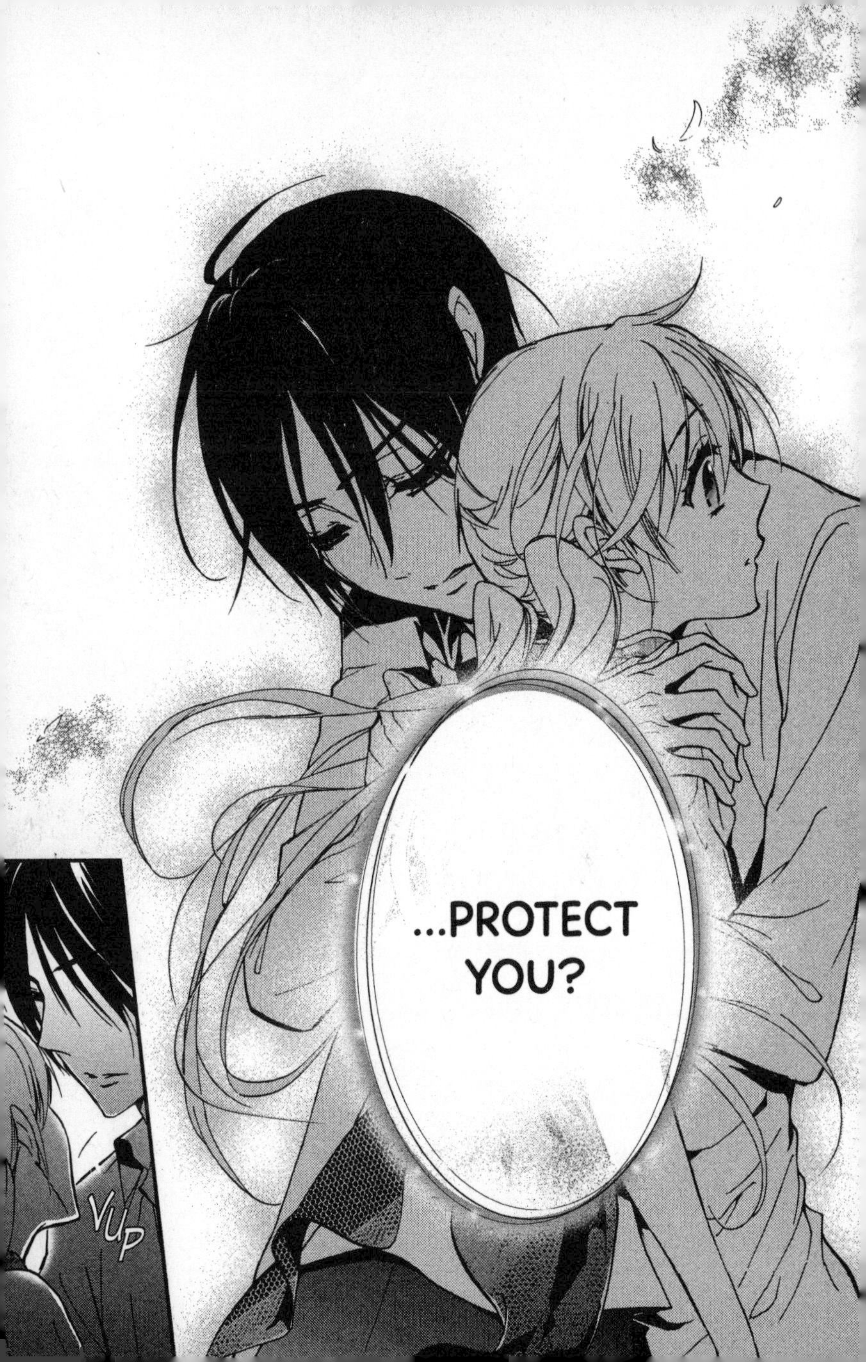
...PROTECT YOU?
VUP

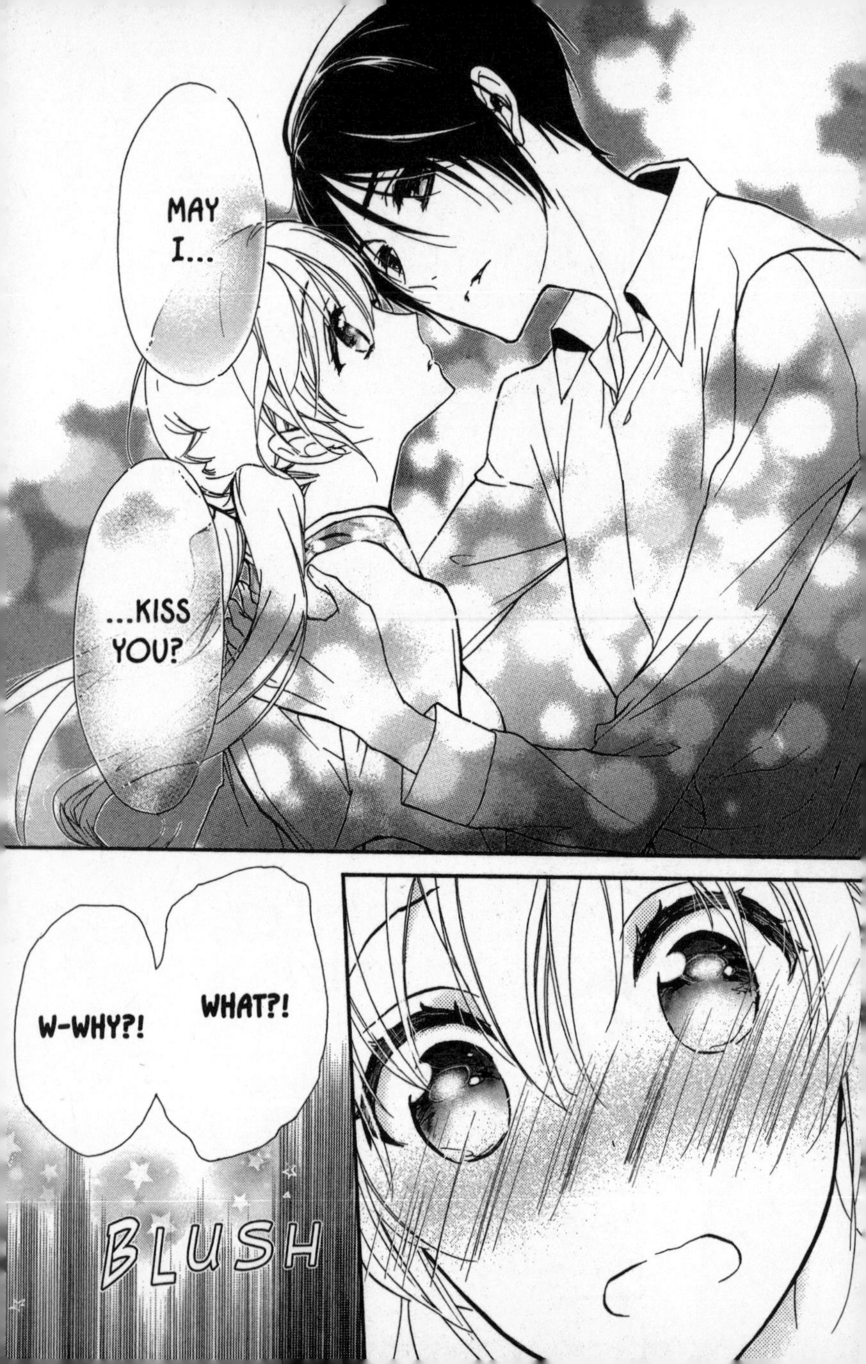
MAY I...
...KISS YOU?
WHAT?!
W-WHY?!
BLUSH

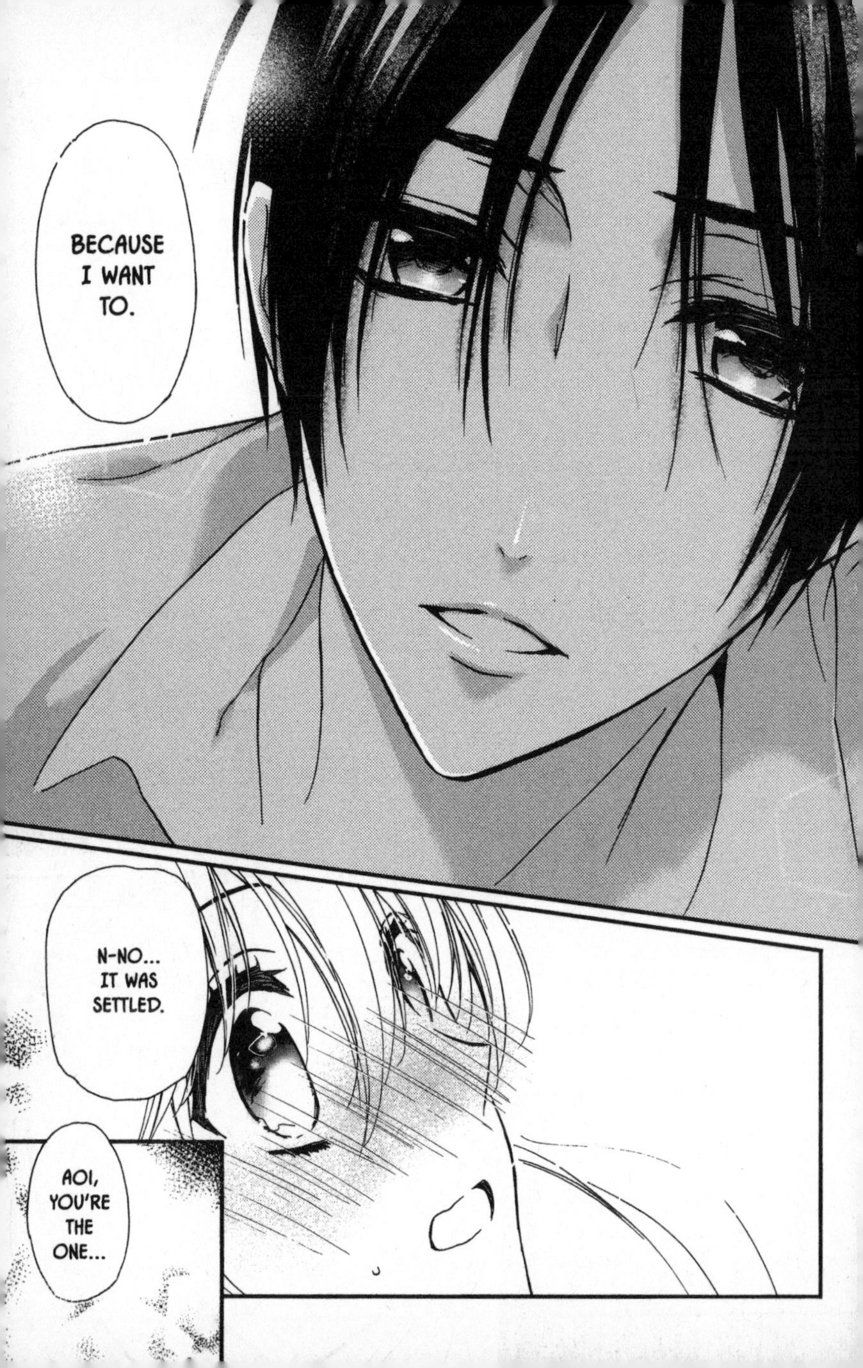
BECAUSE I WANT TO.
N-NO... IT WAS SETTLED.
AOI, YOU'RE THE ONE...

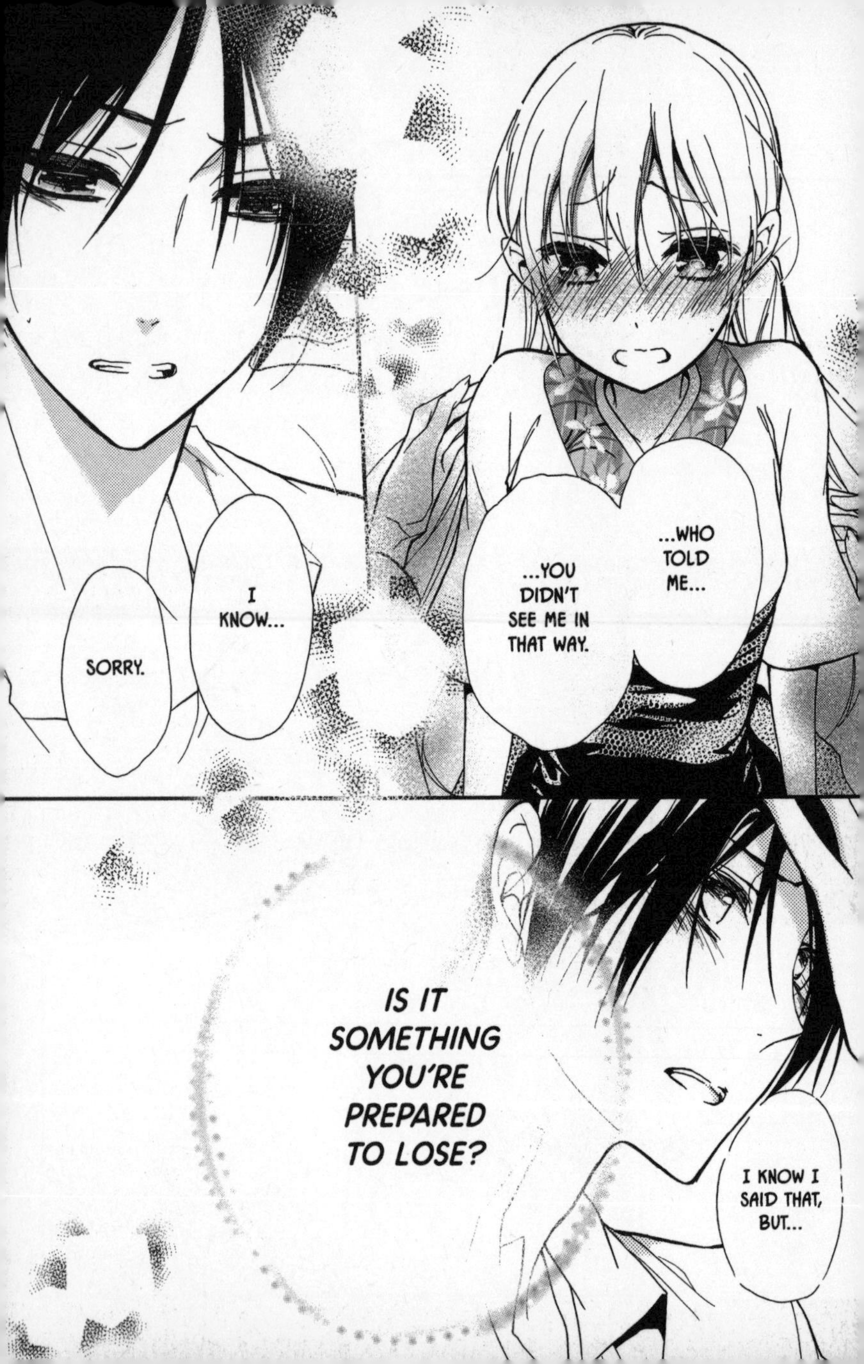
...WHO TOLD ME...
...YOU DIDN'T SEE ME IN THAT WAY.
I KNOW...
SORRY.
I KNOW I SAID THAT, BUT...
IS IT SOMETHING YOU'RE PREPARED TO LOSE?

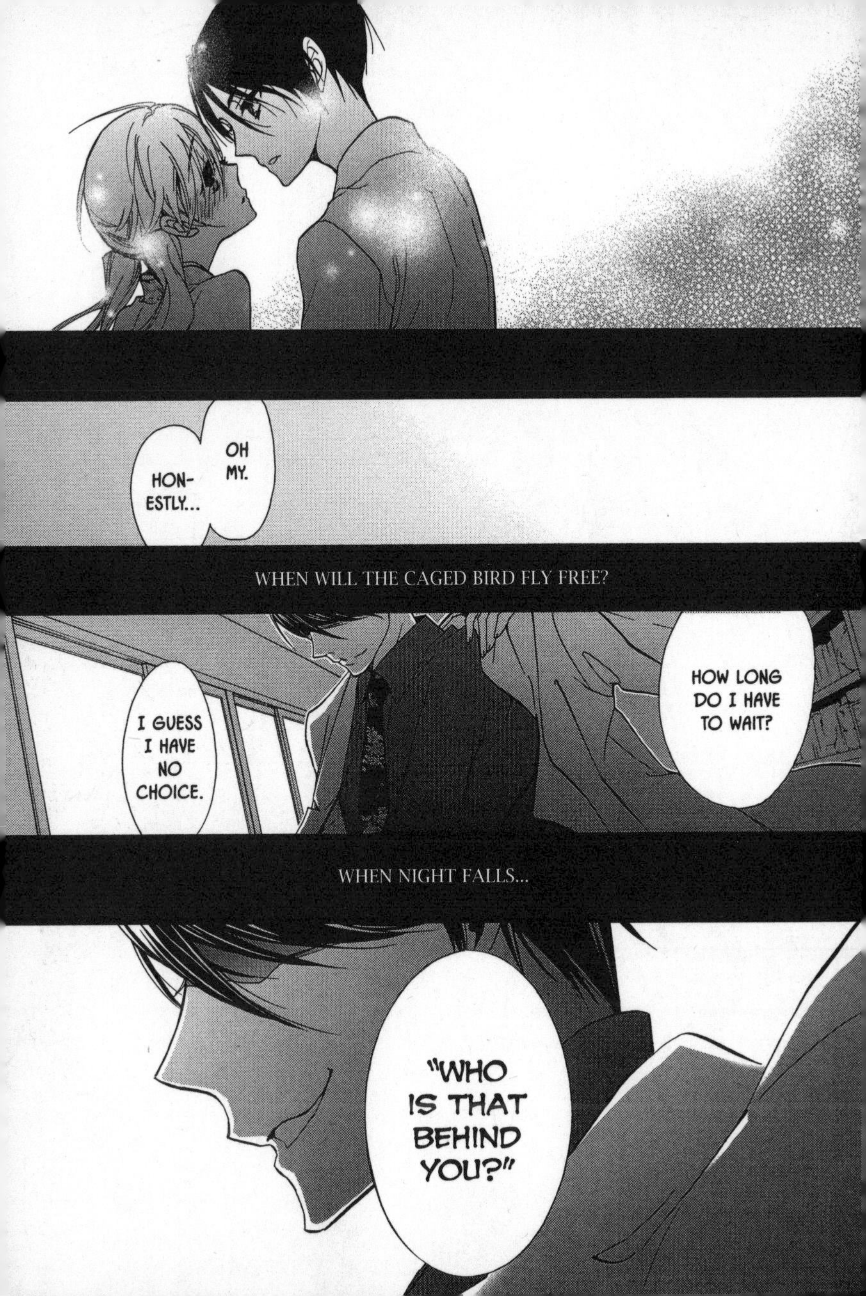
OH MY.
HONESTLY...
WHEN WILL THE CAGED BIRD FLY FREE?
HOW LONG DO I HAVE TO WAIT?
I GUESS I HAVE NO CHOICE.
WHEN NIGHT FALLS...
"WHO IS THAT BEHIND YOU?"

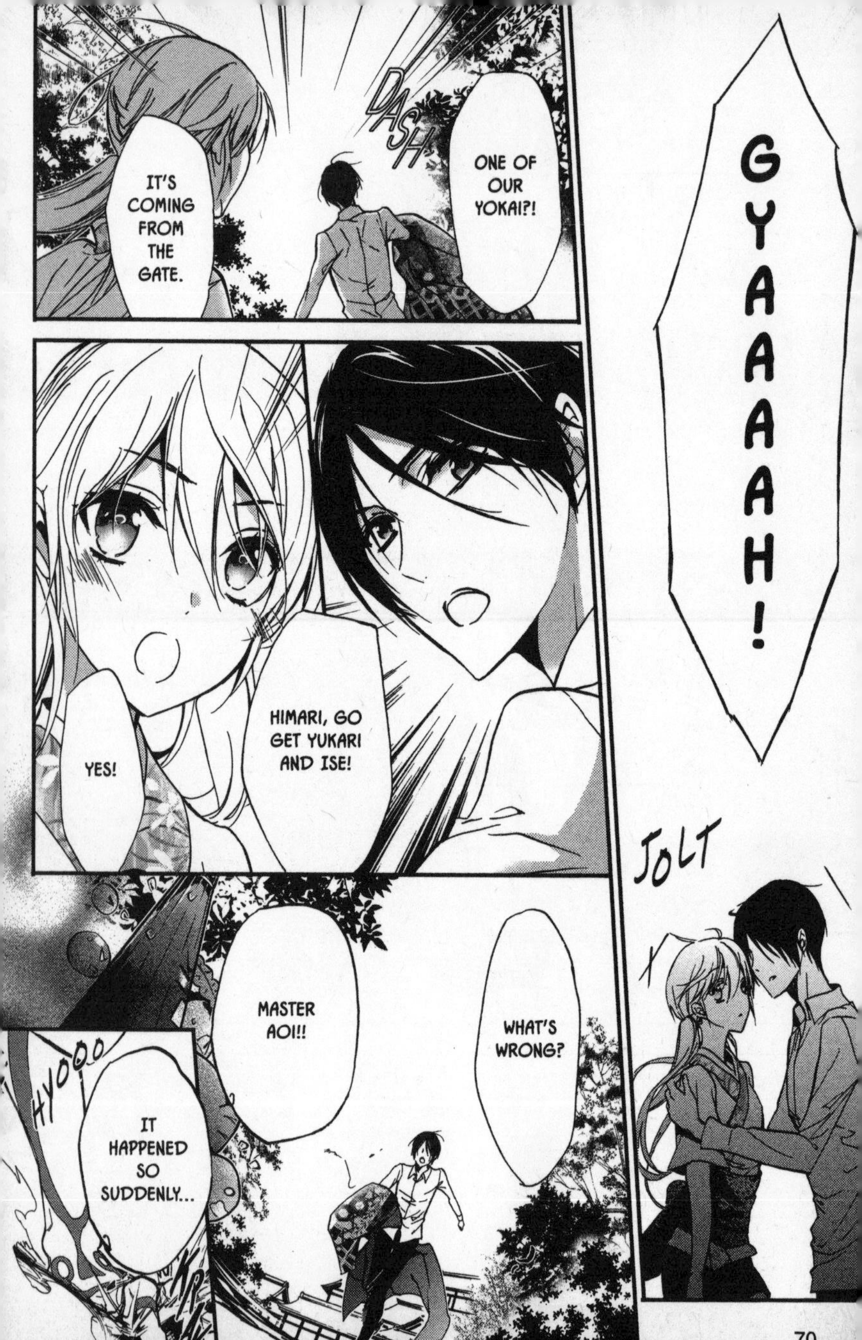
GYAAAAH!
JOLT
DASH
ONE OF OUR YOKAI?!
IT'S COMING FROM THE GATE.
HIMARI, GO GET YUKARI AND ISE!
YES!
WHAT'S WRONG?
MASTER AOI!!
HYOOO
IT HAPPENED SO SUDDENLY...

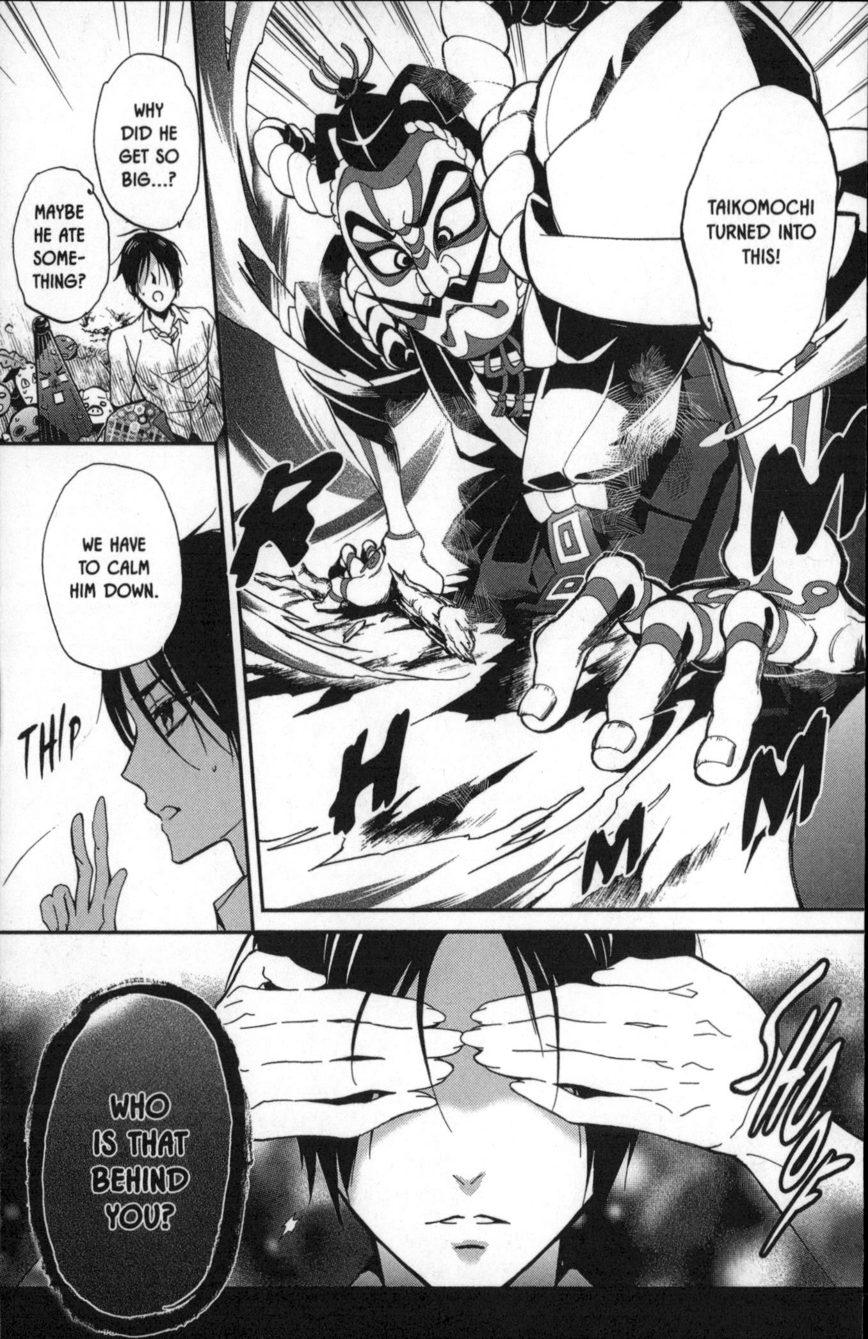
TAIKOMOCHI TURNED INTO THIS!
WHY DID HE GET SO BIG...?
MAYBE HE ATE SOMETHING?
WE HAVE TO CALM HIM DOWN.
THIP
WHO IS THAT BEHIND YOU?

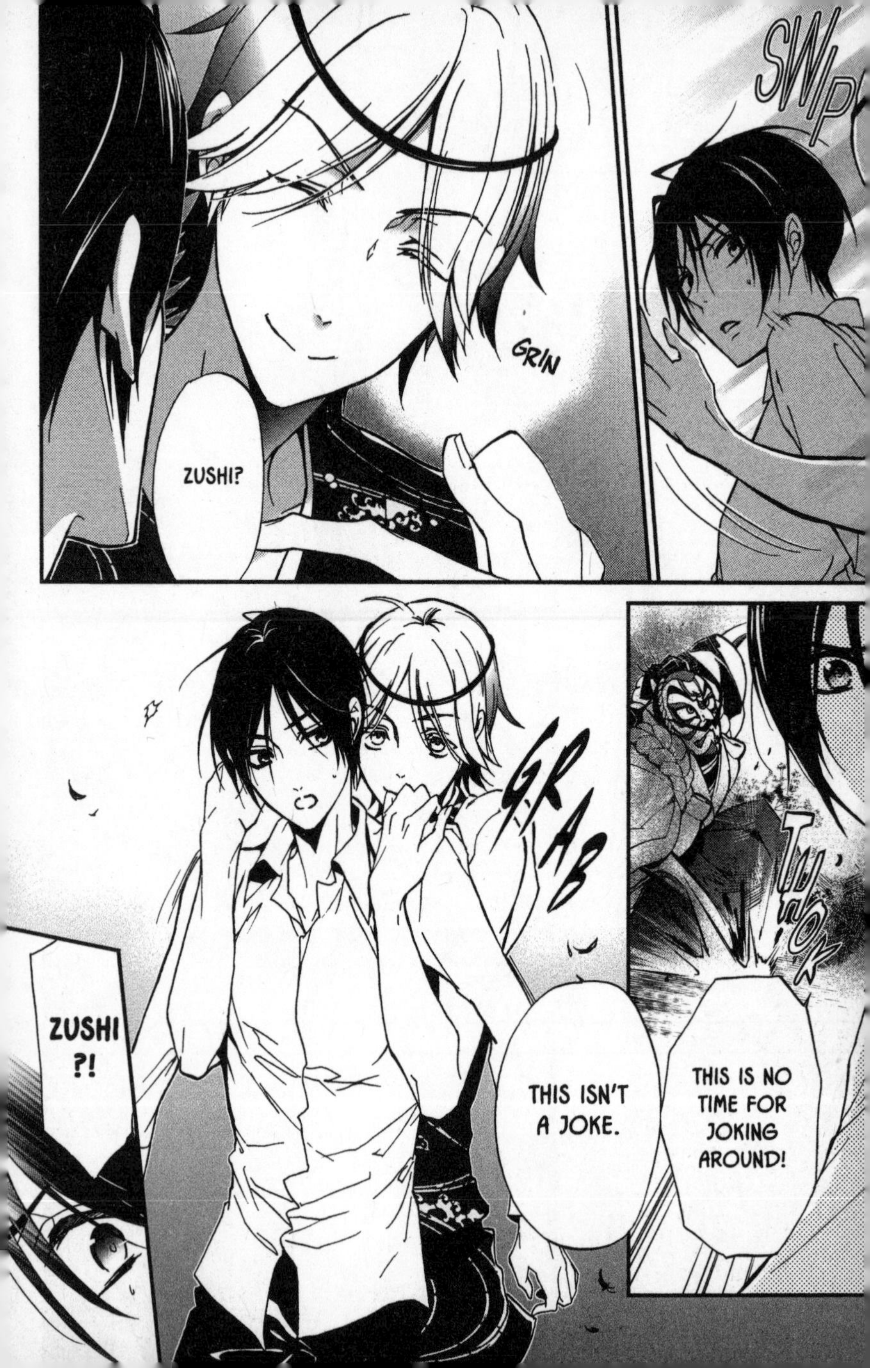
SWIP
GRIN
ZUSHI?
THOK
THIS IS NO TIME FOR JOKING AROUND!
GRAB
THIS ISN'T A JOKE.
ZUSHI ?!

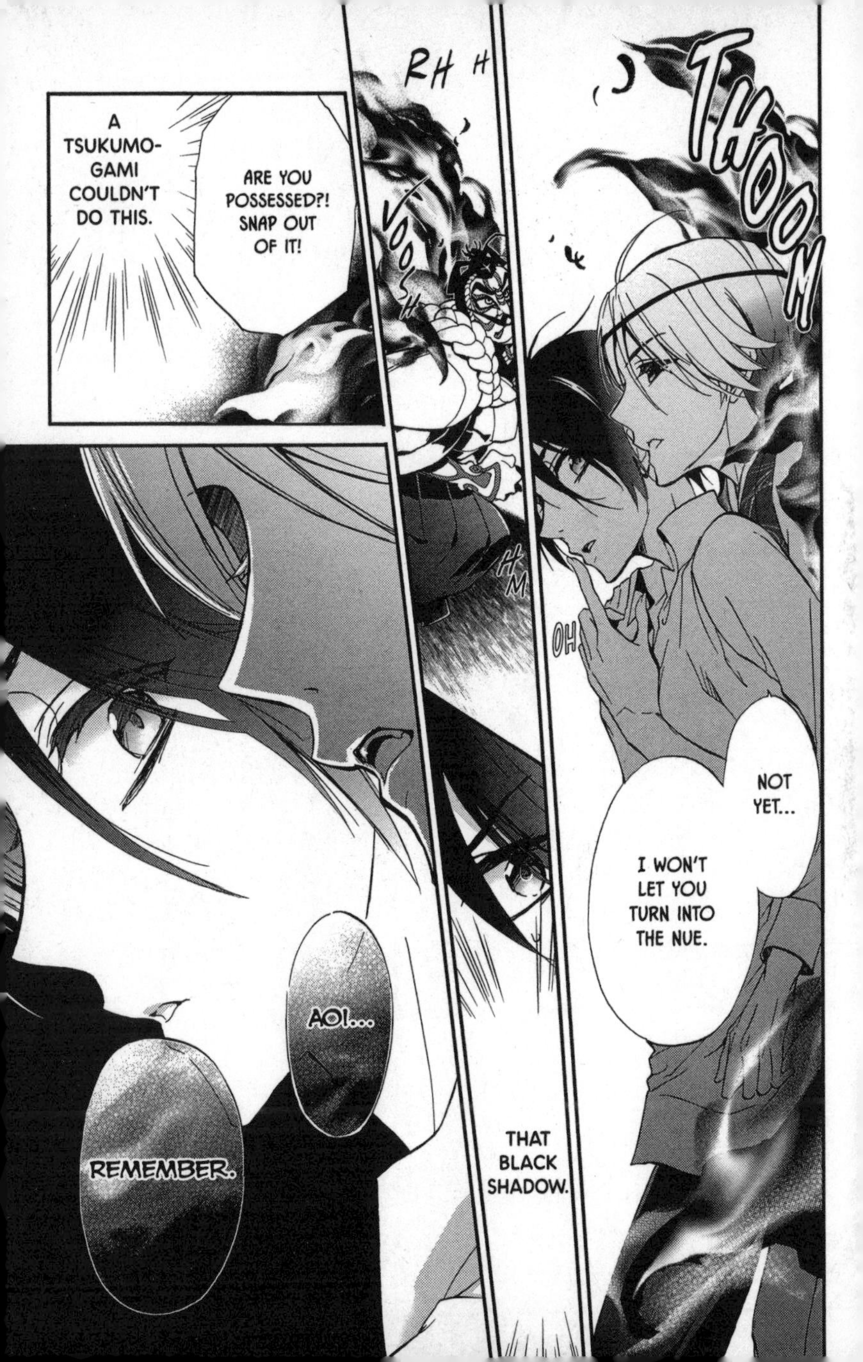
THOOOM
OH
NOT YET...
I WON'T LET YOU TURN INTO THE NUE.
RHH
VOOOSH
HM
THAT BLACK SHADOW.
ARE YOU POSSESSED?! SNAP OUT OF IT!
A TSUKUMO-GAMI COULDN'T DO THIS.
AOI...
REMEMBER.

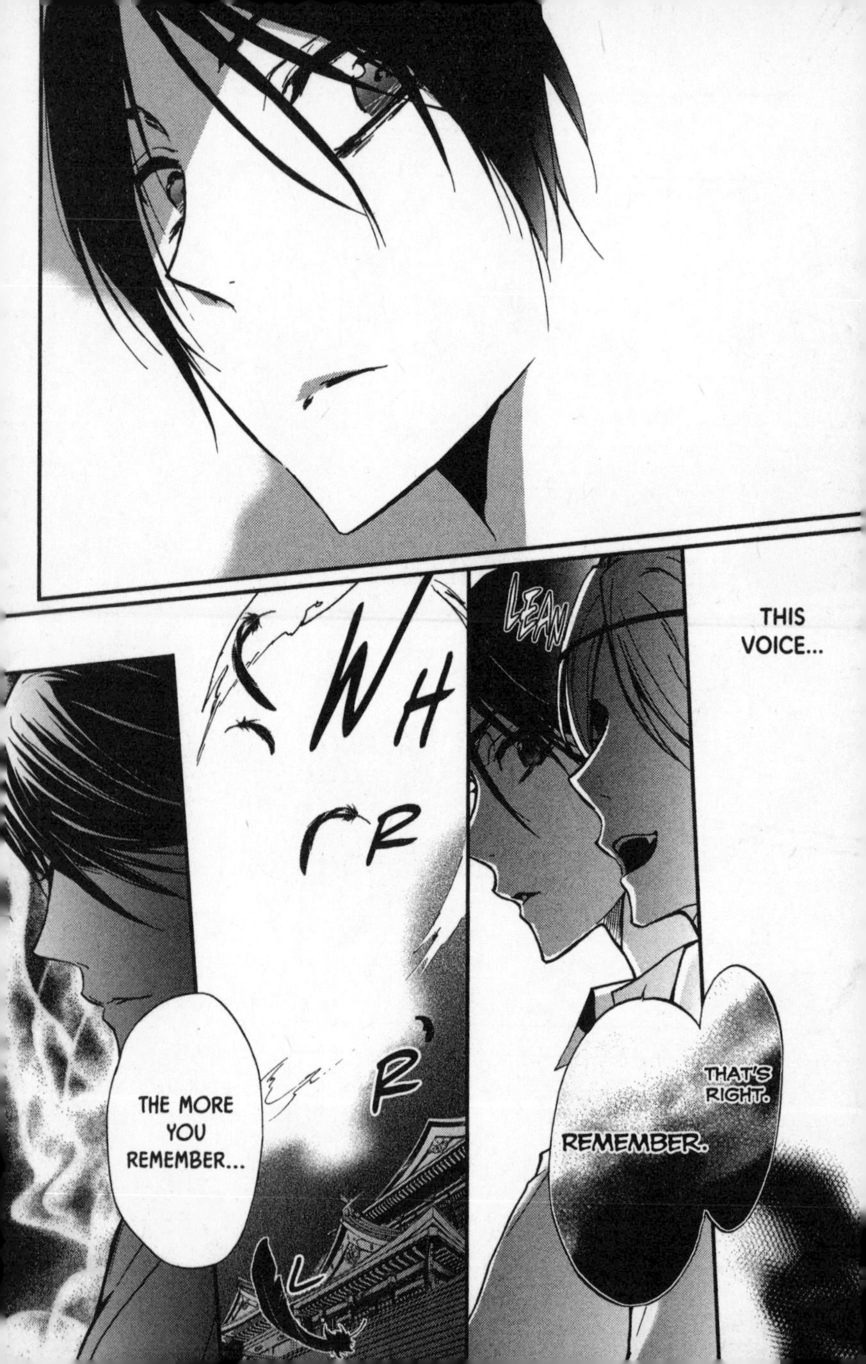
THIS VOICE...
LEAN
THAT'S RIGHT.
REMEMBER.
WHRRL
THE MORE YOU REMEMBER...

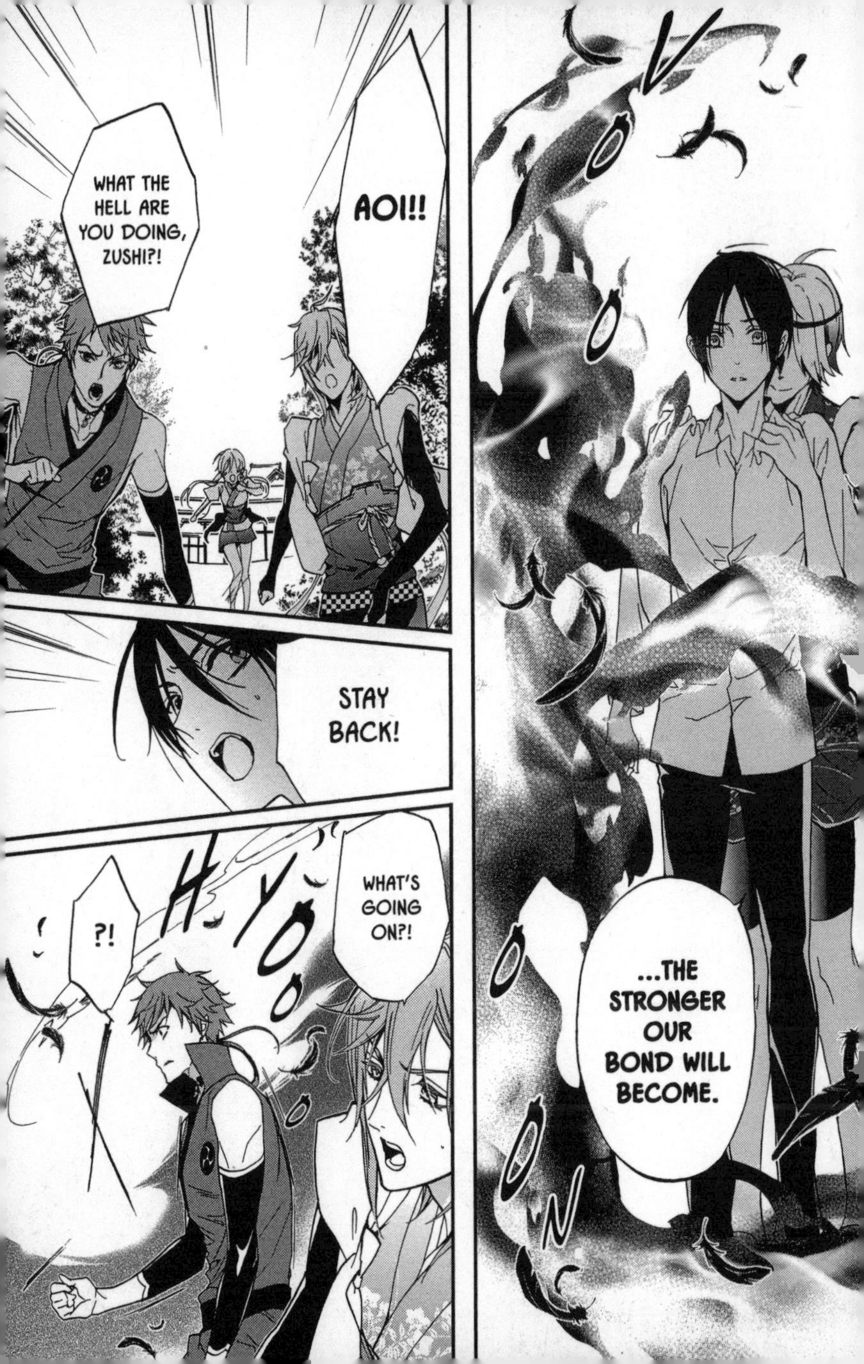
...THE STRONGER OUR BOND WILL BECOME.
AOI!!
WHAT THE HELL ARE YOU DOING, ZUSHI?!
STAY BACK!
WHAT'S GOING ON?!
?!

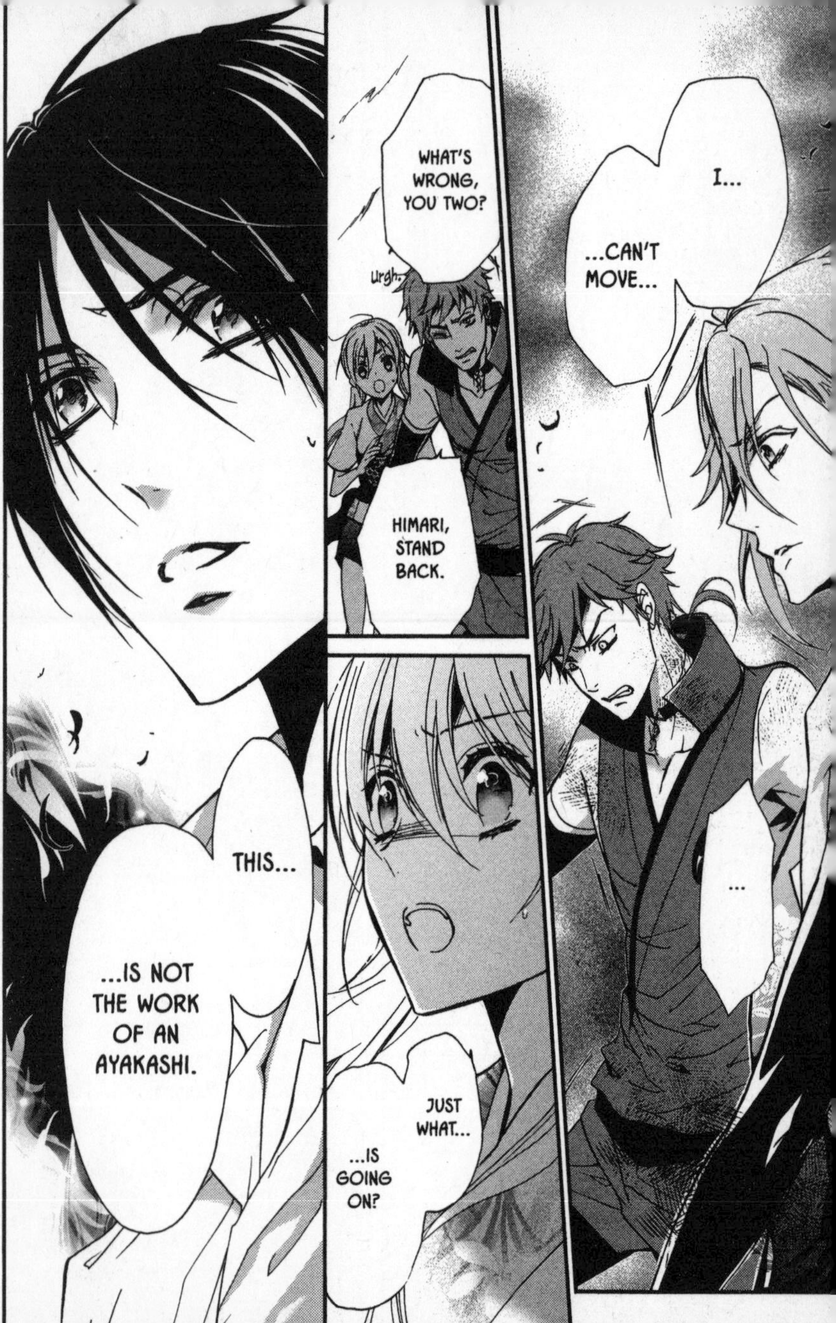
I...
...CAN'T MOVE...
...
WHAT'S WRONG, YOU TWO?
Urgh.
HIMARI, STAND BACK.
JUST WHAT...
...IS GOING ON?
THIS...
...IS NOT THE WORK OF AN AYAKASHI.

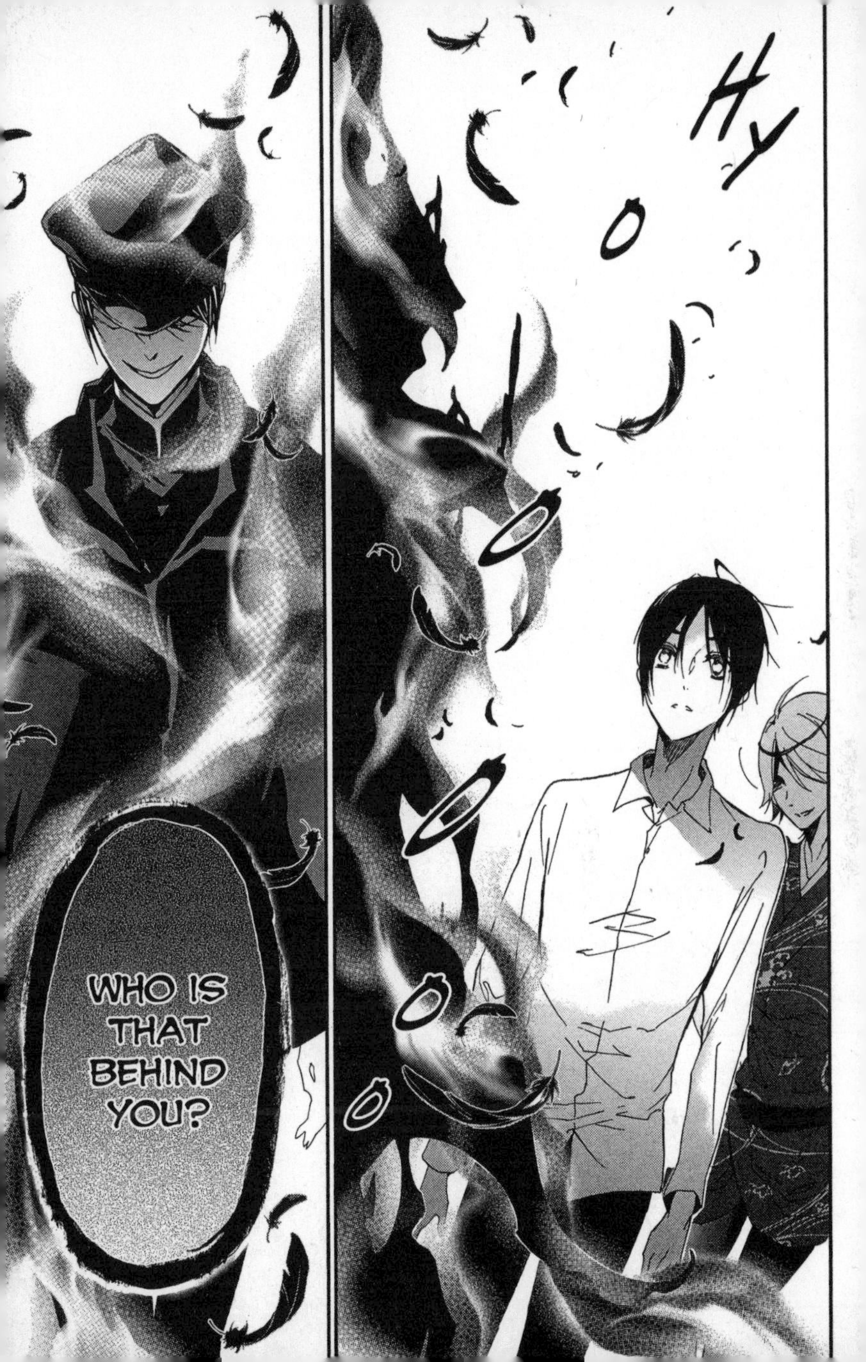
HYO
WHO IS THAT BEHIND YOU?

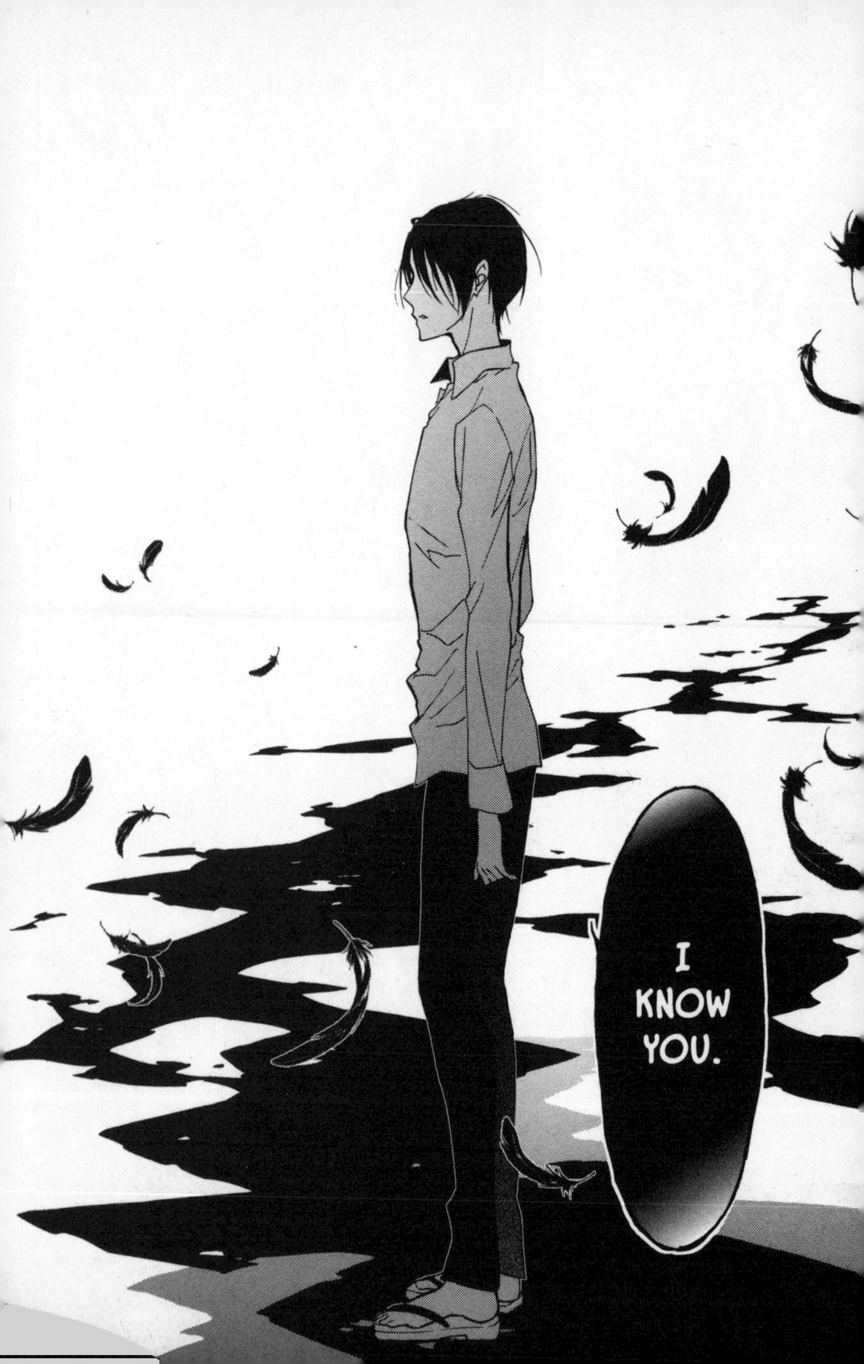
I KNOW YOU.

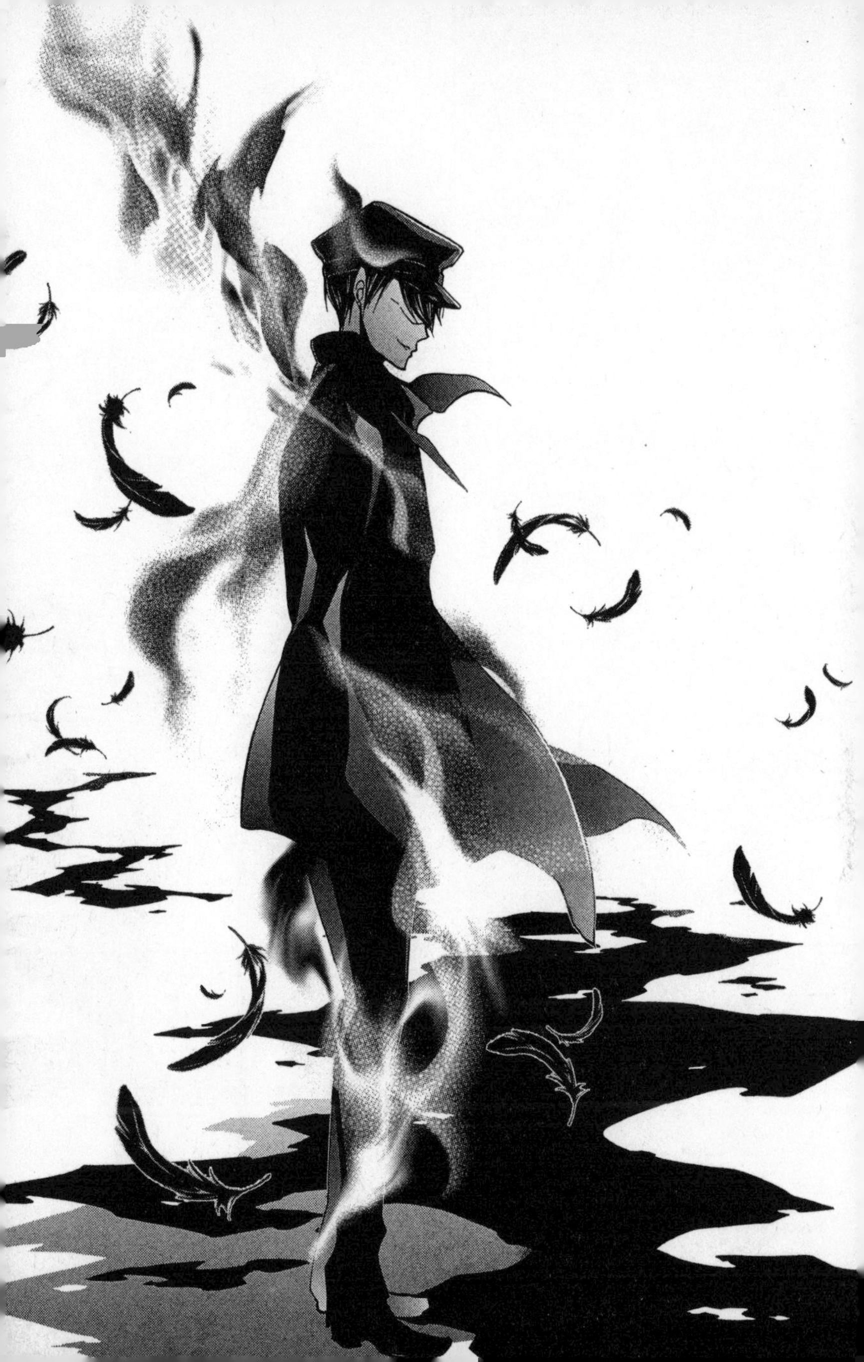

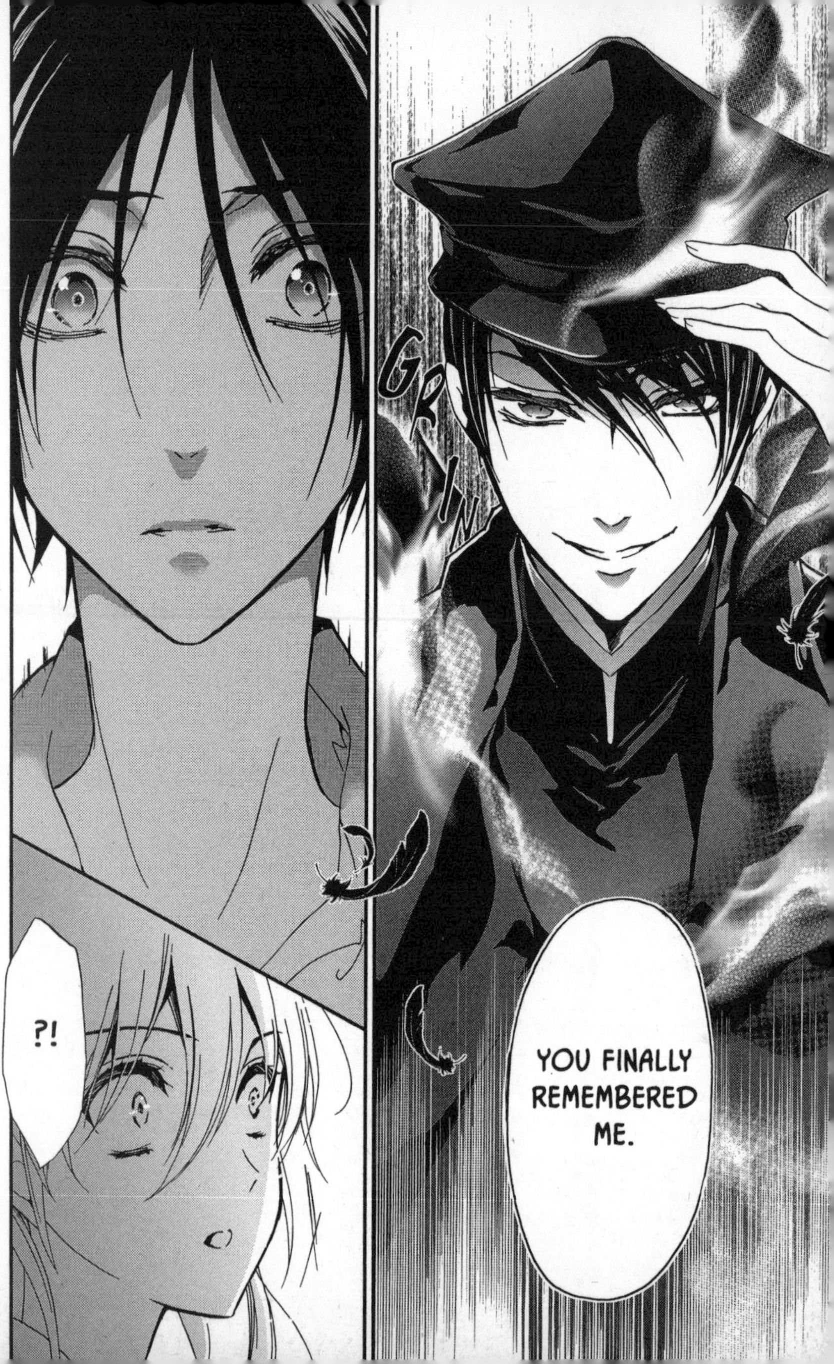
GRIN
YOU FINALLY REMEMBERED ME.
?!

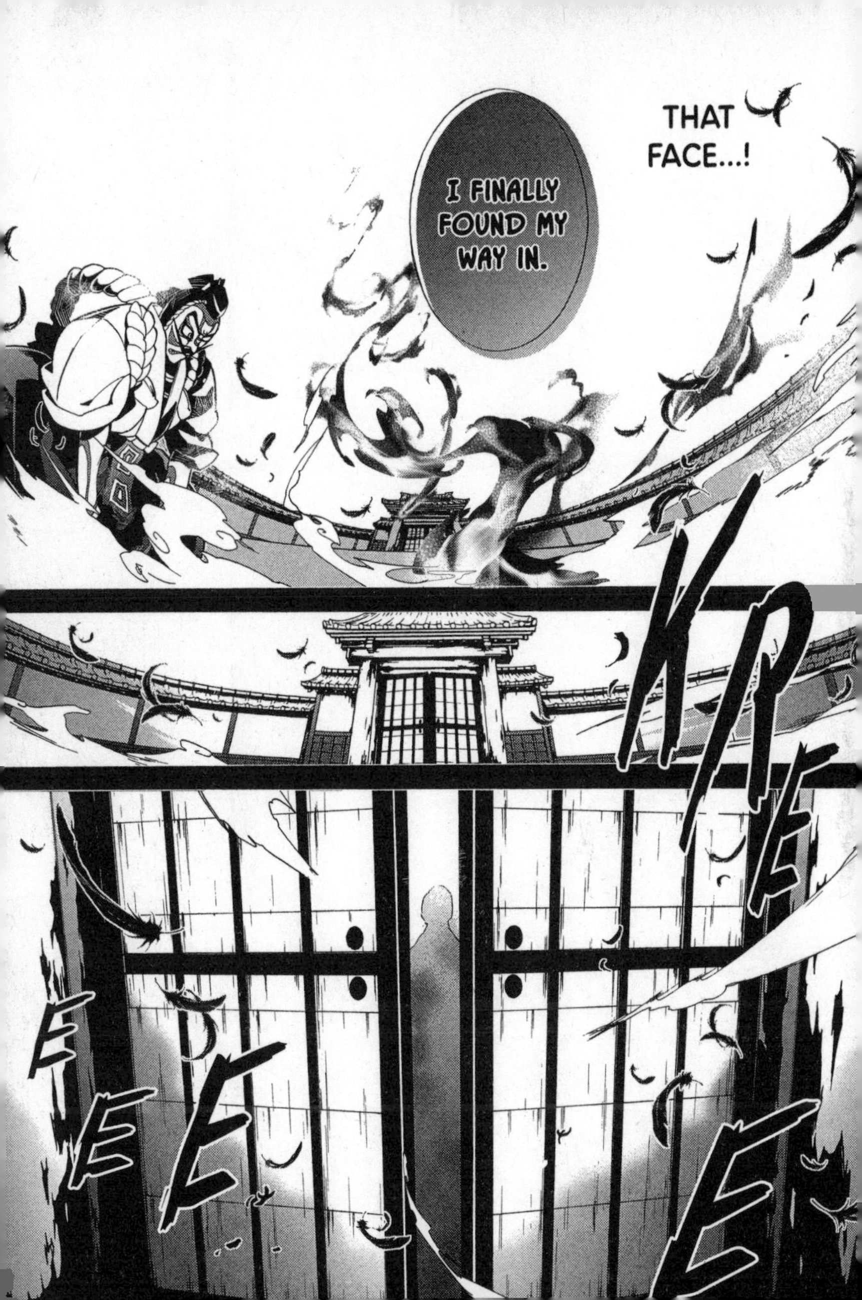
THAT FACE...!
I FINALLY FOUND MY WAY IN.
KREEEEEK

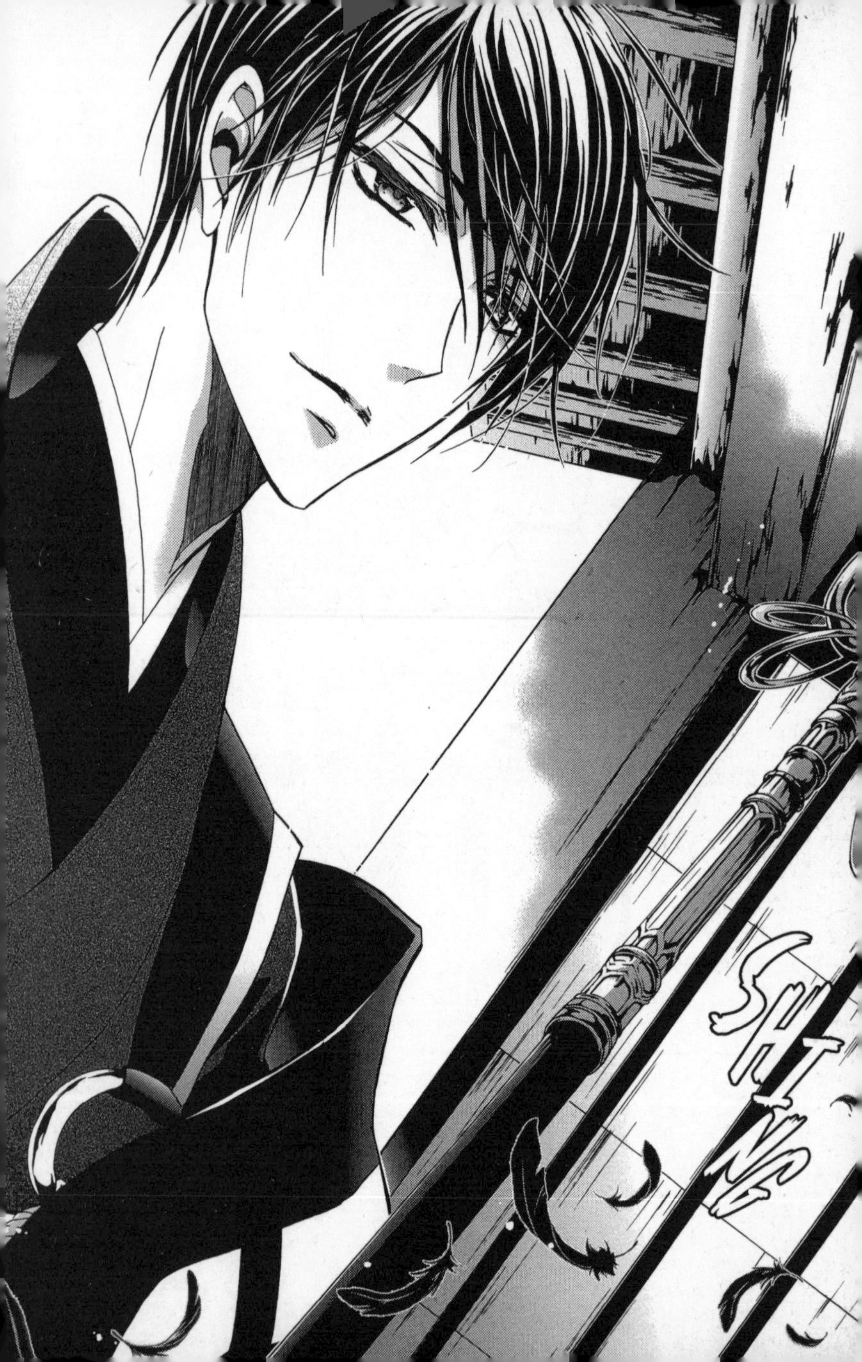
SHING

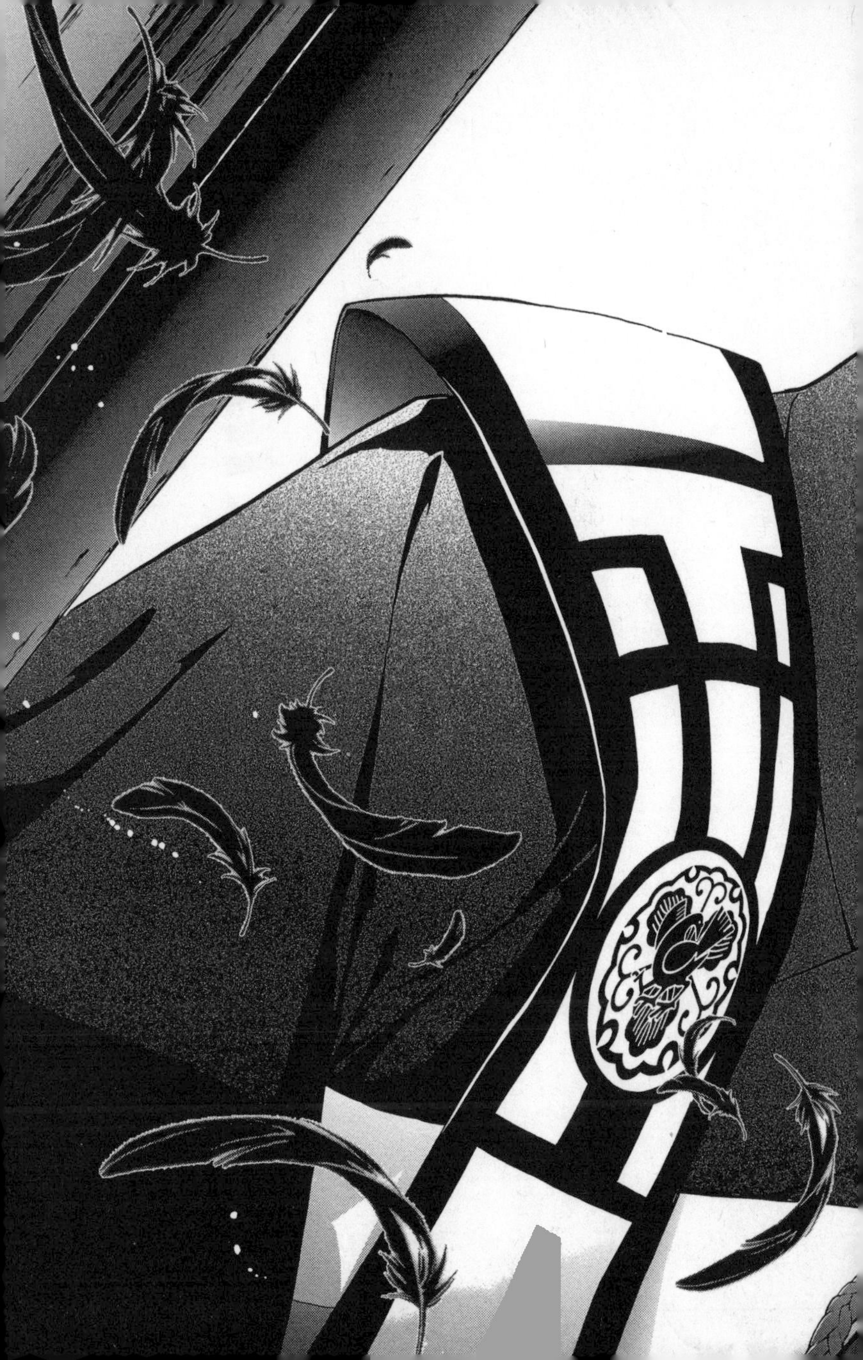

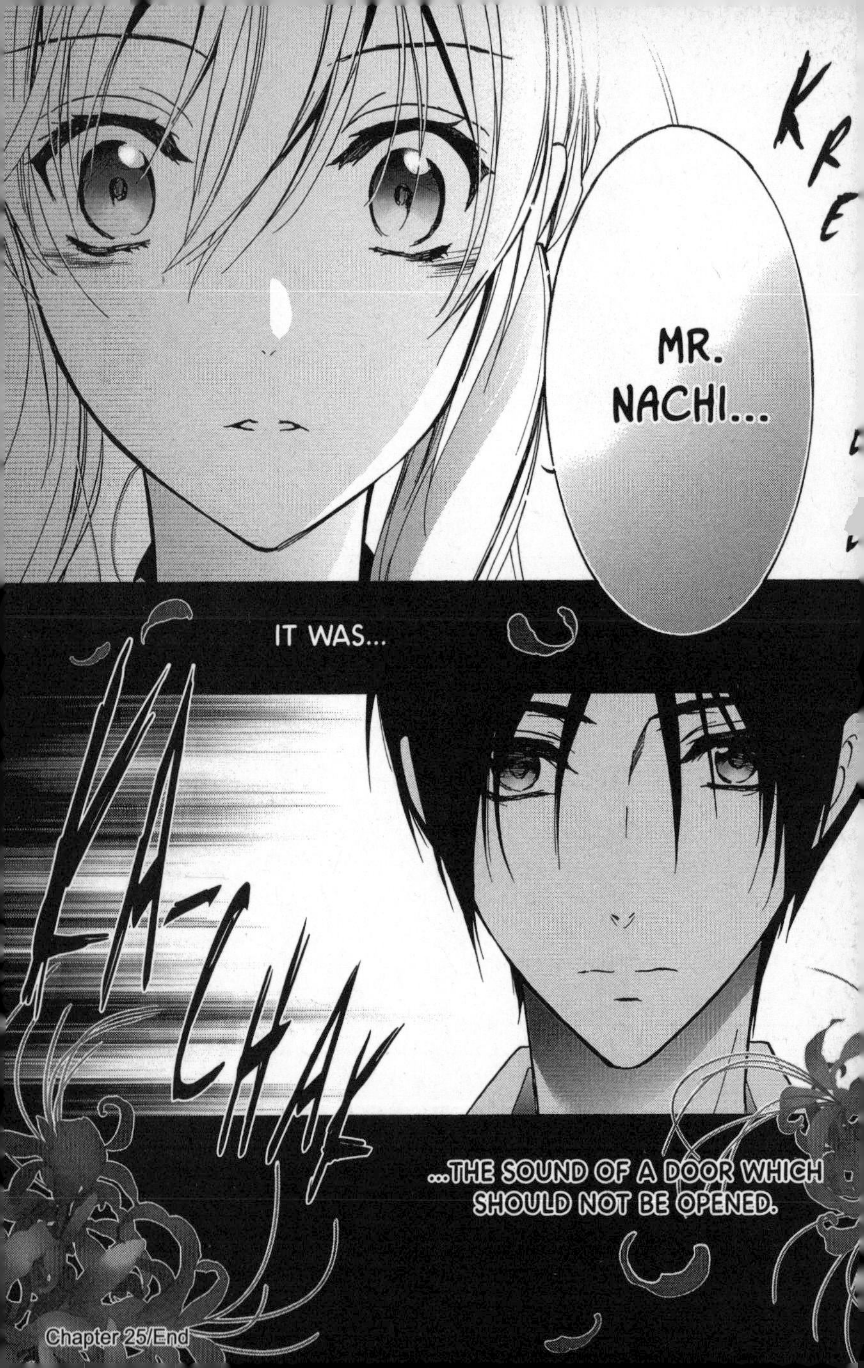
KRE
MR. NACHI...
IT WAS...
...THE SOUND OF A DOOR WHICH SHOULD NOT BE OPENED.
KA-CHAK
Chapter 25/End

the
DEMON
PRINCE
of MOMOCHI
HOUSE

The
DEMON
PRINCE
of MOMOCHI
HOUSE

CHAPTER 26

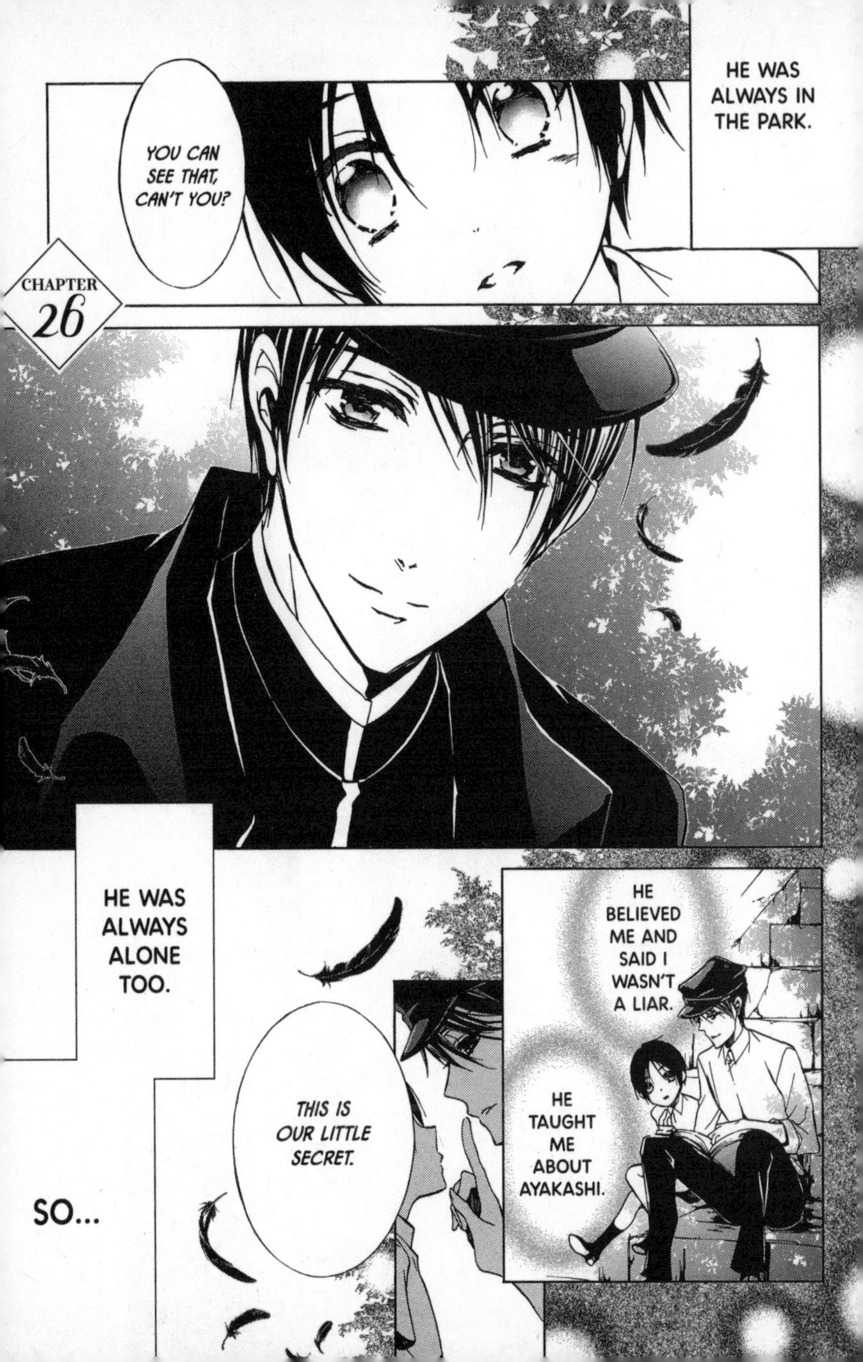
HE WAS ALWAYS IN THE PARK.
YOU CAN SEE THAT, CAN'T YOU?
HE BELIEVED ME AND SAID I WASN'T A LIAR.
HE TAUGHT ME ABOUT AYAKASHI.
THIS IS OUR LITTLE SECRET.
HE WAS ALWAYS ALONE TOO.
SO...

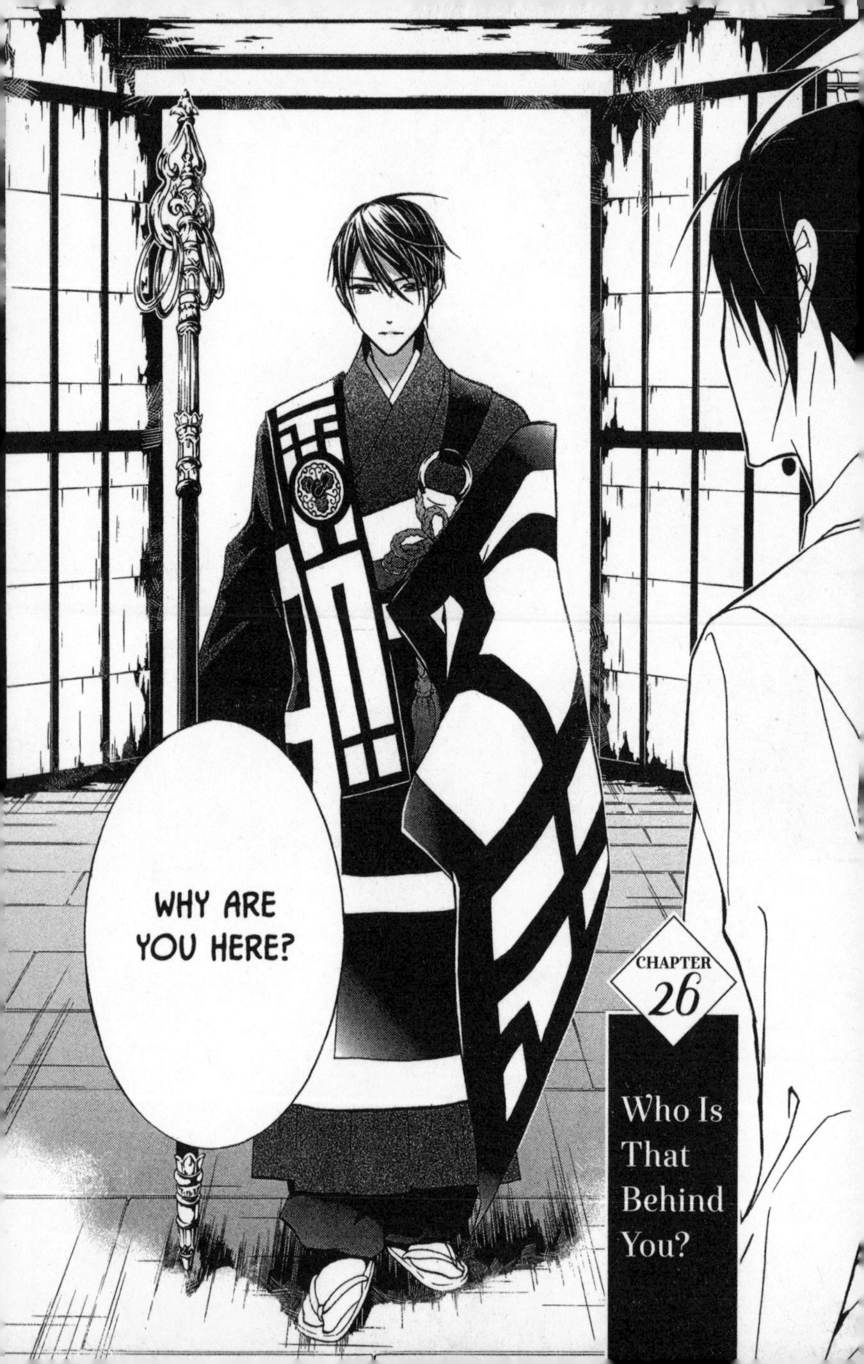
WHY ARE YOU HERE?
CHAPTER 26
Who Is That Behind You?

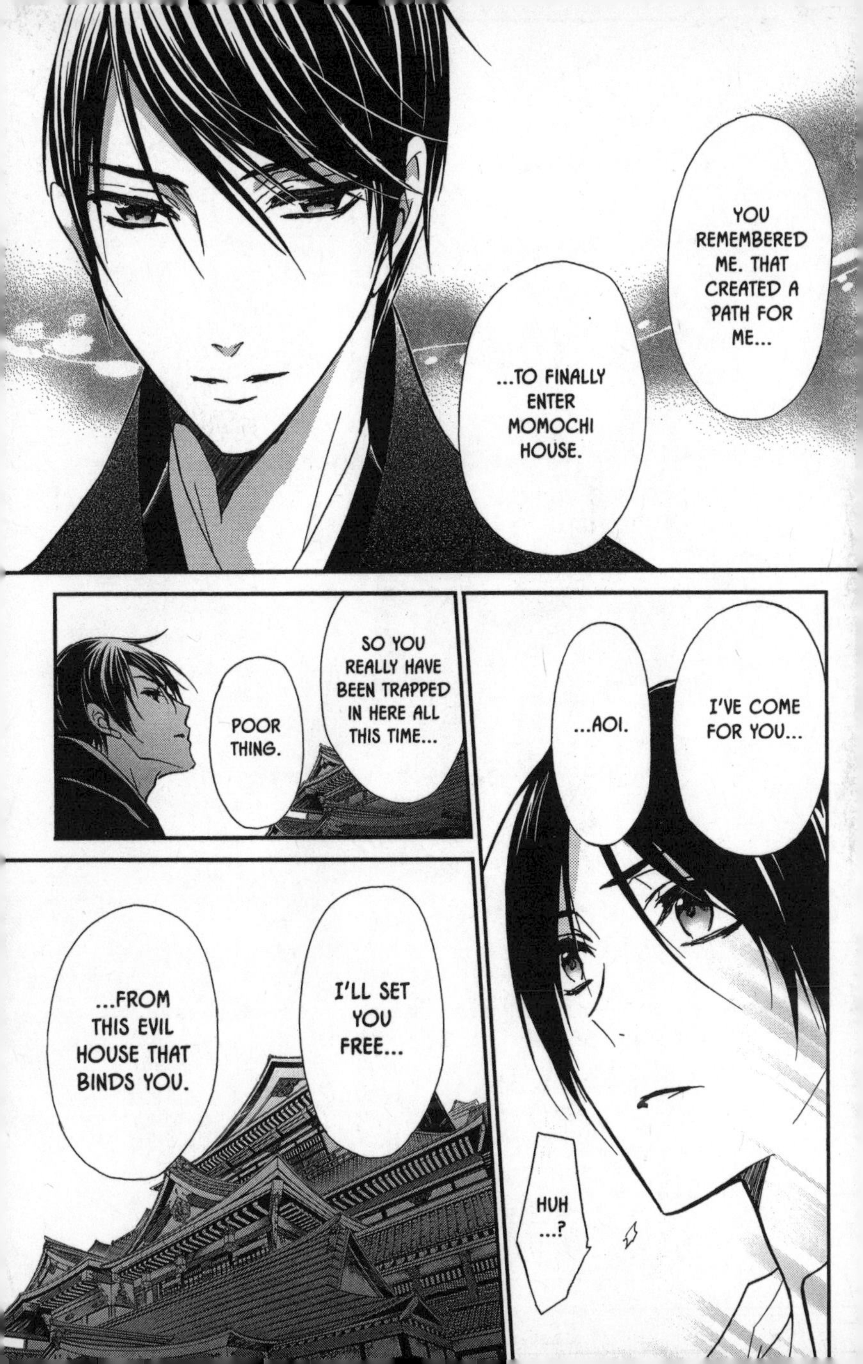
YOU REMEMBERED ME. THAT CREATED A PATH FOR ME...
...TO FINALLY ENTER MOMOCHI HOUSE.
I'VE COME FOR YOU...
...AOI.
HUH ...?
SO YOU REALLY HAVE BEEN TRAPPED IN HERE ALL THIS TIME...
POOR THING.
I'LL SET YOU FREE...
...FROM THIS EVIL HOUSE THAT BINDS YOU.

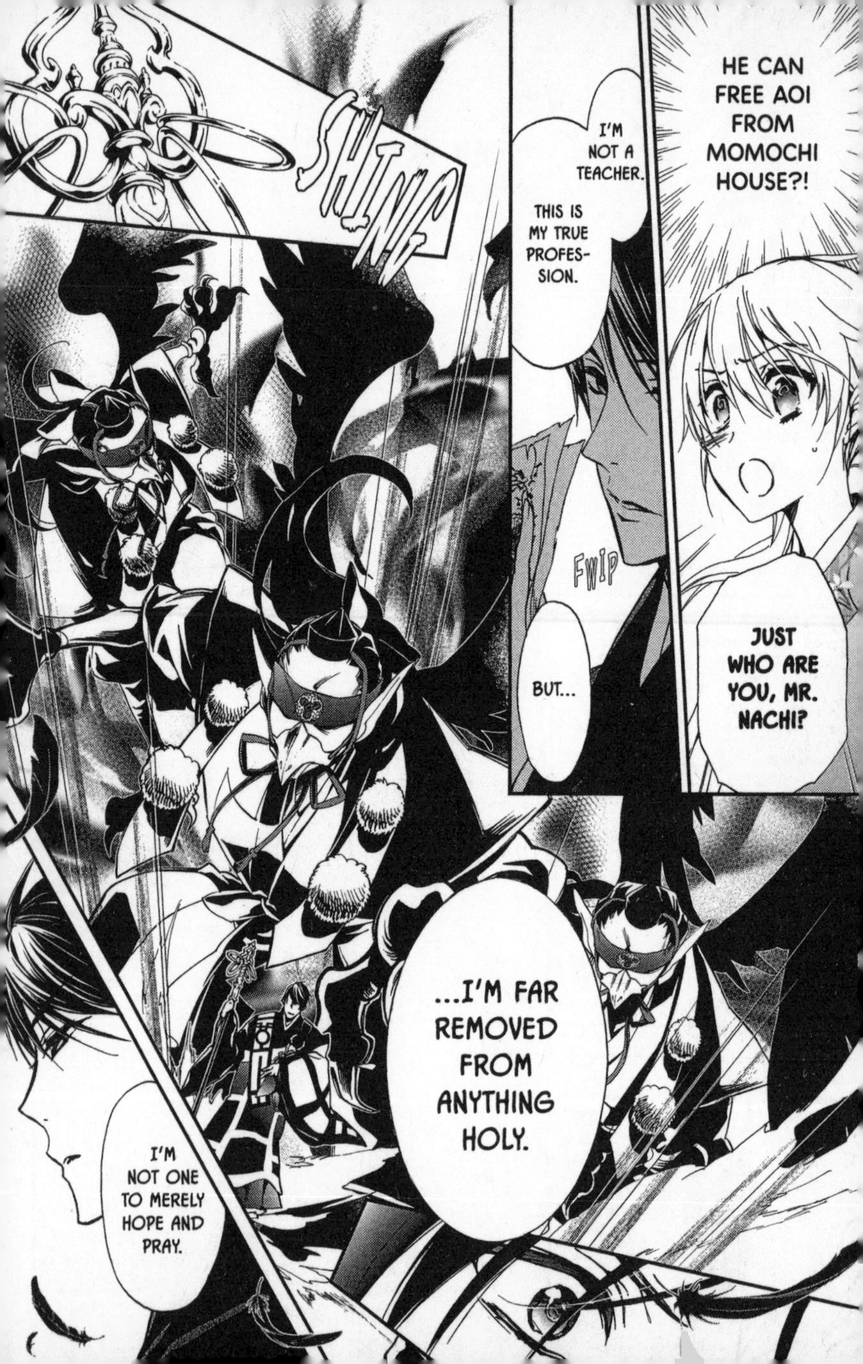
HE CAN FREE AOI FROM MOMOCHI HOUSE?!
JUST WHO ARE YOU, MR. NACHI?
I'M NOT A TEACHER.
THIS IS MY TRUE PROFES-SION.
FWIP
BUT...
SHING
...I'M FAR REMOVED FROM ANYTHING HOLY.
I'M NOT ONE TO MERELY HOPE AND PRAY.

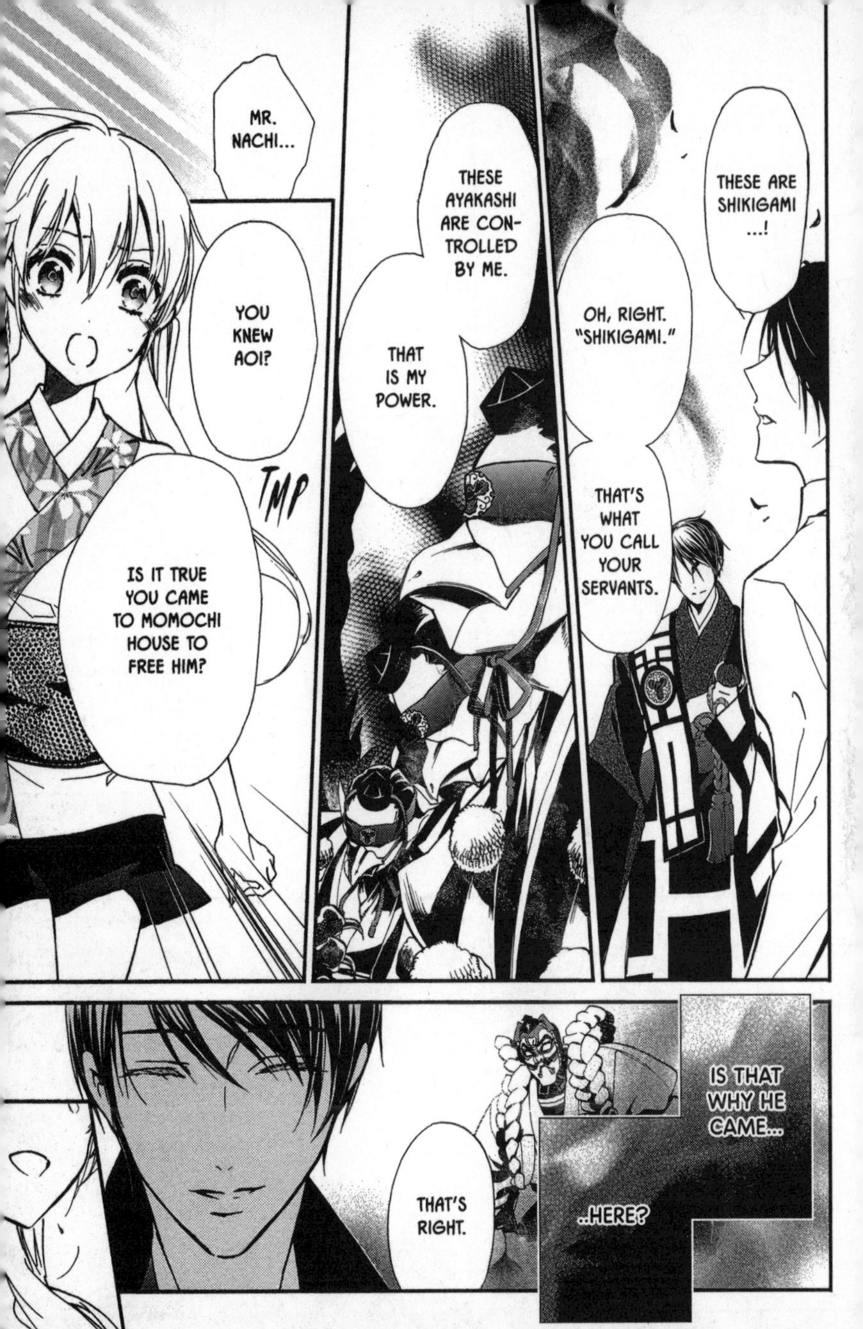
THESE ARE SHIKIGAMI ...!
OH, RIGHT. "SHIKIGAMI."
THAT'S WHAT YOU CALL YOUR SERVANTS.
THESE AYAKASHI ARE CON-TROLLED BY ME.
THAT IS MY POWER.
MR. NACHI...
YOU KNEW AOI?
TMP
IS IT TRUE YOU CAME TO MOMOCHI HOUSE TO FREE HIM?
IS THAT WHY HE CAME...
...HERE?
THAT'S RIGHT.

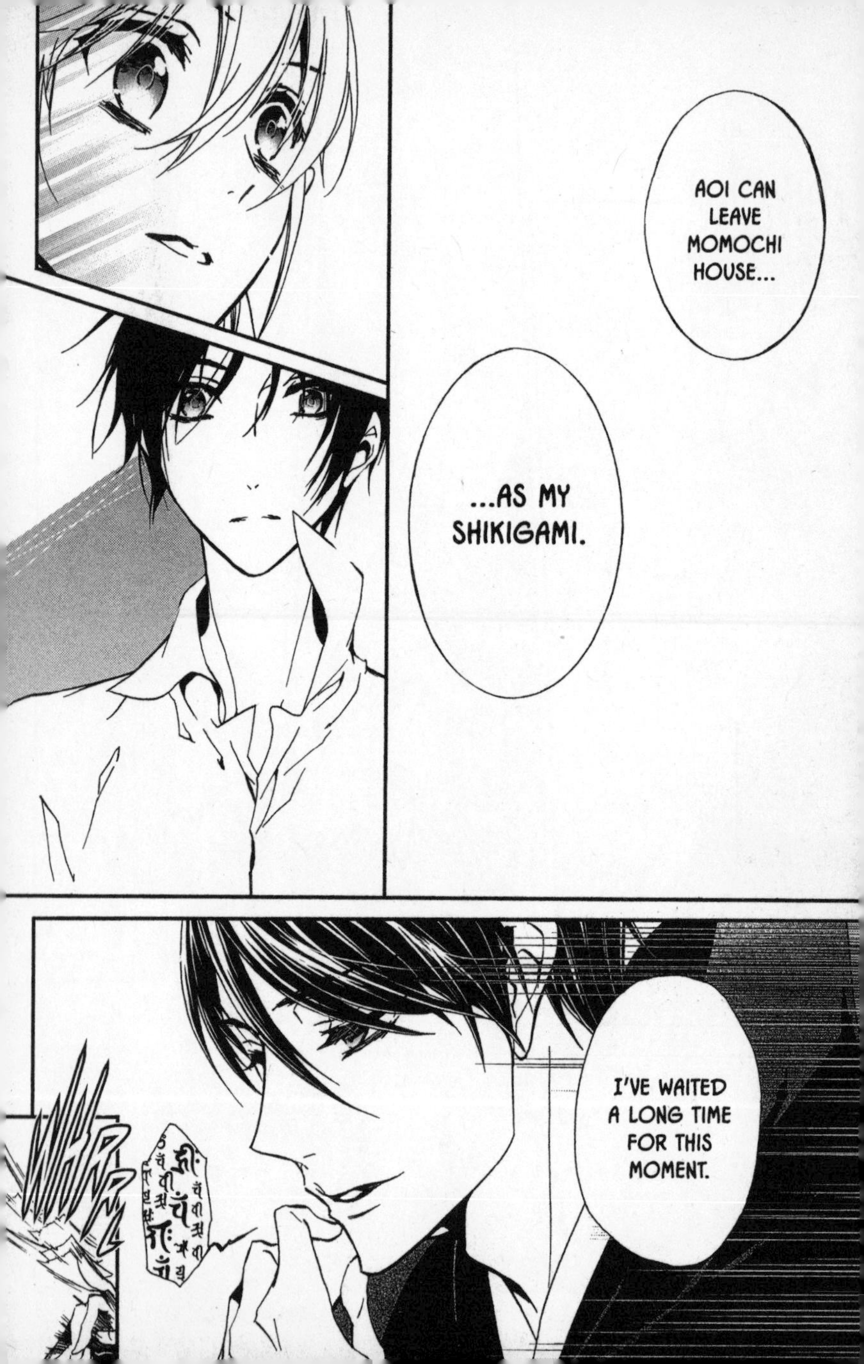
AOI CAN LEAVE MOMOCHI HOUSE...
...AS MY SHIKIGAMI.
I'VE WAITED A LONG TIME FOR THIS MOMENT.

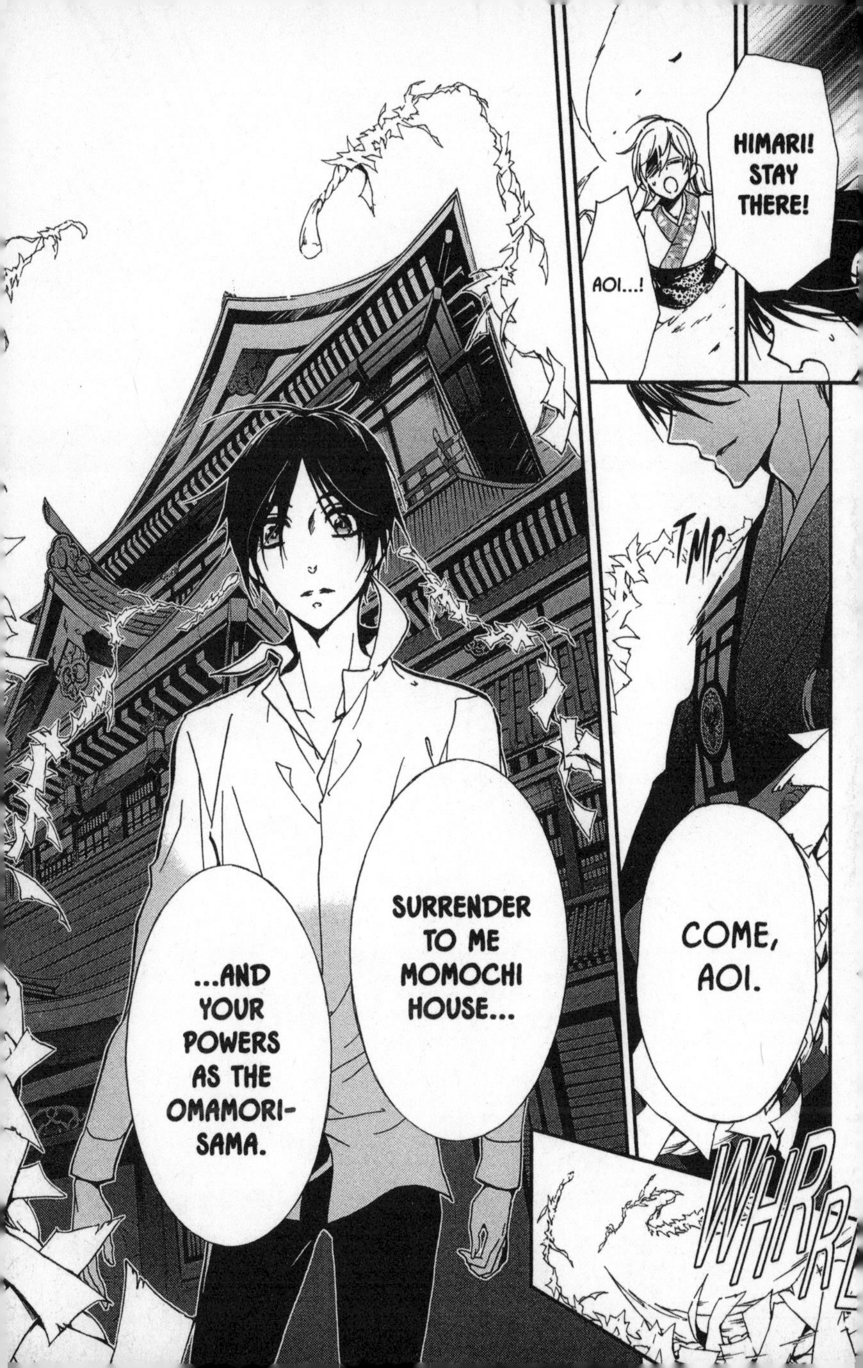
HIMARI! STAY THERE!
AOI...!
TMP
COME, AOI.
WHRRL
SURRENDER TO ME MOMOCHI HOUSE...
...AND YOUR POWERS AS THE OMAMORI-SAMA.

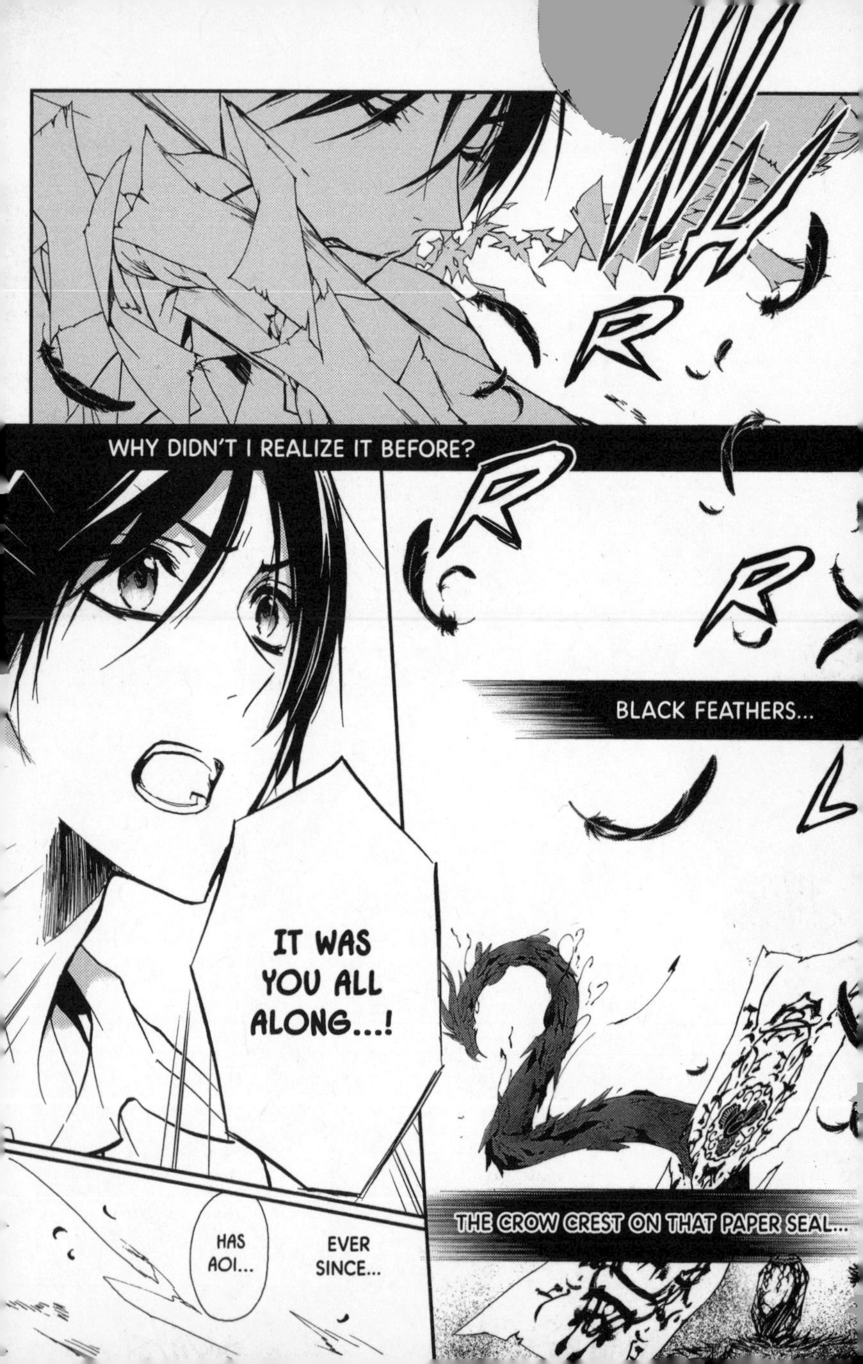
WHY DIDN'T I REALIZE IT BEFORE?
BLACK FEATHERS...
THE CROW CREST ON THAT PAPER SEAL...
IT WAS YOU ALL ALONG...!
EVER SINCE...
HAS AOI...

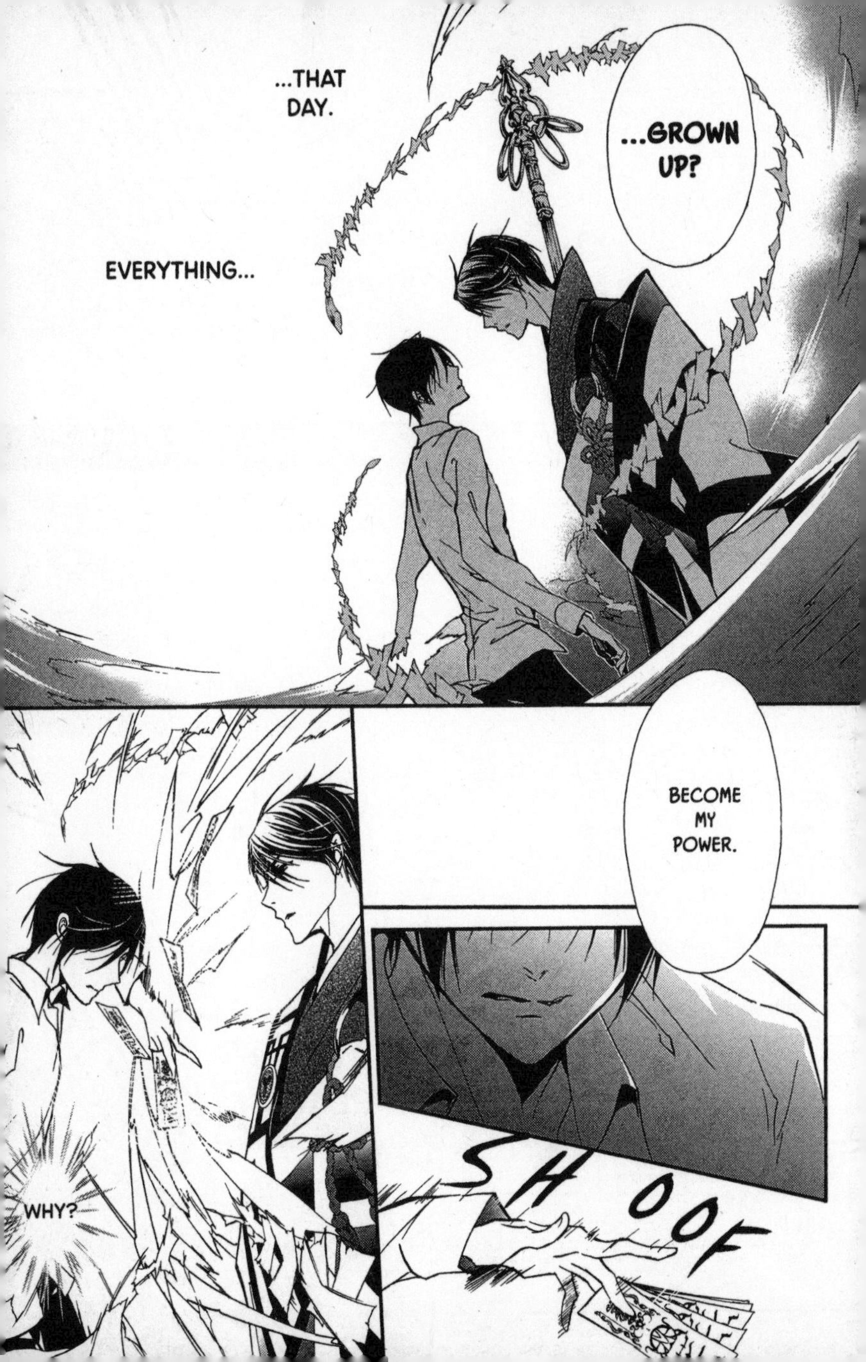
...GROWN UP?
...THAT DAY.
EVERYTHING...
BECOME MY POWER.
SHOOF
WHY?

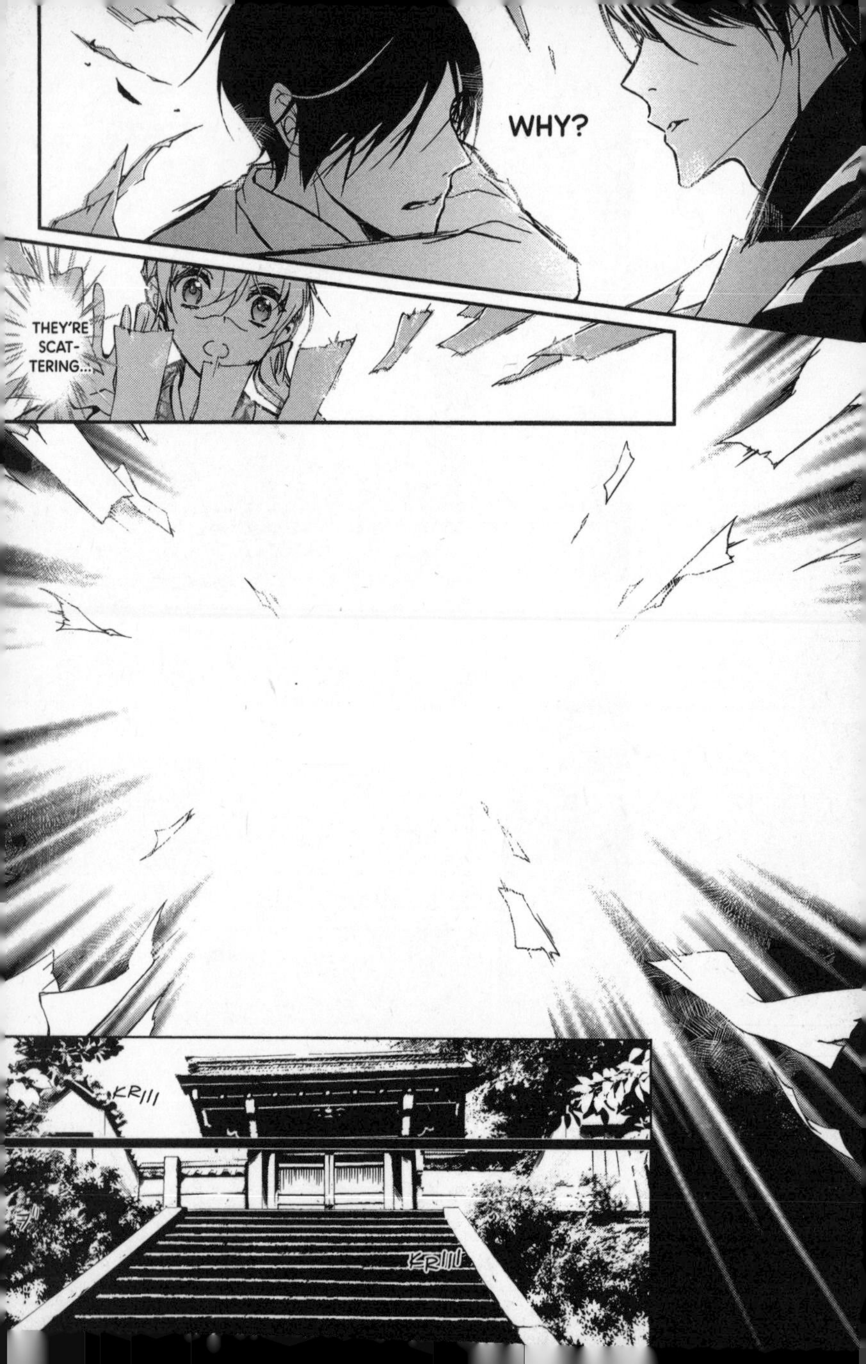
WHY?
THEY'RE SCAT-TERING...
KRIII
KRIII

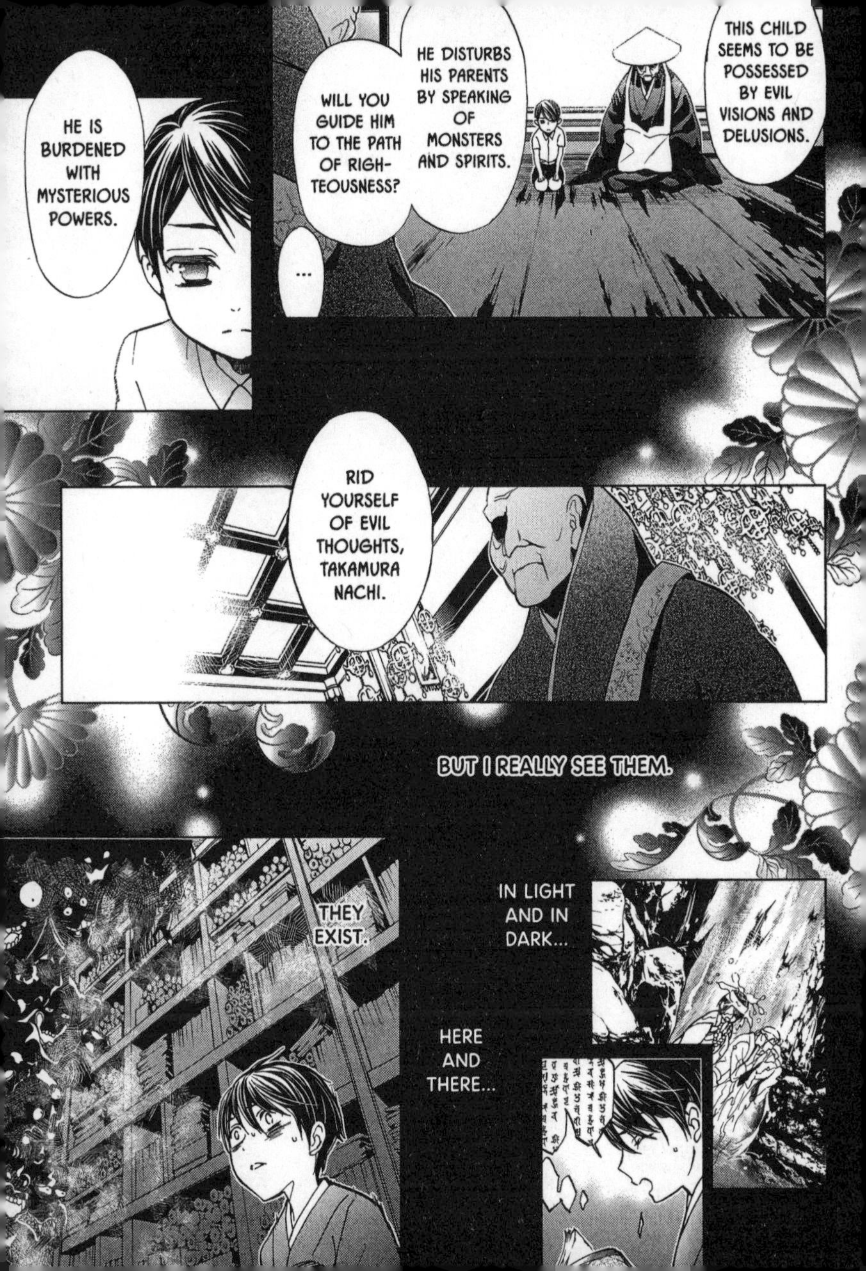
THIS CHILD SEEMS TO BE POSSESSED BY EVIL VISIONS AND DELUSIONS.
HE DISTURBS HIS PARENTS BY SPEAKING OF MONSTERS AND SPIRITS.
WILL YOU GUIDE HIM TO THE PATH OF RIGH-TEOUSNESS?
...
HE IS BURDENED WITH MYSTERIOUS POWERS.
RID YOURSELF OF EVIL THOUGHTS, TAKAMURA NACHI.
BUT I REALLY SEE THEM.
IN LIGHT AND IN DARK...
HERE AND THERE...
THEY EXIST.

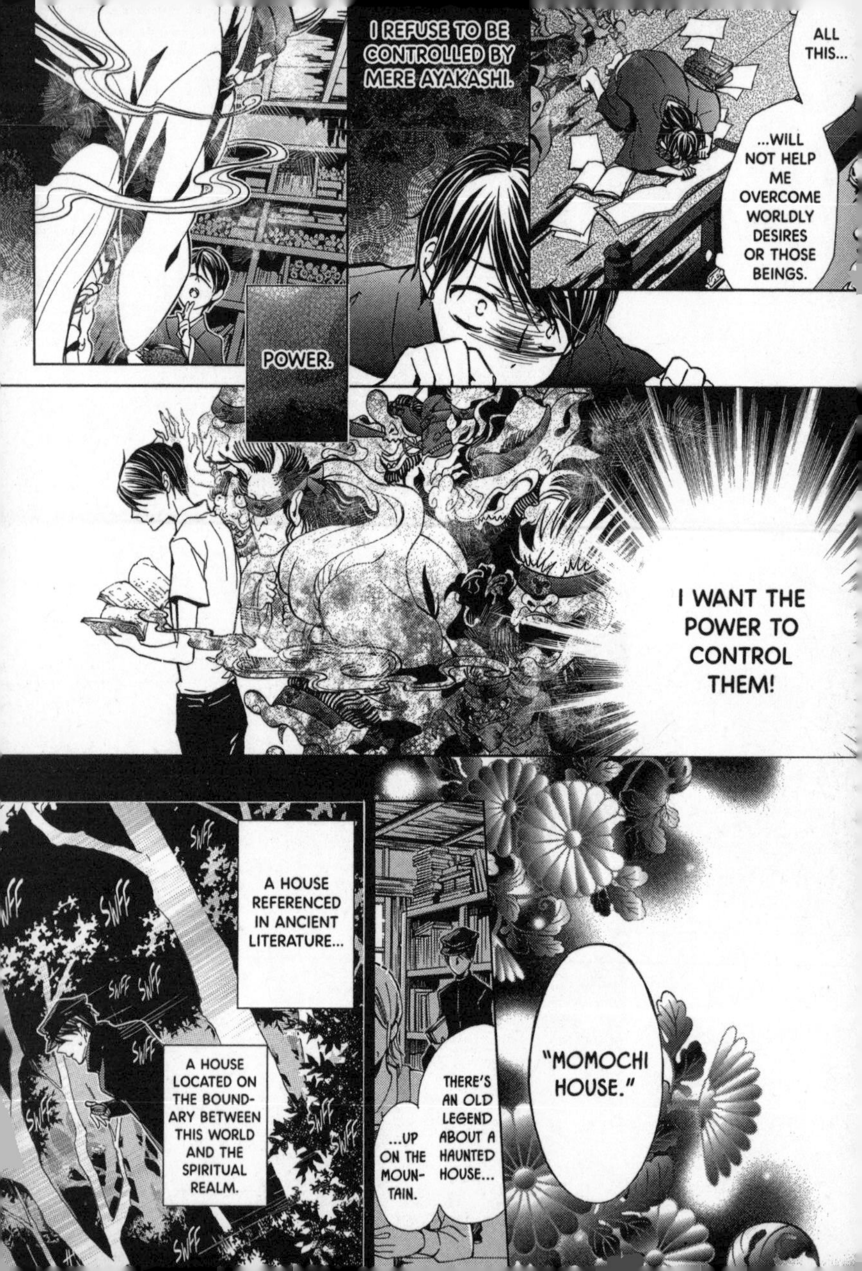
ALL THIS...
...WILL NOT HELP ME OVERCOME WORLDLY DESIRES OR THOSE BEINGS.
I REFUSE TO BE CONTROLLED BY MERE AYAKASHI.
POWER.
I WANT THE POWER TO CONTROL THEM!
THERE'S AN OLD LEGEND ABOUT A HAUNTED HOUSE...
...UP ON THE MOUNTAIN.
"MOMOCHI HOUSE."
A HOUSE REFERENCED IN ANCIENT LITERATURE...
A HOUSE LOCATED ON THE BOUND-ARY BETWEEN THIS WORLD AND THE SPIRITUAL REALM.
SWFF SWFF SWFF SWFF SWFF SWFF SWFF SWFF

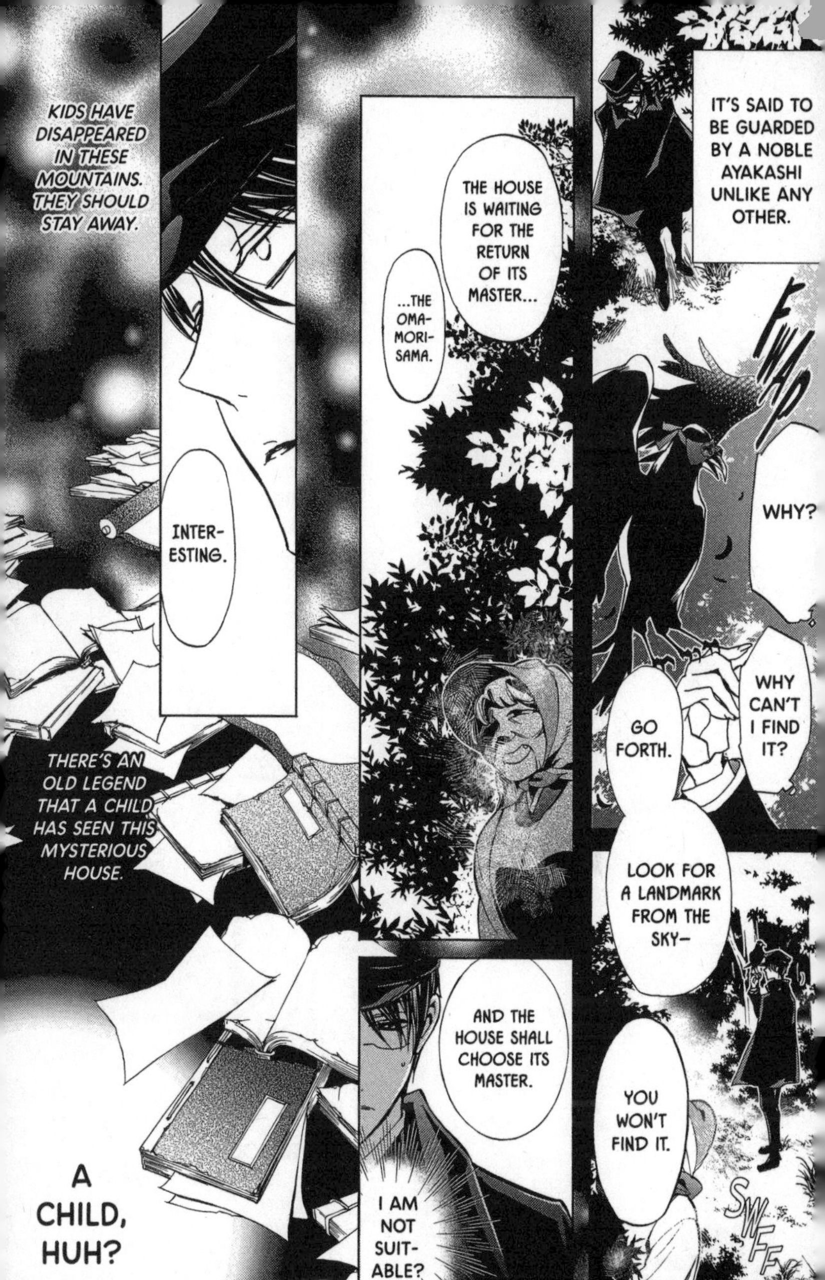
IT'S SAID TO BE GUARDED BY A NOBLE AYAKASHI UNLIKE ANY OTHER.
FWAP
WHY?
WHY CAN'T I FIND IT?
GO FORTH.
LOOK FOR A LANDMARK FROM THE SKY—
YOU WON'T FIND IT.
SWFF
THE HOUSE IS WAITING FOR THE RETURN OF ITS MASTER...
...THE OMAMORI-SAMA.
AND THE HOUSE SHALL CHOOSE ITS MASTER.
I AM NOT SUITABLE?
KIDS HAVE DISAPPEARED IN THESE MOUNTAINS. THEY SHOULD STAY AWAY.
INTERESTING.
THERE'S AN OLD LEGEND THAT A CHILD HAS SEEN THIS MYSTERIOUS HOUSE.
A CHILD, HUH?

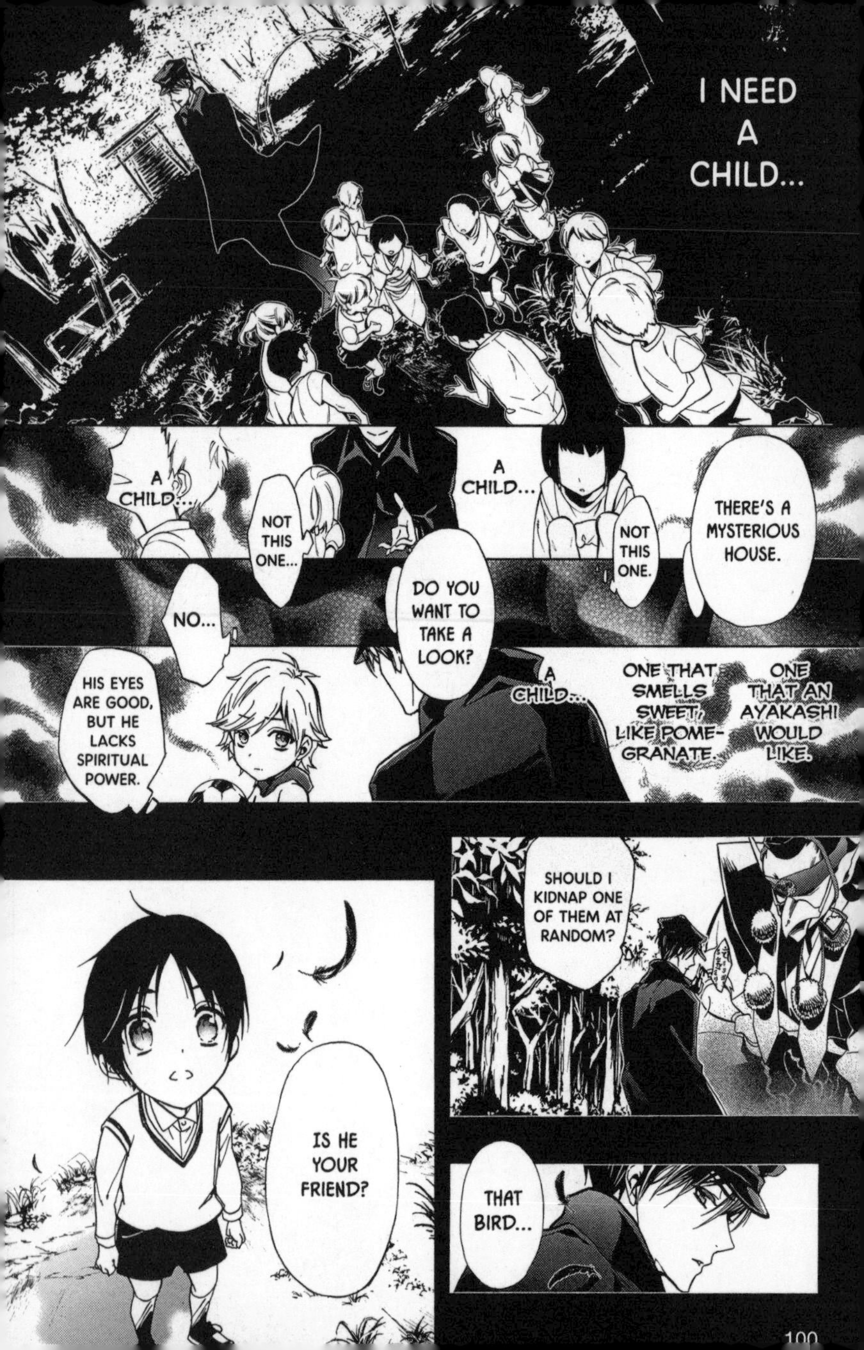
I NEED A CHILD...
A CHILD...
NOT THIS ONE.
THERE'S A MYSTERIOUS HOUSE.
A CHILD...
NOT THIS ONE...
DO YOU WANT TO TAKE A LOOK?
NO...
ONE THAT AN AYAKASHI WOULD LIKE.
ONE THAT SMELLS SWEET, LIKE POMEGRANATE.
A CHILD...
HIS EYES ARE GOOD, BUT HE LACKS SPIRITUAL POWER.
SHOULD I KIDNAP ONE OF THEM AT RANDOM?
THAT BIRD...
IS HE YOUR FRIEND?

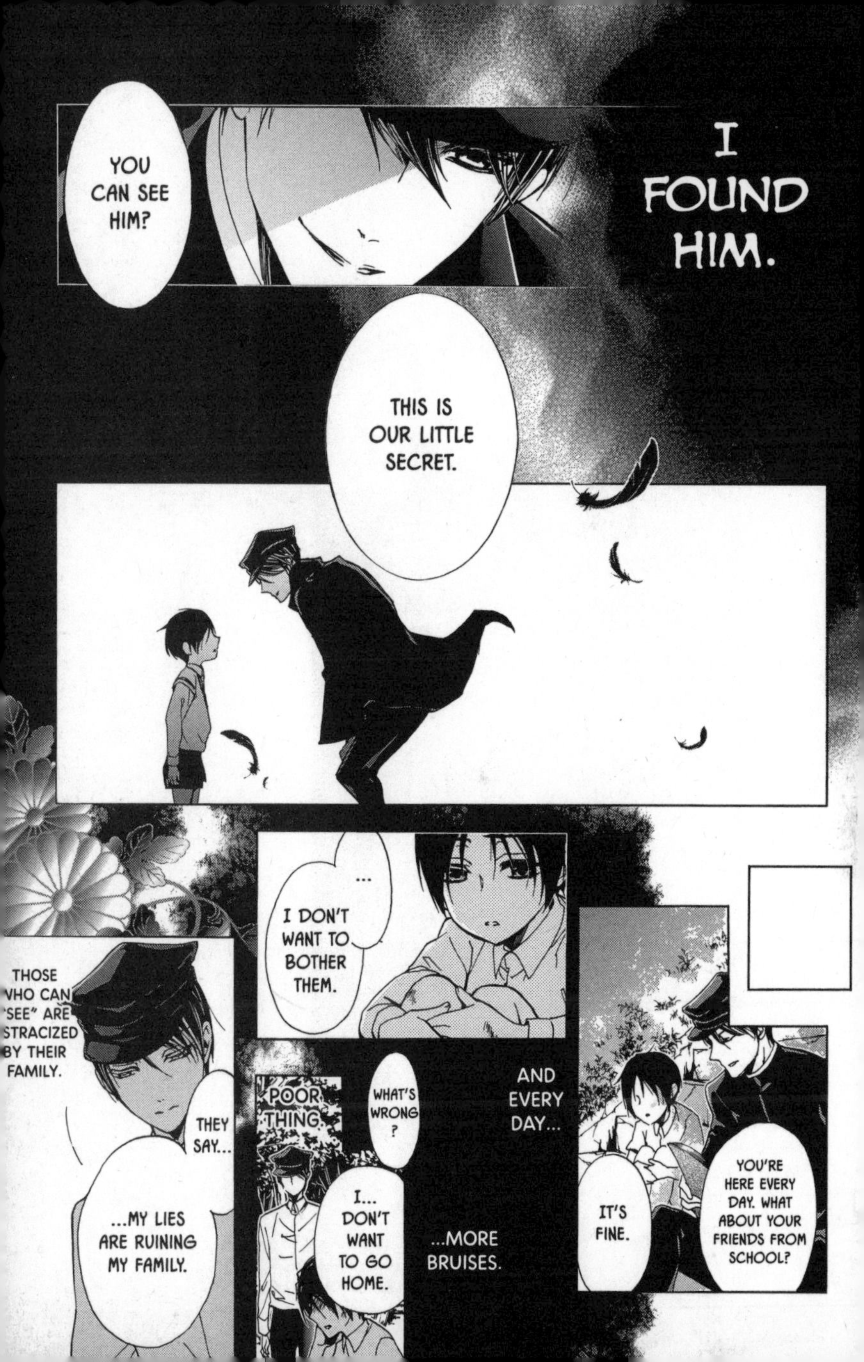
I FOUND HIM.
YOU CAN SEE HIM?
THIS IS OUR LITTLE SECRET.
... I DON'T WANT TO BOTHER THEM.
YOU'RE HERE EVERY DAY. WHAT ABOUT YOUR FRIENDS FROM SCHOOL?
IT'S FINE.
AND EVERY DAY...
...MORE BRUISES.
WHAT'S WRONG?
POOR THING.
I... DON'T WANT TO GO HOME.
THOSE VHO CAN "SEE" ARE STRACIZED BY THEIR FAMILY.
THEY SAY...
...MY LIES ARE RUINING MY FAMILY.

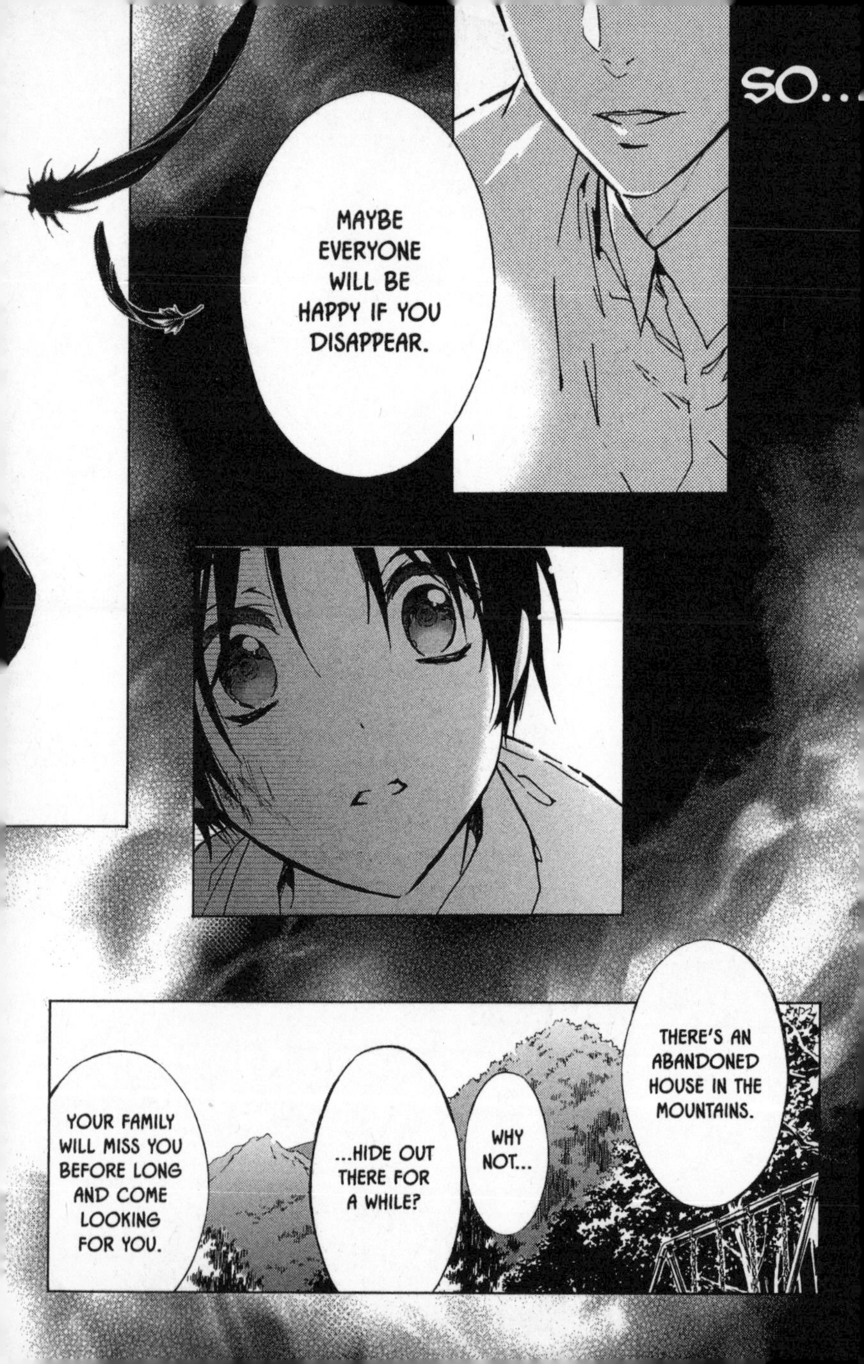
SO...
MAYBE EVERYONE WILL BE HAPPY IF YOU DISAPPEAR.
THERE'S AN ABANDONED HOUSE IN THE MOUNTAINS.
WHY NOT...
...HIDE OUT THERE FOR A WHILE?
YOUR FAMILY WILL MISS YOU BEFORE LONG AND COME LOOKING FOR YOU.

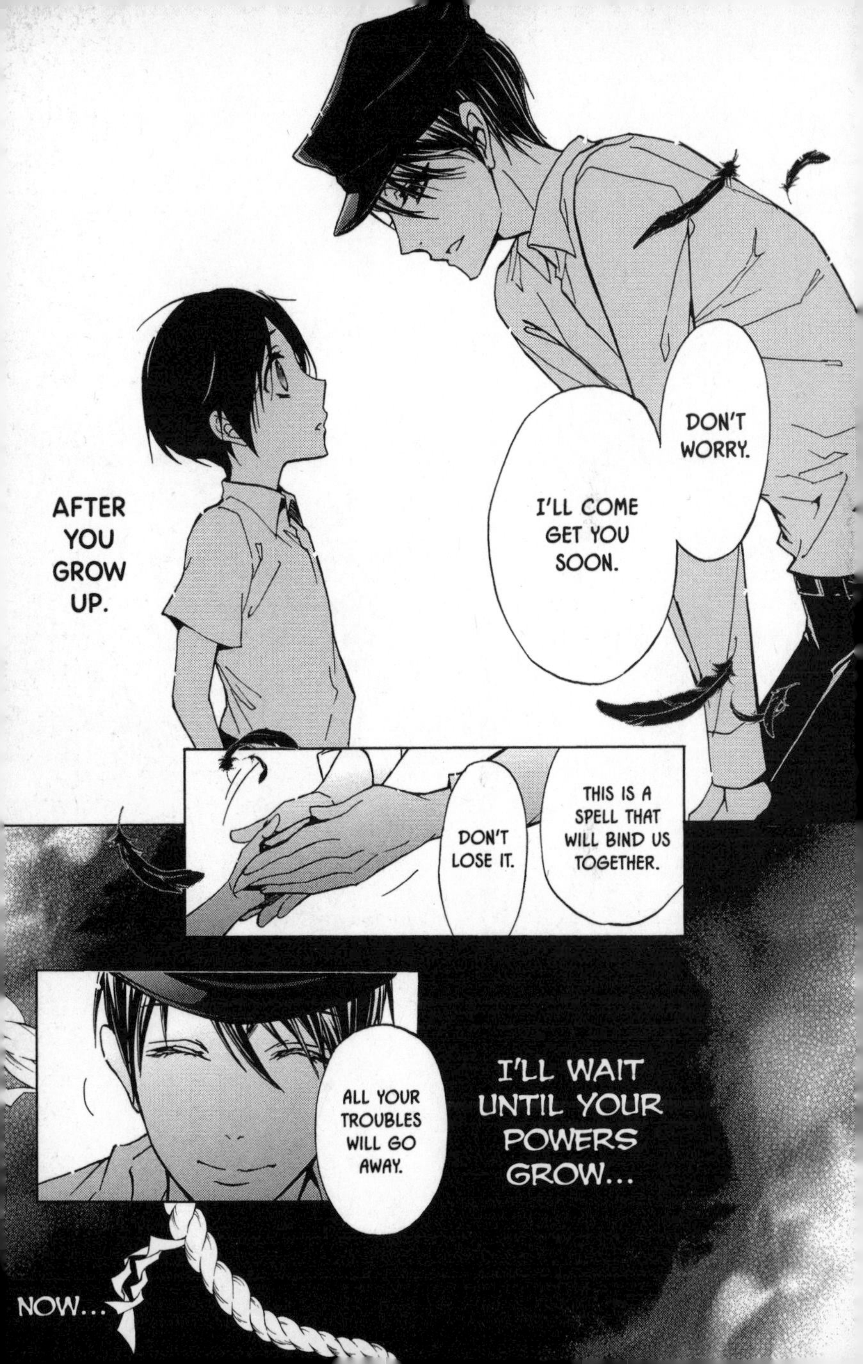
DON'T WORRY.
I'LL COME GET YOU SOON.
AFTER YOU GROW UP.
THIS IS A SPELL THAT WILL BIND US TOGETHER.
DON'T LOSE IT.
I'LL WAIT UNTIL YOUR POWERS GROW...
ALL YOUR TROUBLES WILL GO AWAY.
NOW...

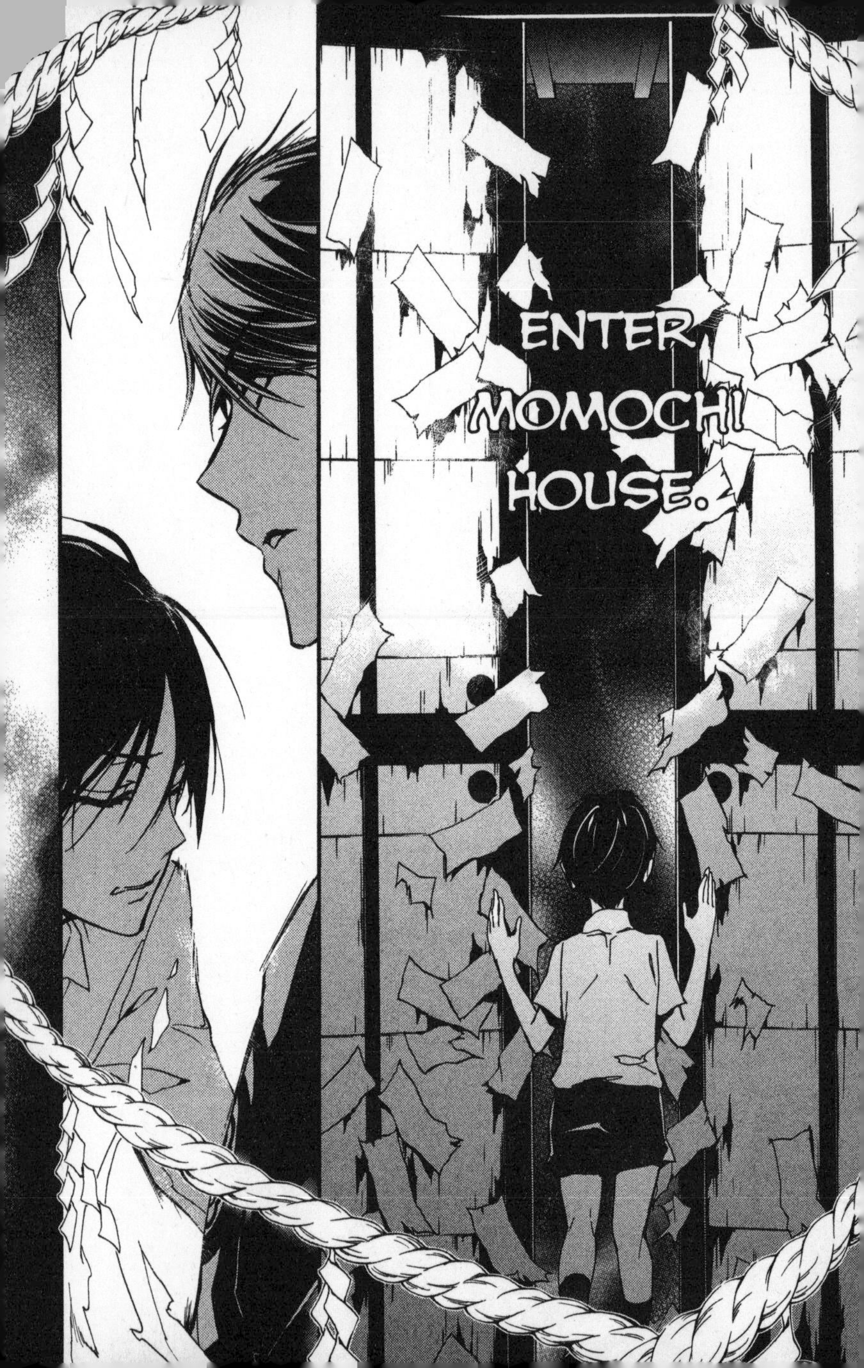
ENTER MOMOCHI HOUSE.

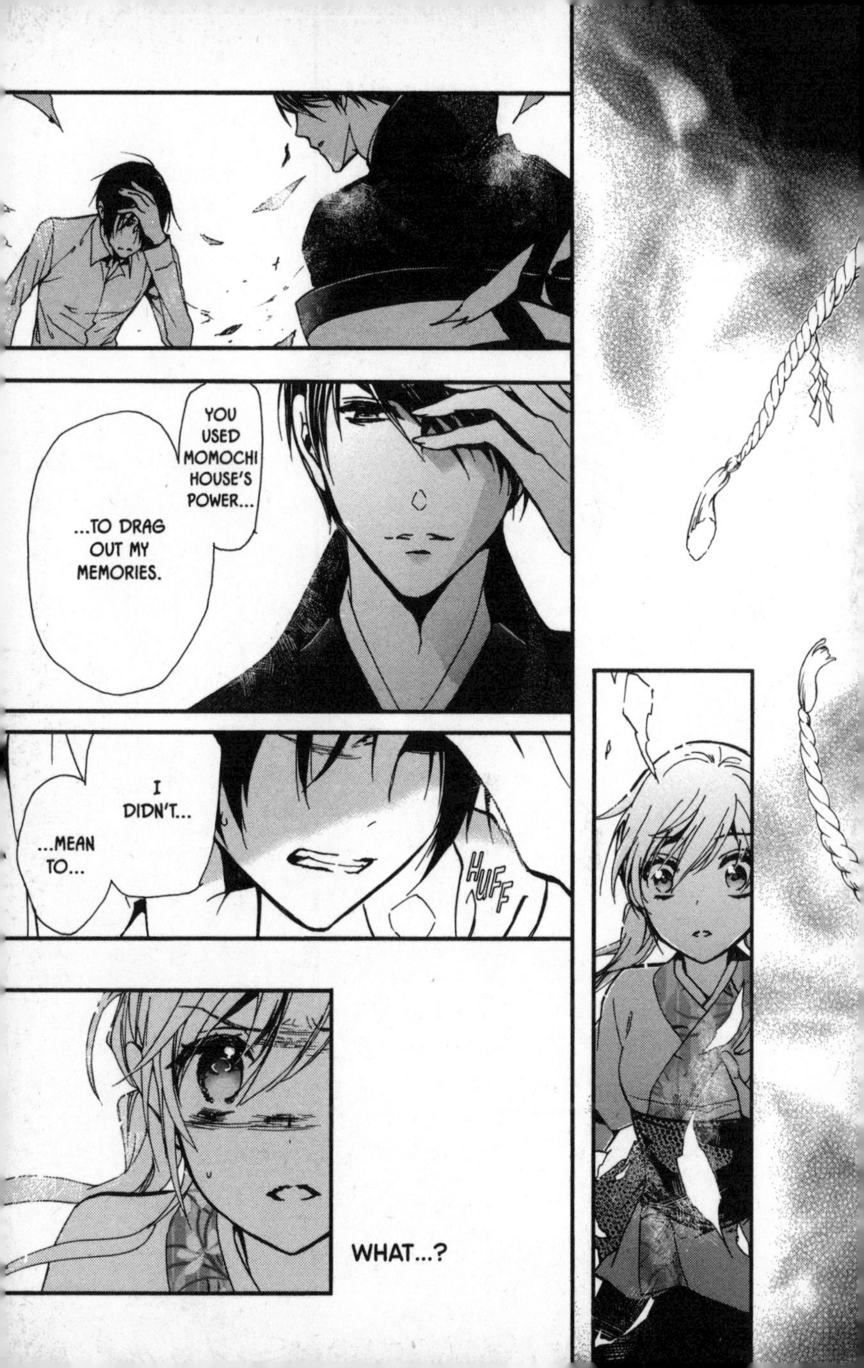
YOU USED MOMOCHI HOUSE'S POWER...
...TO DRAG OUT MY MEMORIES.
I DIDN'T...
...MEAN TO...
HUFF
WHAT...?

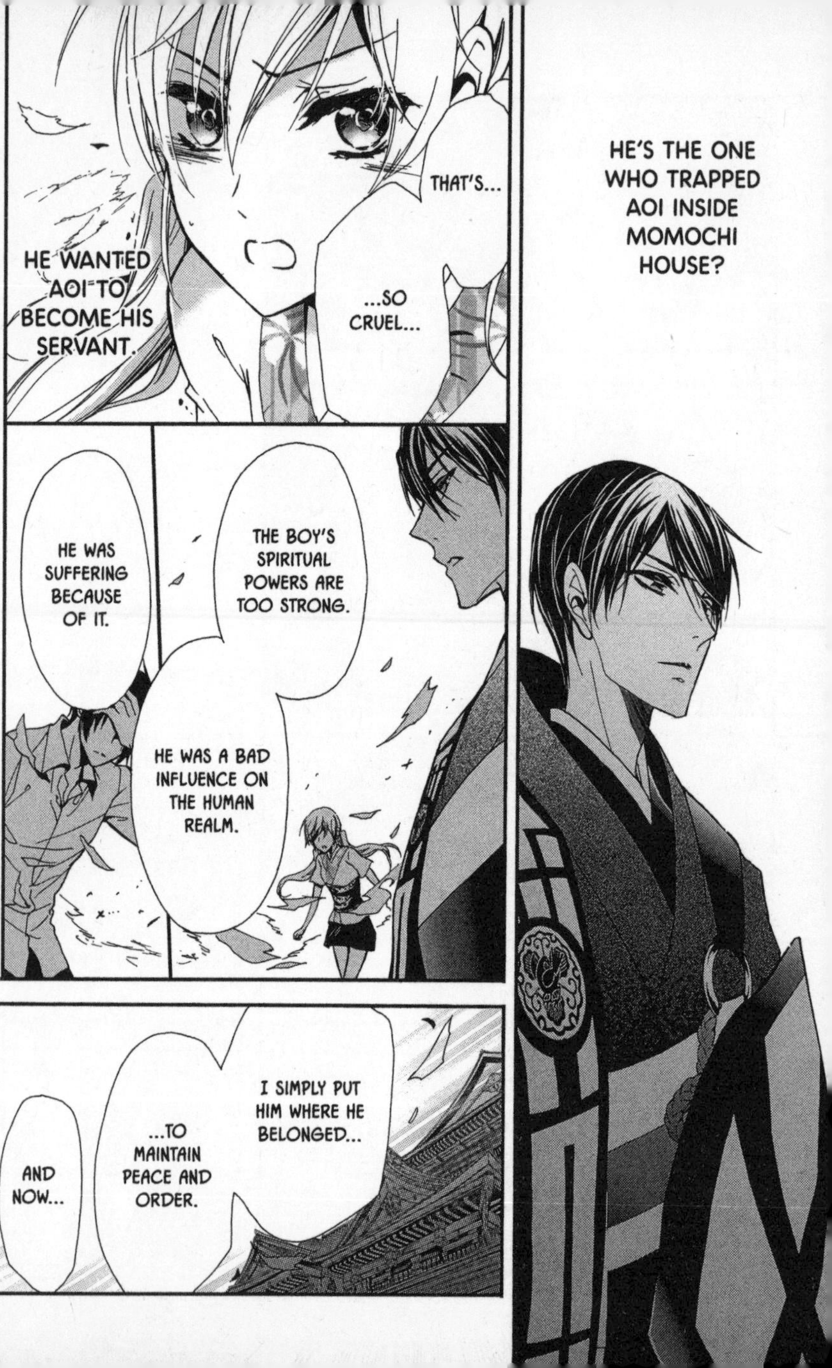
HE'S THE ONE WHO TRAPPED AOI INSIDE MOMOCHI HOUSE?
THAT'S...
...SO CRUEL...
HE WANTED AOI TO BECOME HIS SERVANT.
THE BOY'S SPIRITUAL POWERS ARE TOO STRONG.
HE WAS A BAD INFLUENCE ON THE HUMAN REALM.
HE WAS SUFFERING BECAUSE OF IT.
I SIMPLY PUT HIM WHERE HE BELONGED...
...TO MAINTAIN PEACE AND ORDER.
AND NOW...

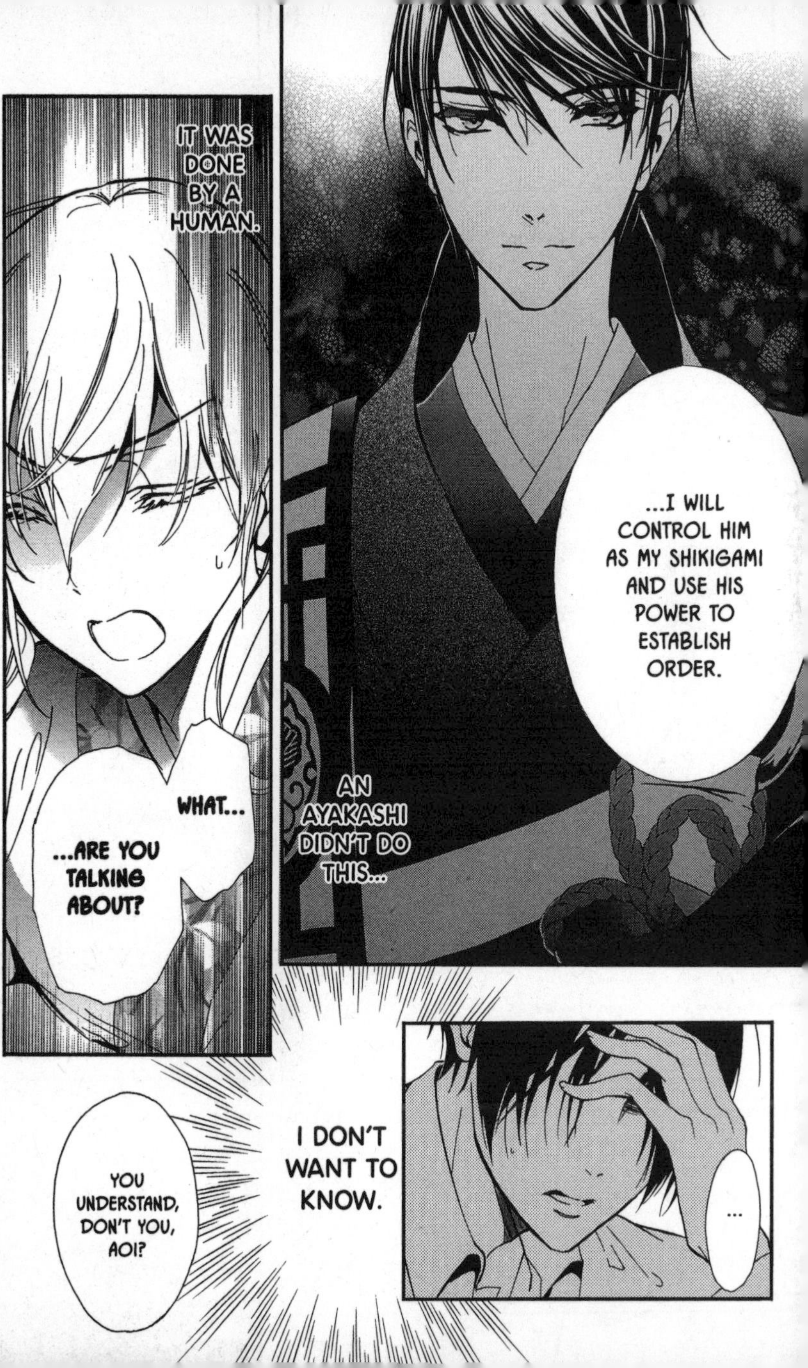
...I WILL CONTROL HIM AS MY SHIKIGAMI AND USE HIS POWER TO ESTABLISH ORDER.
AN AYAKASHI DIDN'T DO THIS...
IT WAS DONE BY A HUMAN.
WHAT...
...ARE YOU TALKING ABOUT?
...
I DON'T WANT TO KNOW.
YOU UNDERSTAND, DON'T YOU, AOI?

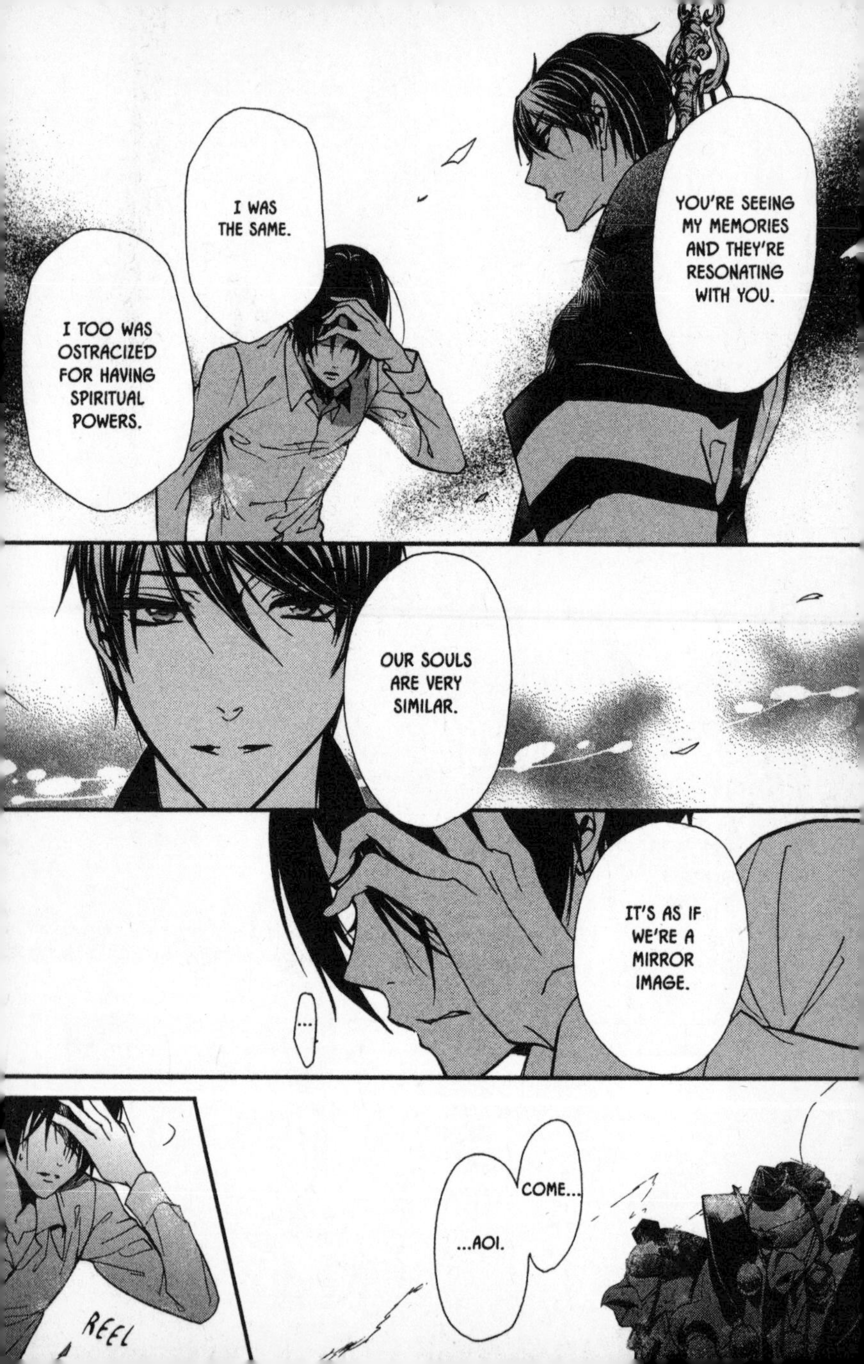
YOU'RE SEEING MY MEMORIES AND THEY'RE RESONATING WITH YOU.
I WAS THE SAME.
I TOO WAS OSTRACIZED FOR HAVING SPIRITUAL POWERS.
OUR SOULS ARE VERY SIMILAR.
IT'S AS IF WE'RE A MIRROR IMAGE.
...
COME...
...AOI.
REEL

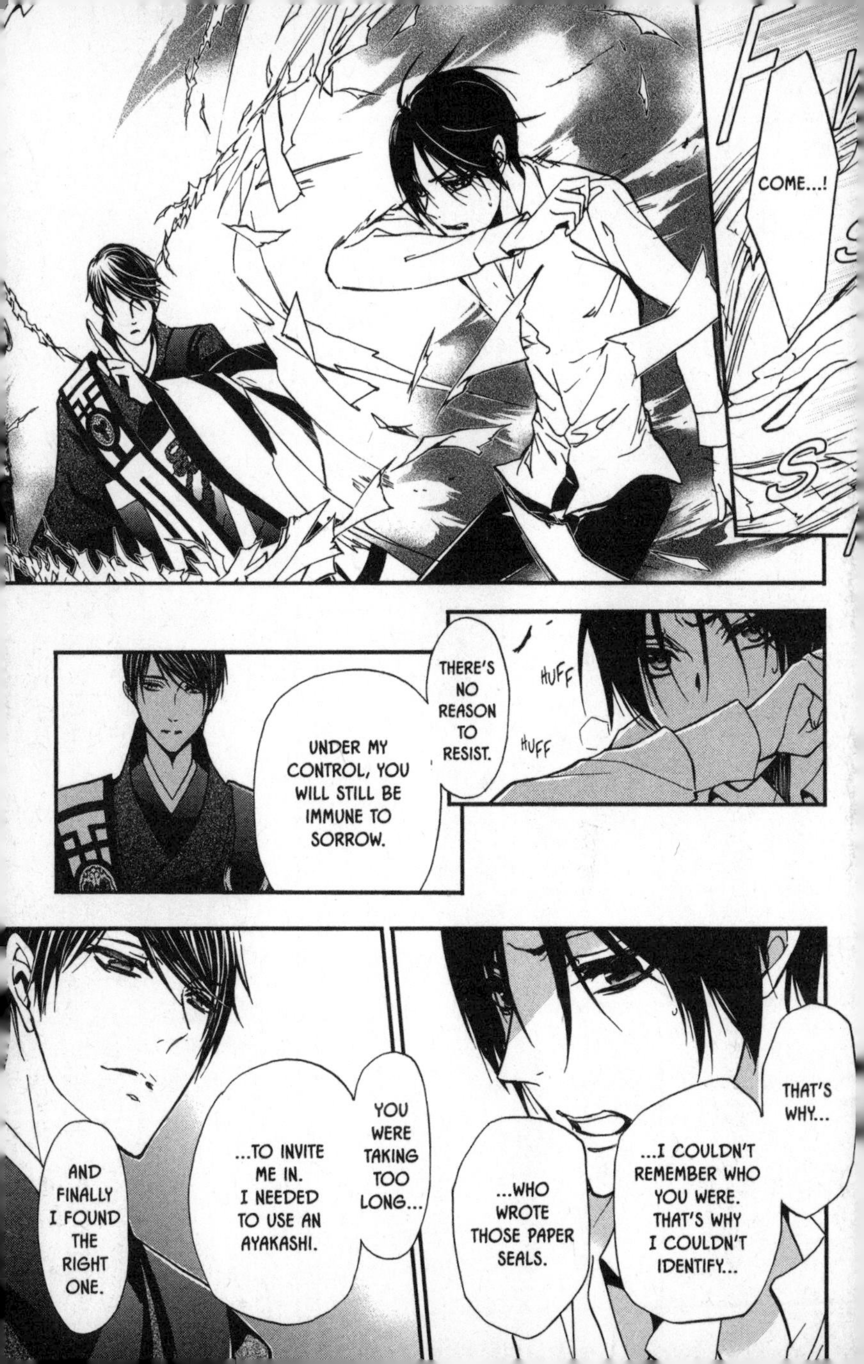
COME...!
HUFF
HUFF
THERE'S NO REASON TO RESIST.
UNDER MY CONTROL, YOU WILL STILL BE IMMUNE TO SORROW.
THAT'S WHY...
...I COULDN'T REMEMBER WHO YOU WERE. THAT'S WHY I COULDN'T IDENTIFY...
...WHO WROTE THOSE PAPER SEALS.
YOU WERE TAKING TOO LONG...
...TO INVITE ME IN. I NEEDED TO USE AN AYAKASHI.
AND FINALLY I FOUND THE RIGHT ONE.

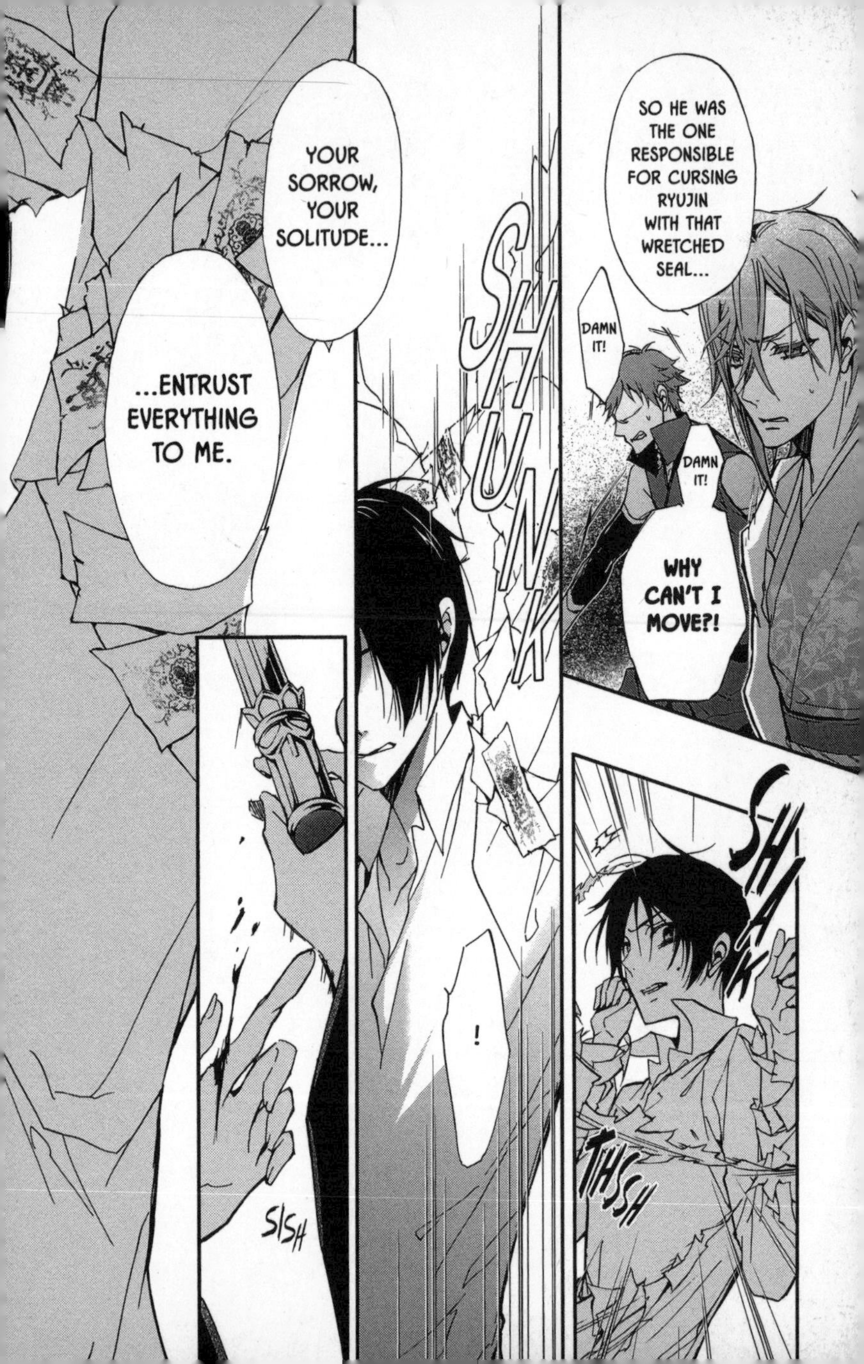
SO HE WAS THE ONE RESPONSIBLE FOR CURSING RYUJIN WITH THAT WRETCHED SEAL...
DAMN IT!
DAMN IT!
WHY CAN'T I MOVE?!
SHAK
THSSH
SHUNK
!
YOUR SORROW, YOUR SOLITUDE...
...ENTRUST EVERYTHING TO ME.
SISH

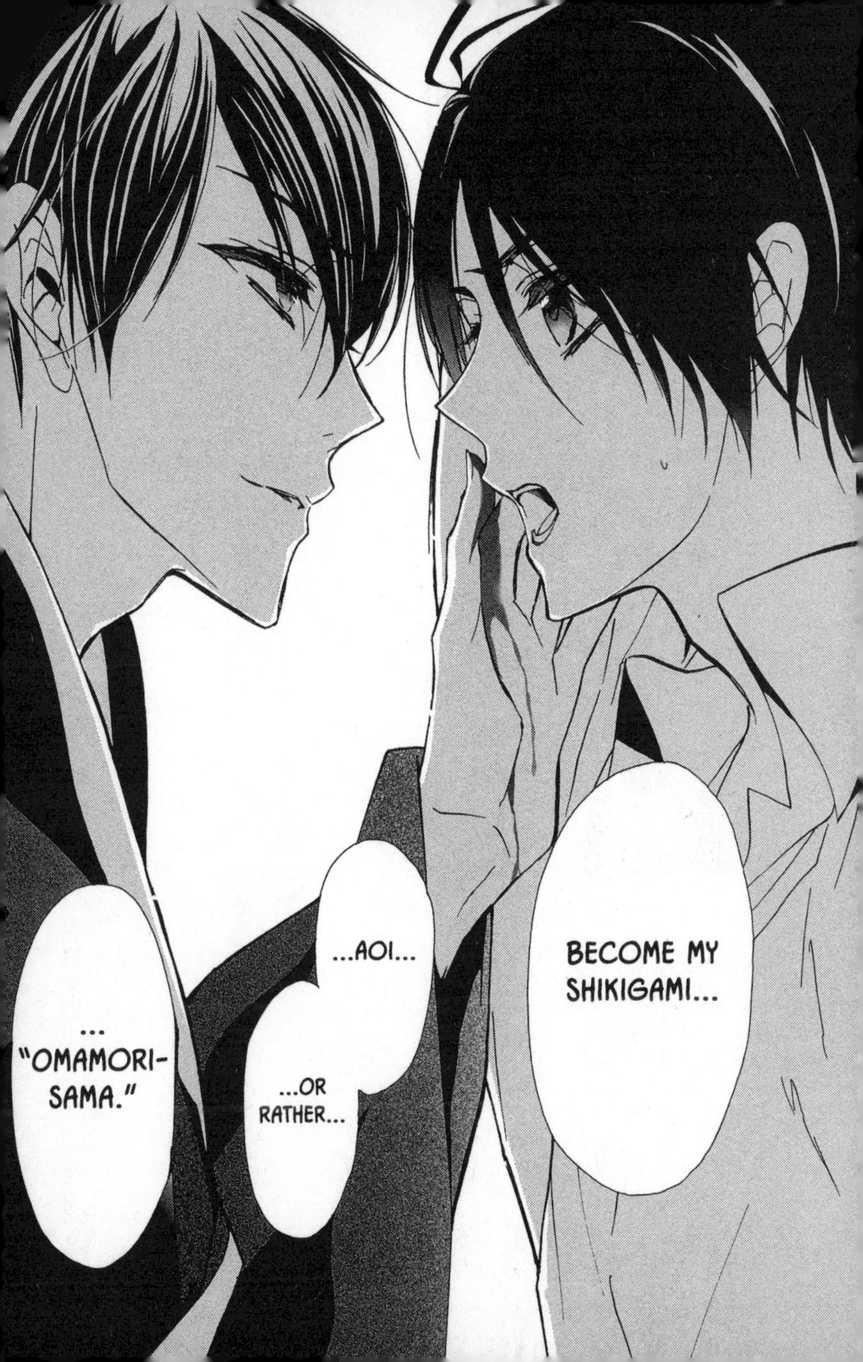
BECOME MY SHIKIGAMI...
...AOI...
...OR RATHER...
... "OMAMORI-SAMA."

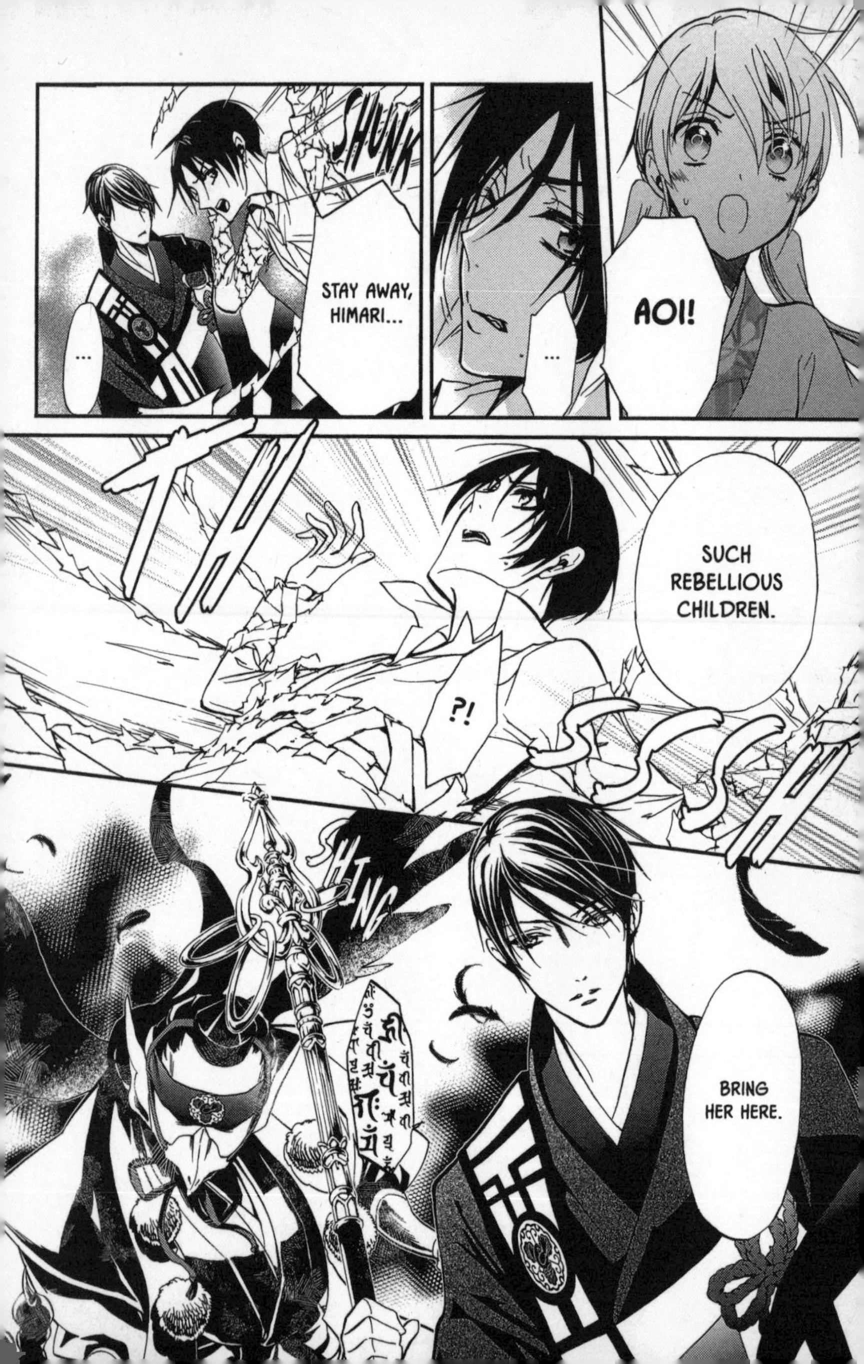
AOI!
...
SHUNK
STAY AWAY, HIMARI...
...
SUCH REBELLIOUS CHILDREN.
?!
BRING HER HERE.
SHING

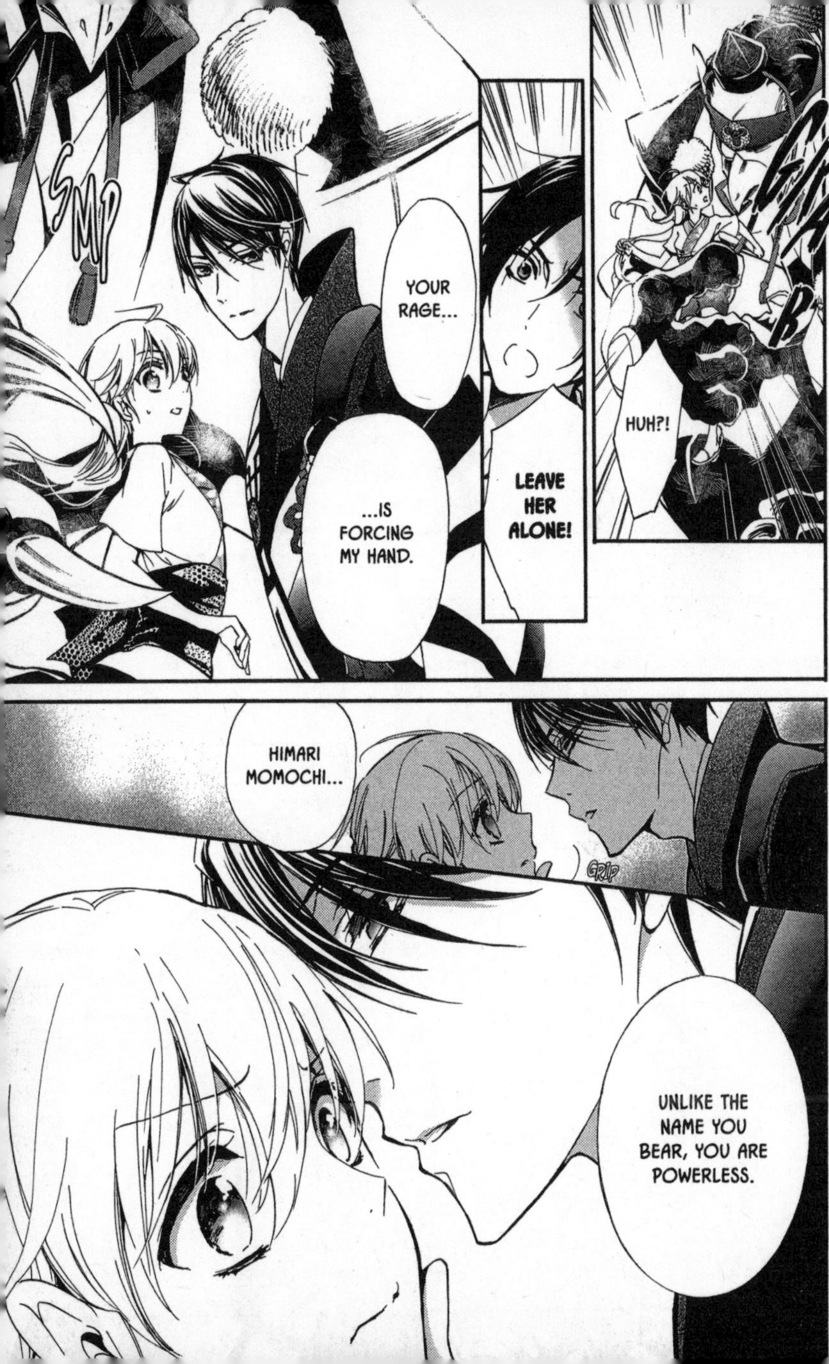
GRAB
HUH?!
LEAVE HER ALONE!
YOUR RAGE...
...IS FORCING MY HAND.
SMP
HIMARI MOMOCHI...
GRIP
UNLIKE THE NAME YOU BEAR, YOU ARE POWERLESS.

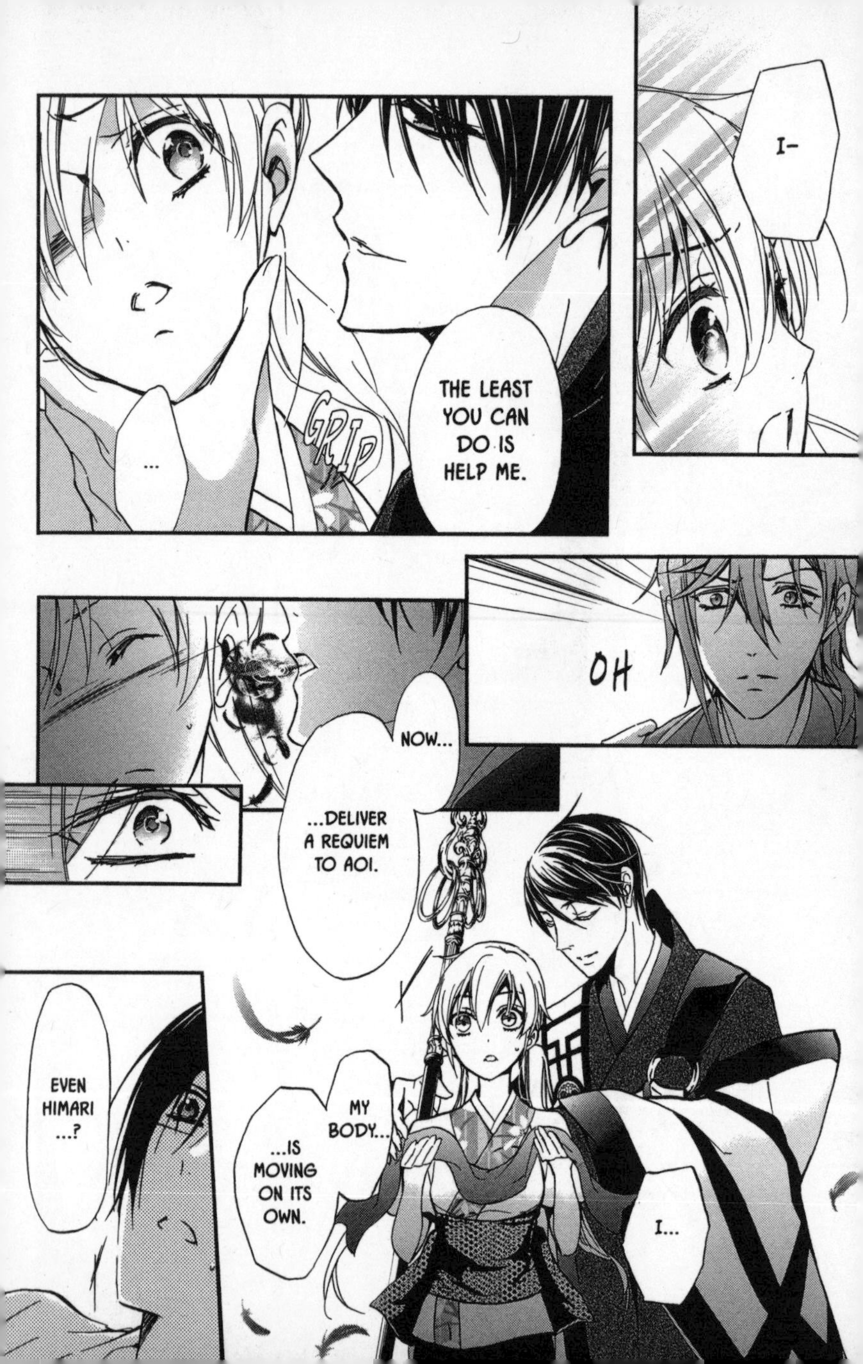
I–
THE LEAST YOU CAN DO IS HELP ME.
GRIP
...
OH
NOW...
...DELIVER A REQUIEM TO AOI.
I...
MY BODY...
...IS MOVING ON ITS OWN.
EVEN HIMARI ...?

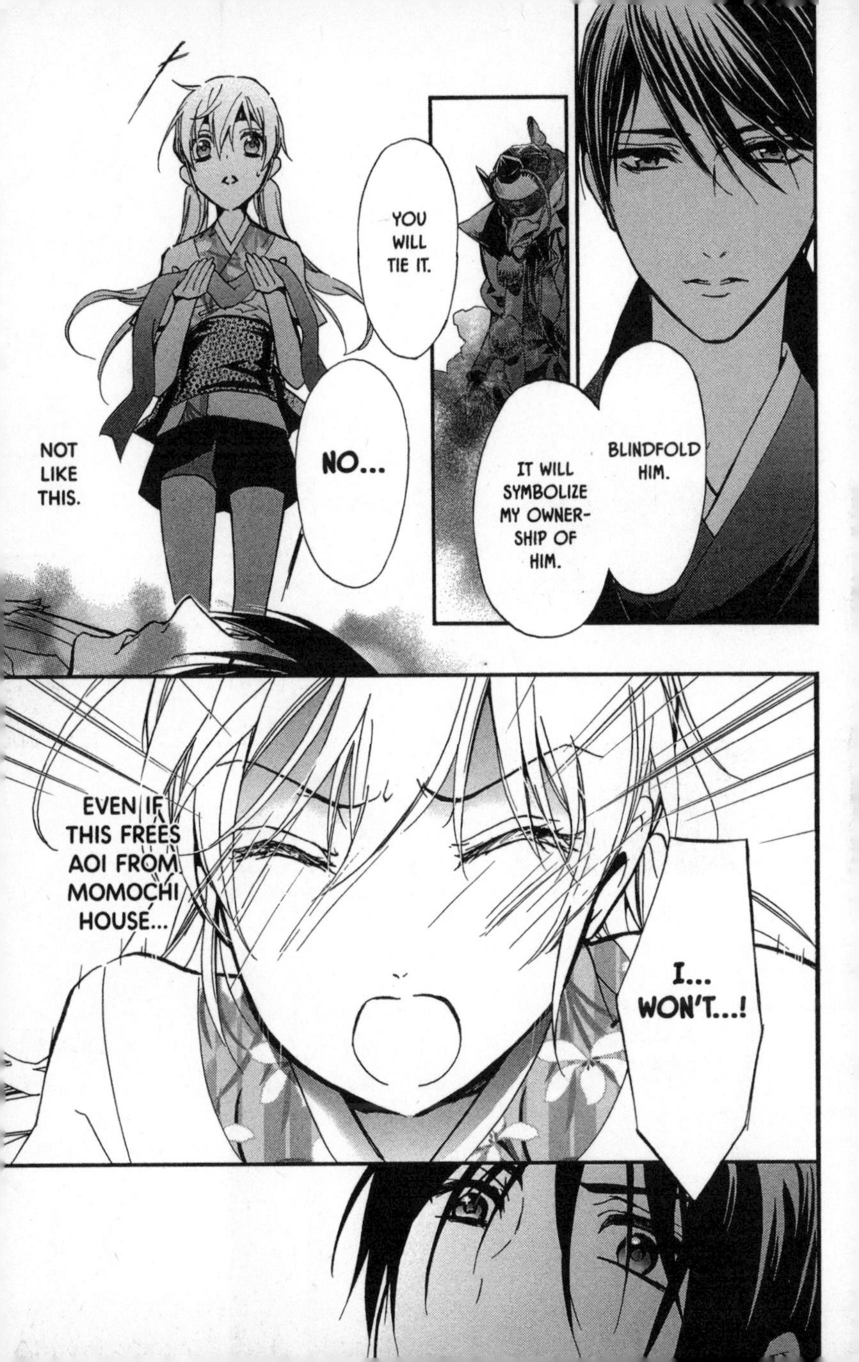
BLINDFOLD HIM.
IT WILL SYMBOLIZE MY OWNERSHIP OF HIM.
YOU WILL TIE IT.
NO...
NOT LIKE THIS.
EVEN IF THIS FREES AOI FROM MOMOCHI HOUSE...
I... WON'T...!

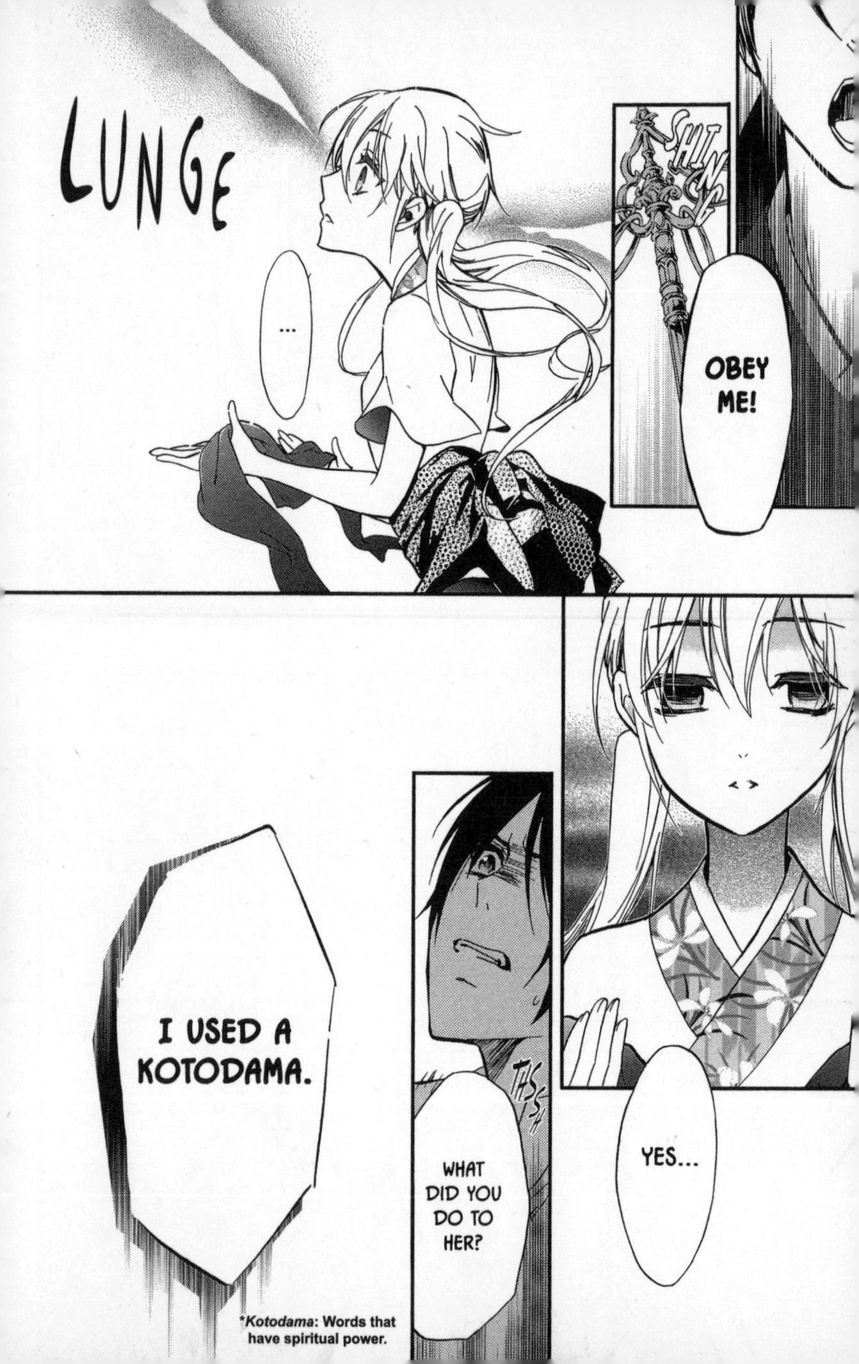
SHIN
OBEY ME!
LUNGE
...
YES...
THSSH
WHAT DID YOU DO TO HER?
I USED A KOTODAMA.

*Kotodama: Words that have spiritual power.

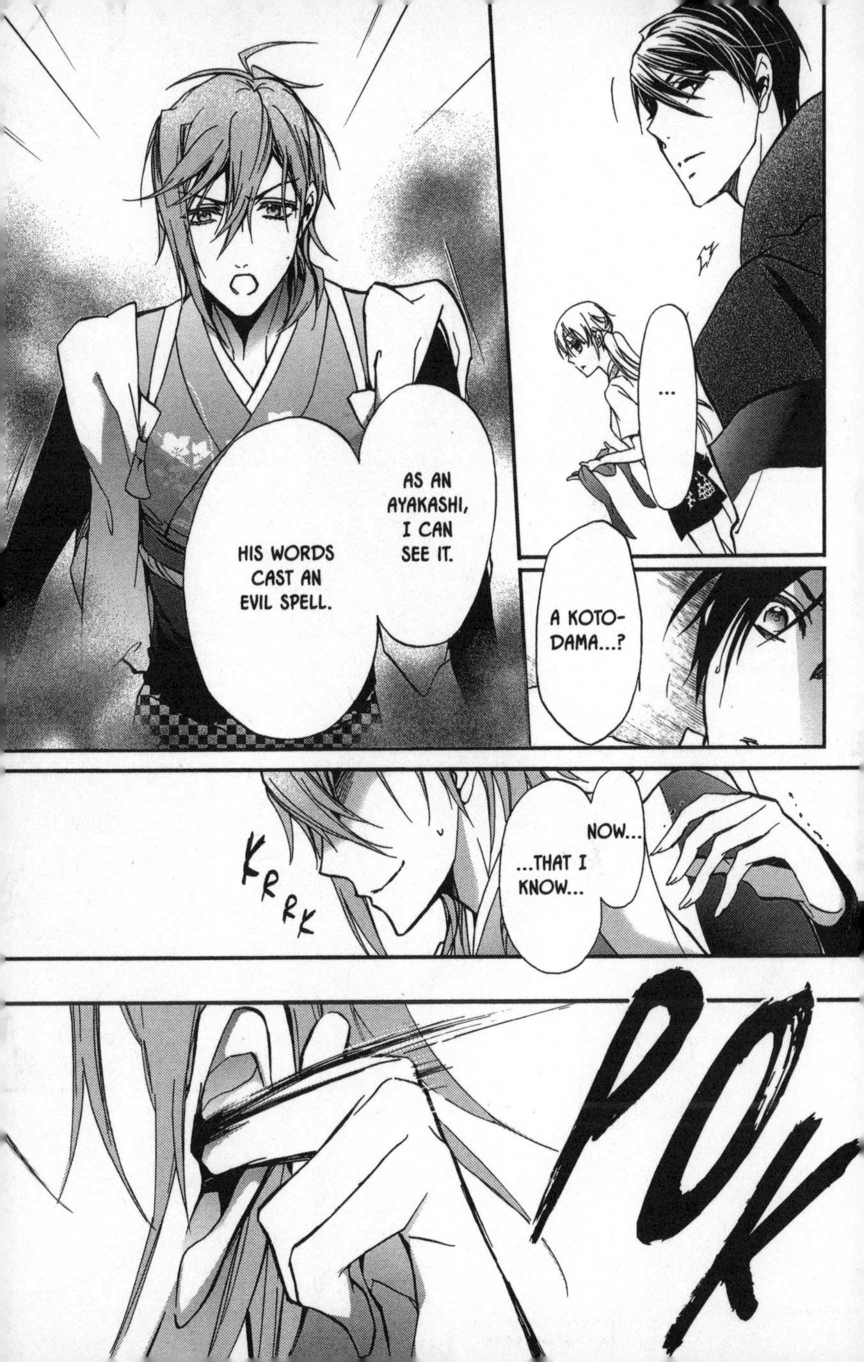
...
A KOTO-DAMA...?
AS AN AYAKASHI, I CAN SEE IT.
HIS WORDS CAST AN EVIL SPELL.
NOW... ...THAT I KNOW...
KRRK
POK

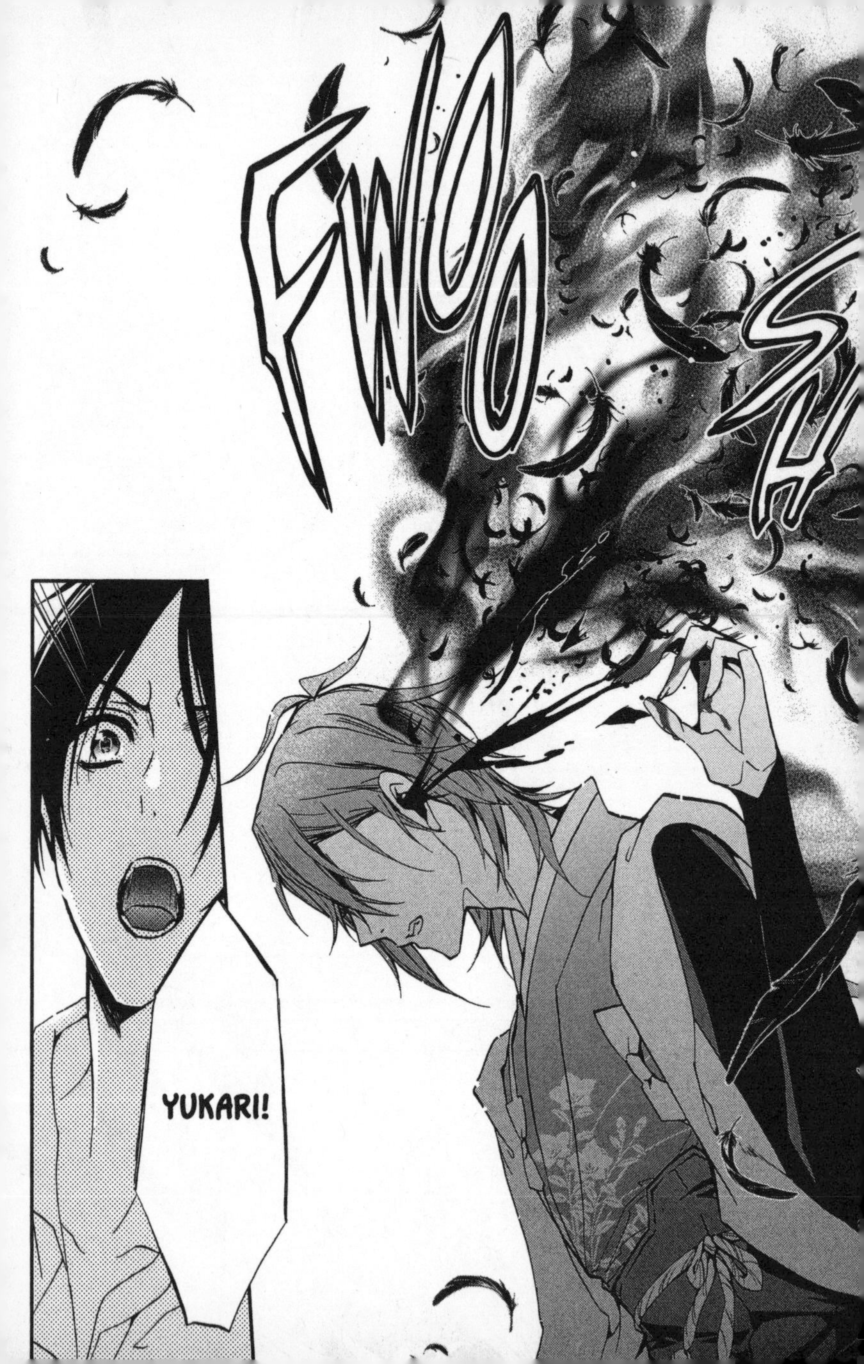
FWOOSH
YUKARI!

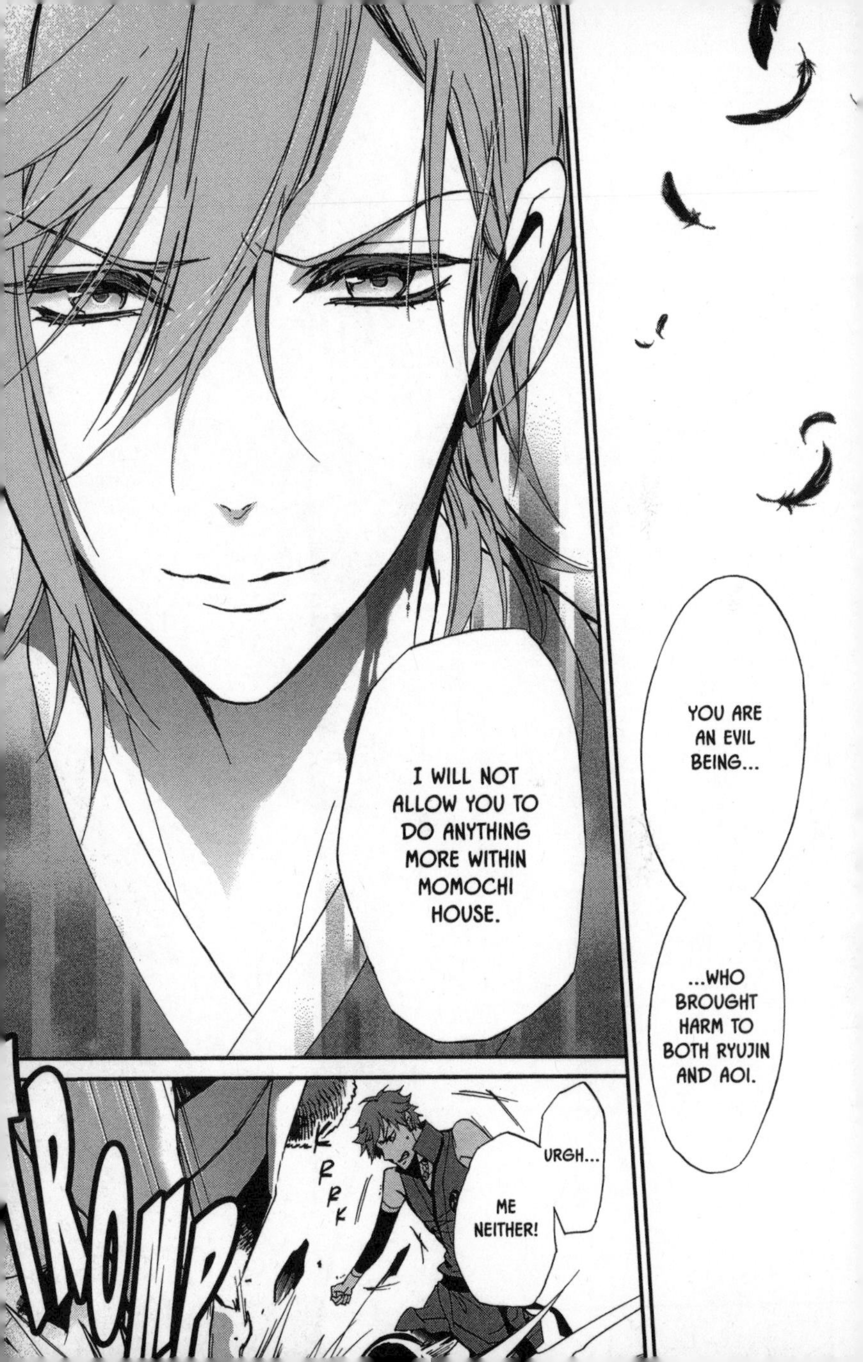
YOU ARE AN EVIL BEING...
...WHO BROUGHT HARM TO BOTH RYUJIN AND AOI.
I WILL NOT ALLOW YOU TO DO ANYTHING MORE WITHIN MOMOCHI HOUSE.
URGH...
ME NEITHER!
RRK

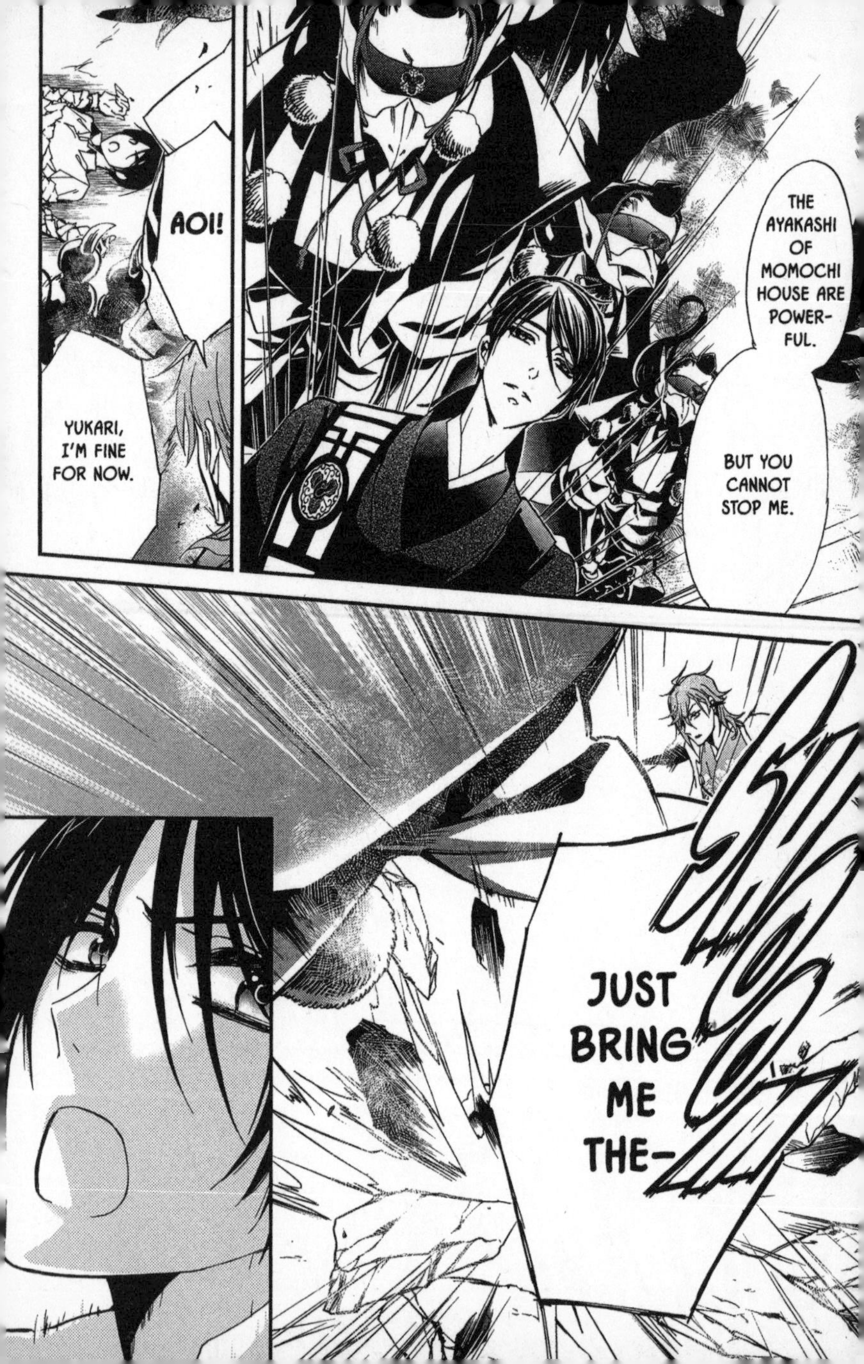
THE AYAKASHI OF MOMOCHI HOUSE ARE POWER-FUL.
BUT YOU CANNOT STOP ME.
AOI!
YUKARI, I'M FINE FOR NOW.
JUST BRING ME THE—

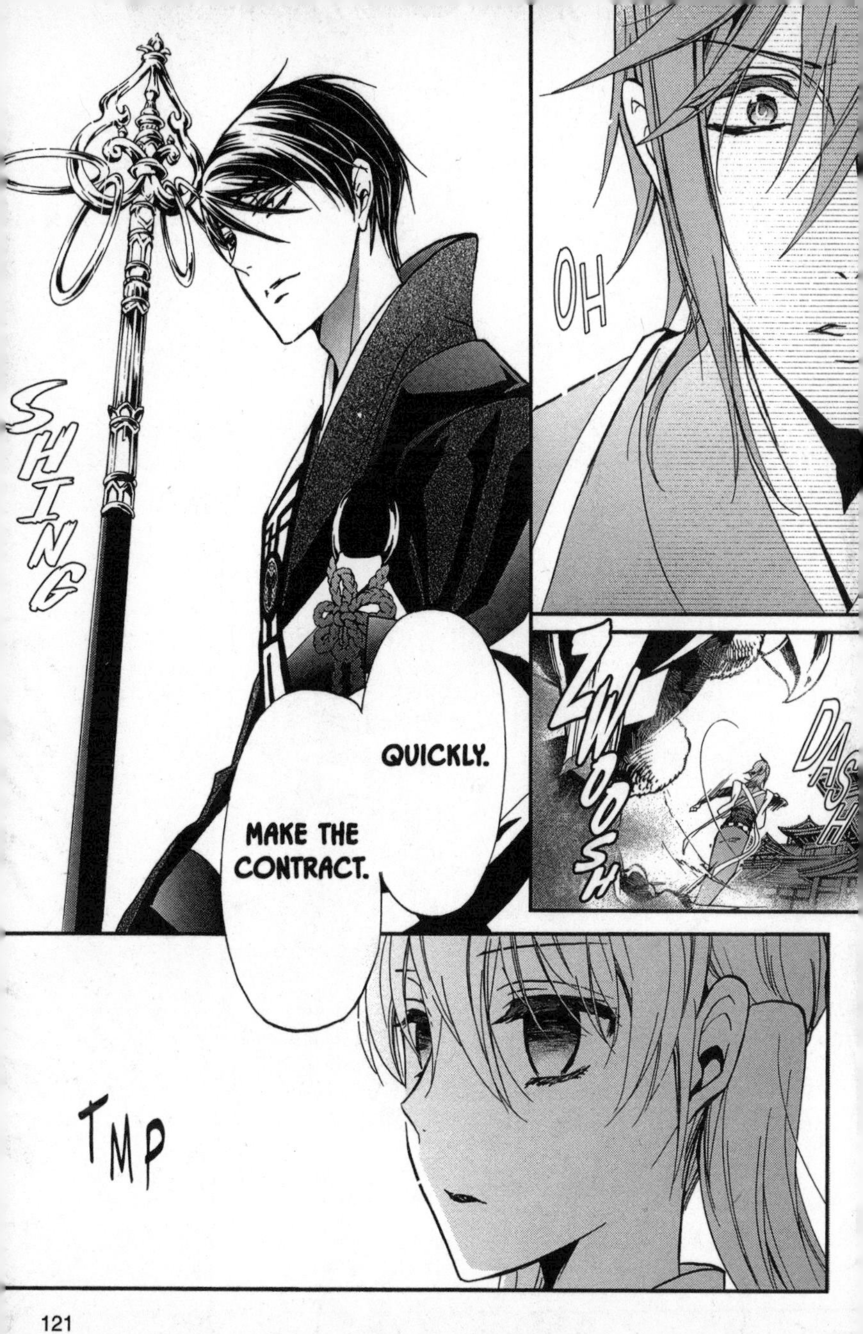
OH
ZWOOSH
DASH
SHING
QUICKLY.
MAKE THE CONTRACT.
TMP

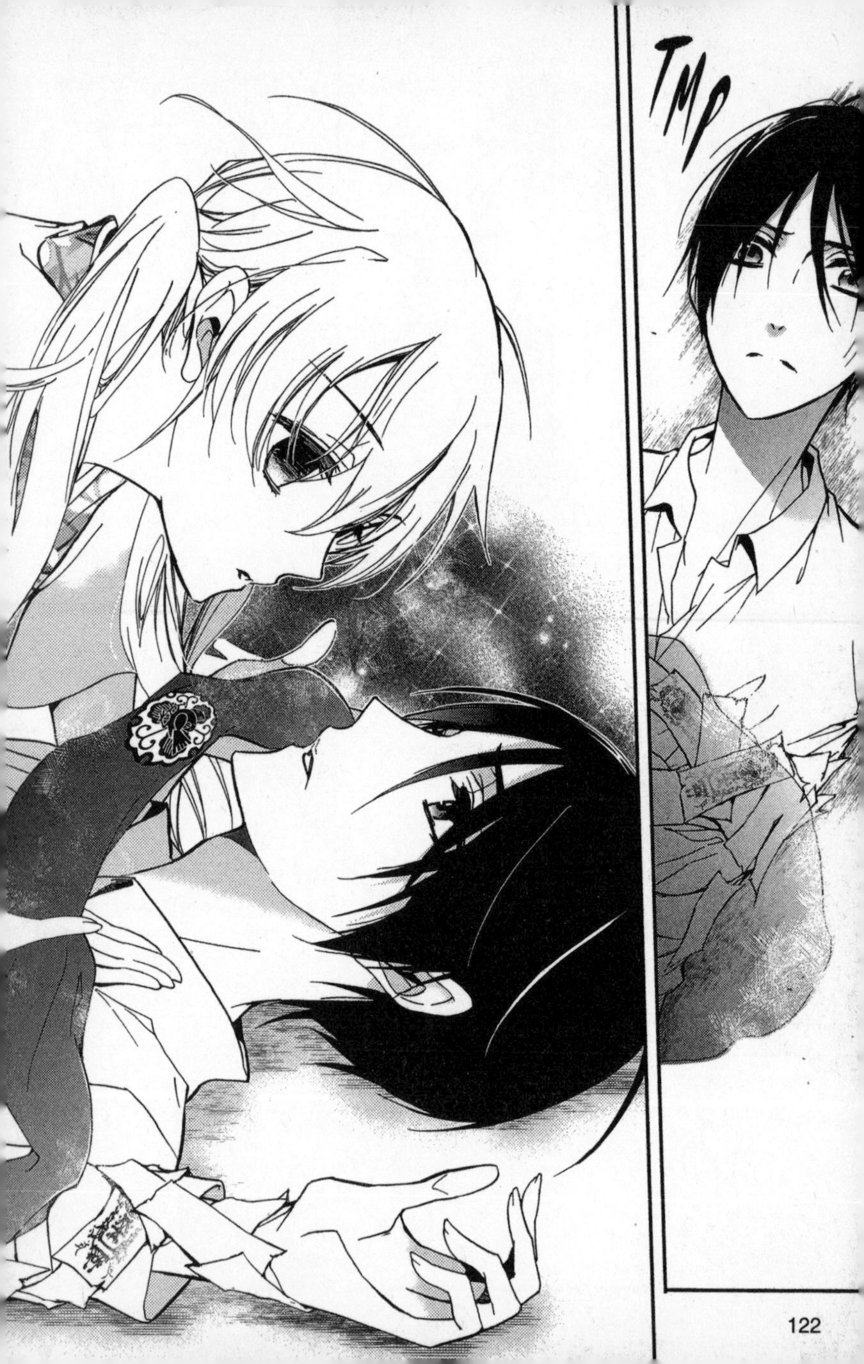
TMP

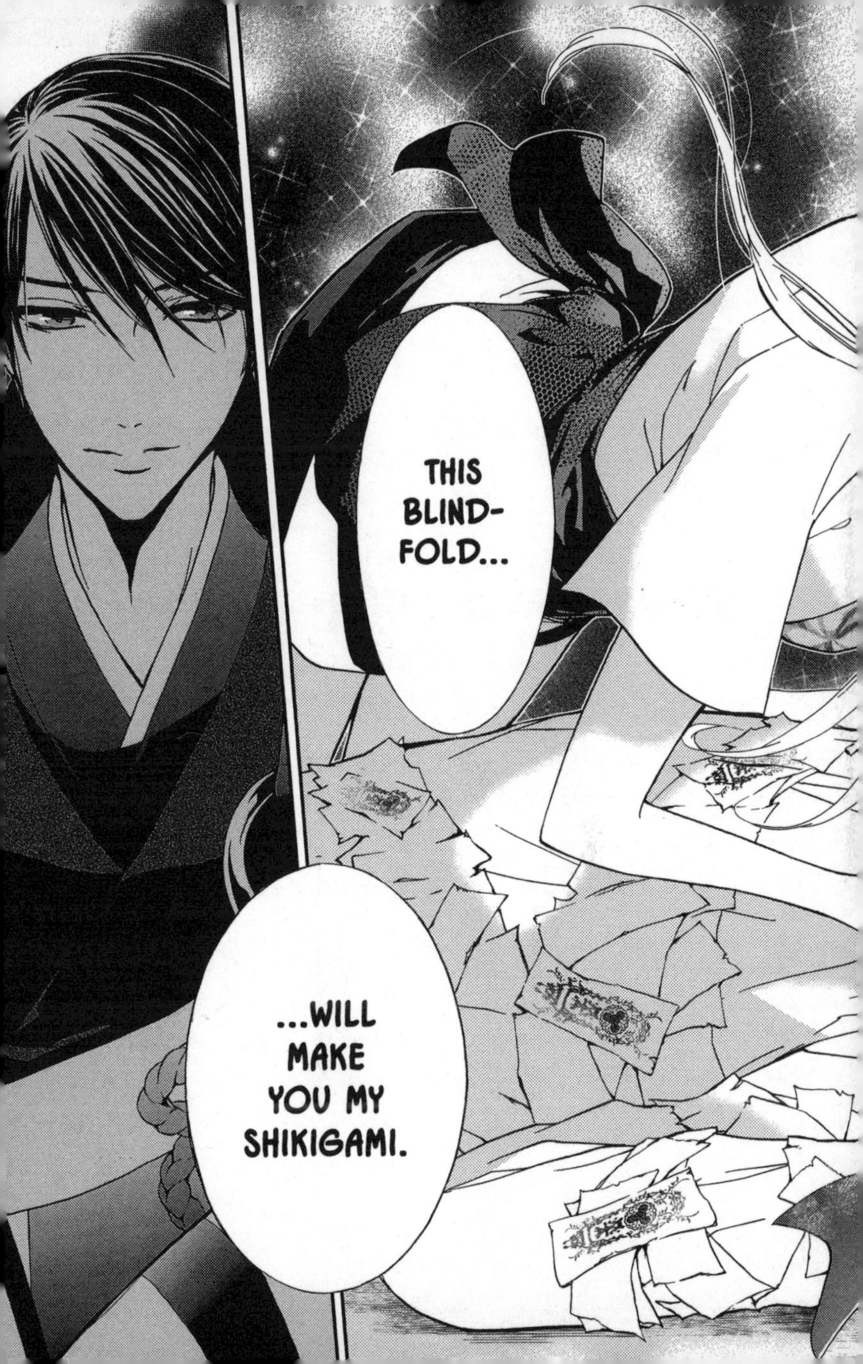
THIS BLIND-FOLD...
...WILL MAKE YOU MY SHIKIGAMI.

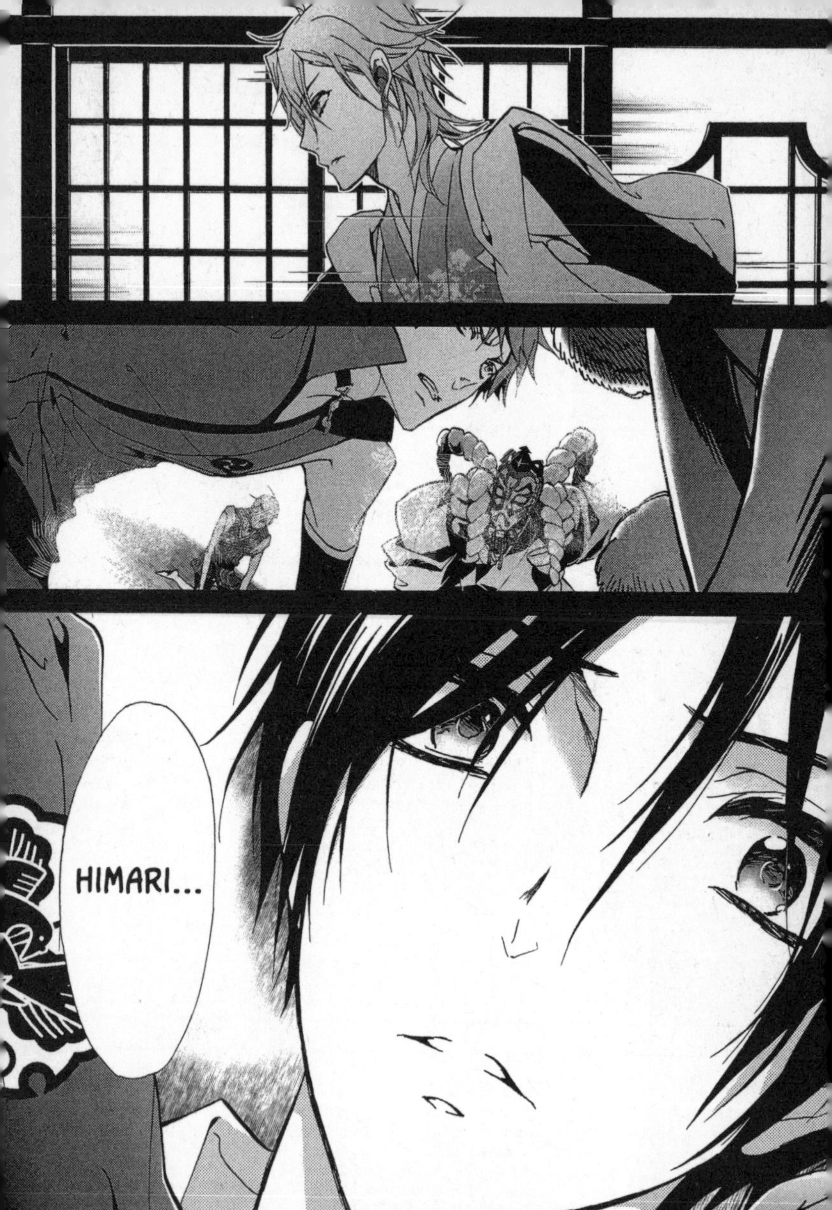
HIMARI...

The
DEMON
PRINCE
of MOMOCHI
HOUSE

The
DEMON
PRINCE
of MOMOCHI
HOUSE

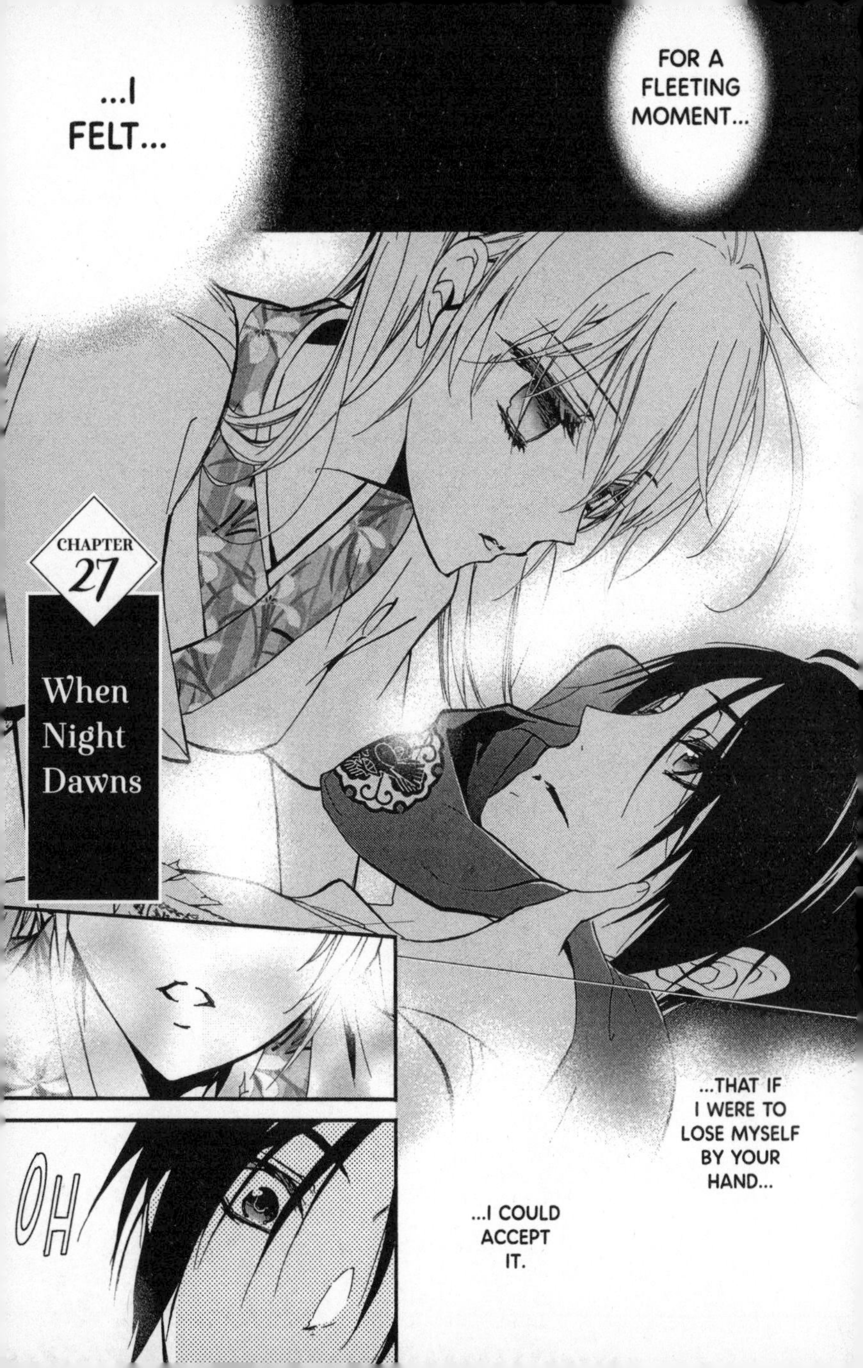
FOR A FLEETING MOMENT...
...I FELT...
CHAPTER 27
When Night Dawns
...THAT IF I WERE TO LOSE MYSELF BY YOUR HAND...
...I COULD ACCEPT IT.
OH

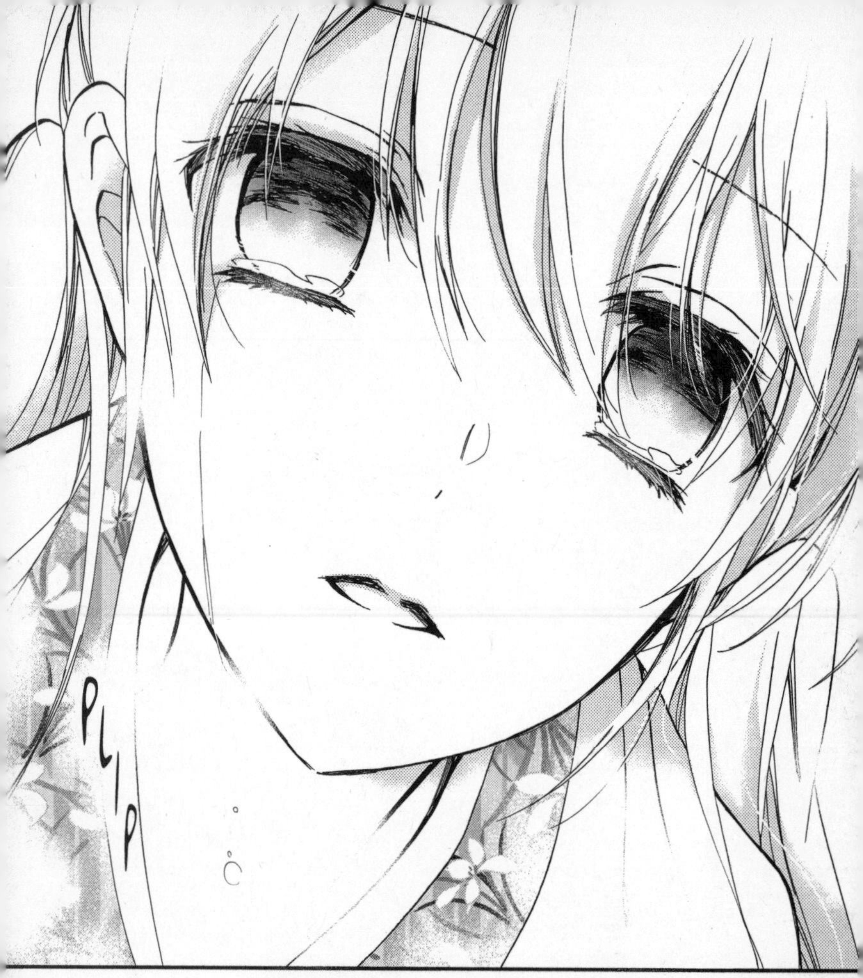
PLIP
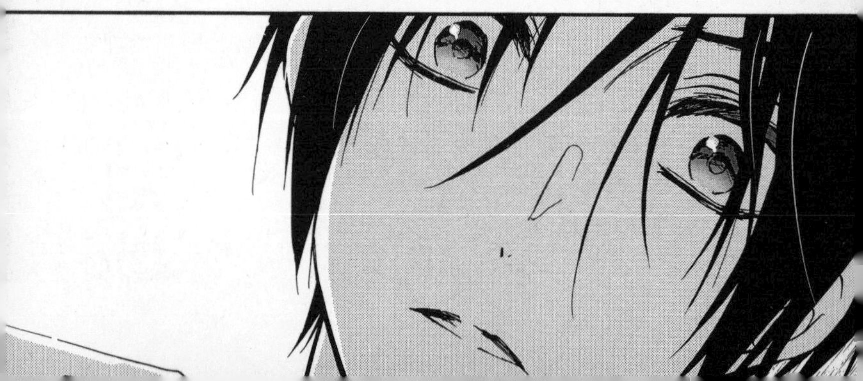

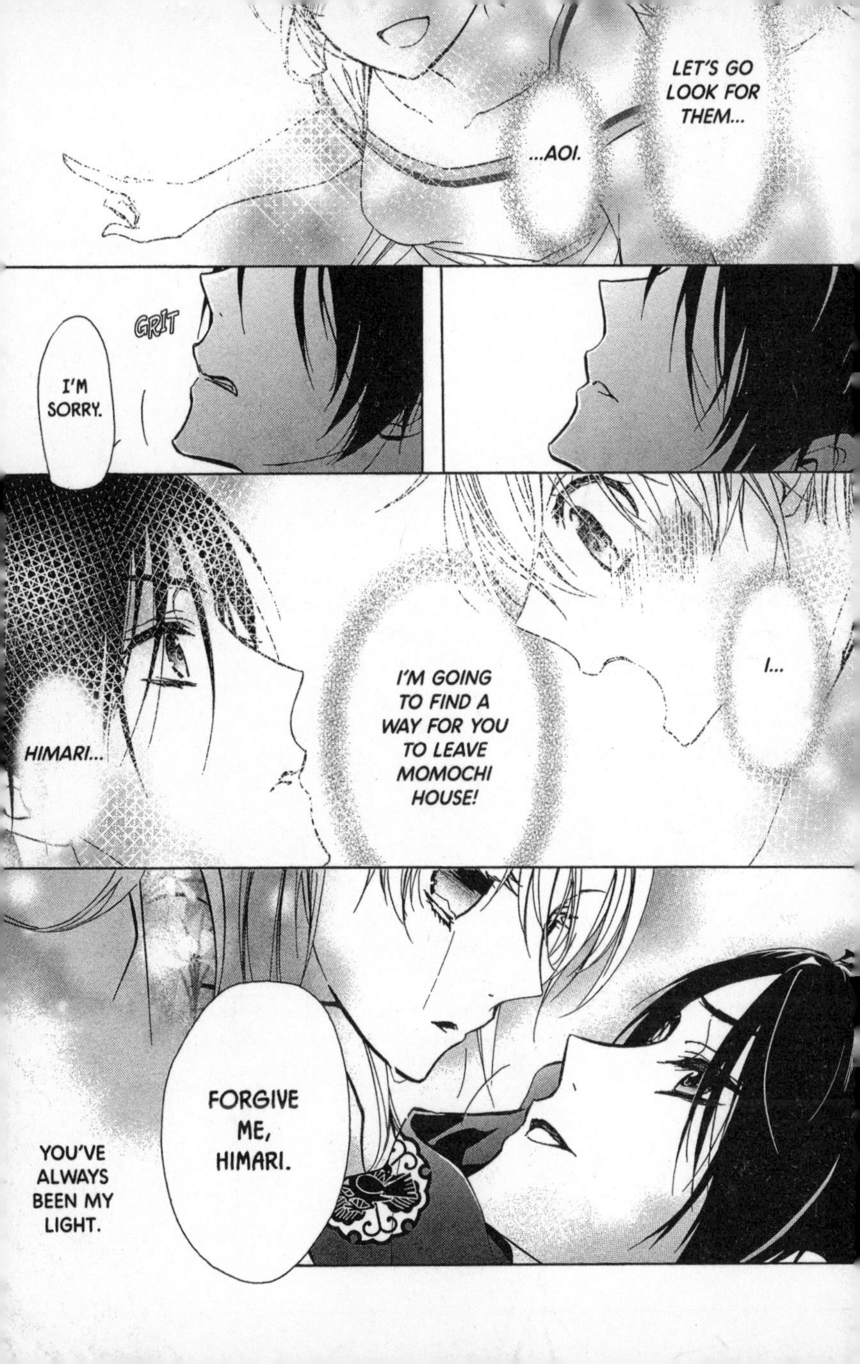
LET'S GO LOOK FOR THEM...
...AOI.
GRIT
I'M SORRY.
I...
I'M GOING TO FIND A WAY FOR YOU TO LEAVE MOMOCHI HOUSE!
HIMARI...
FORGIVE ME, HIMARI.
YOU'VE ALWAYS BEEN MY LIGHT.

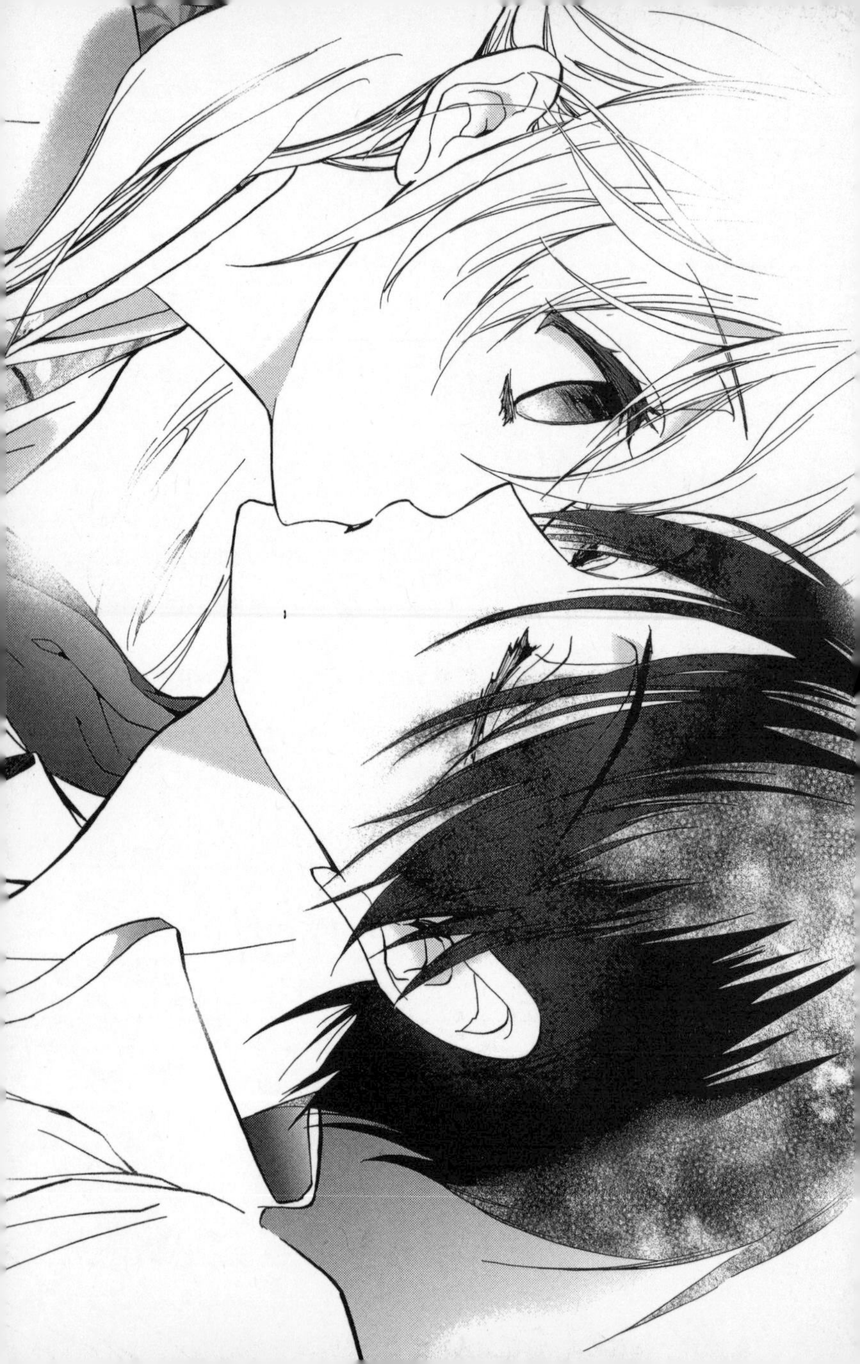

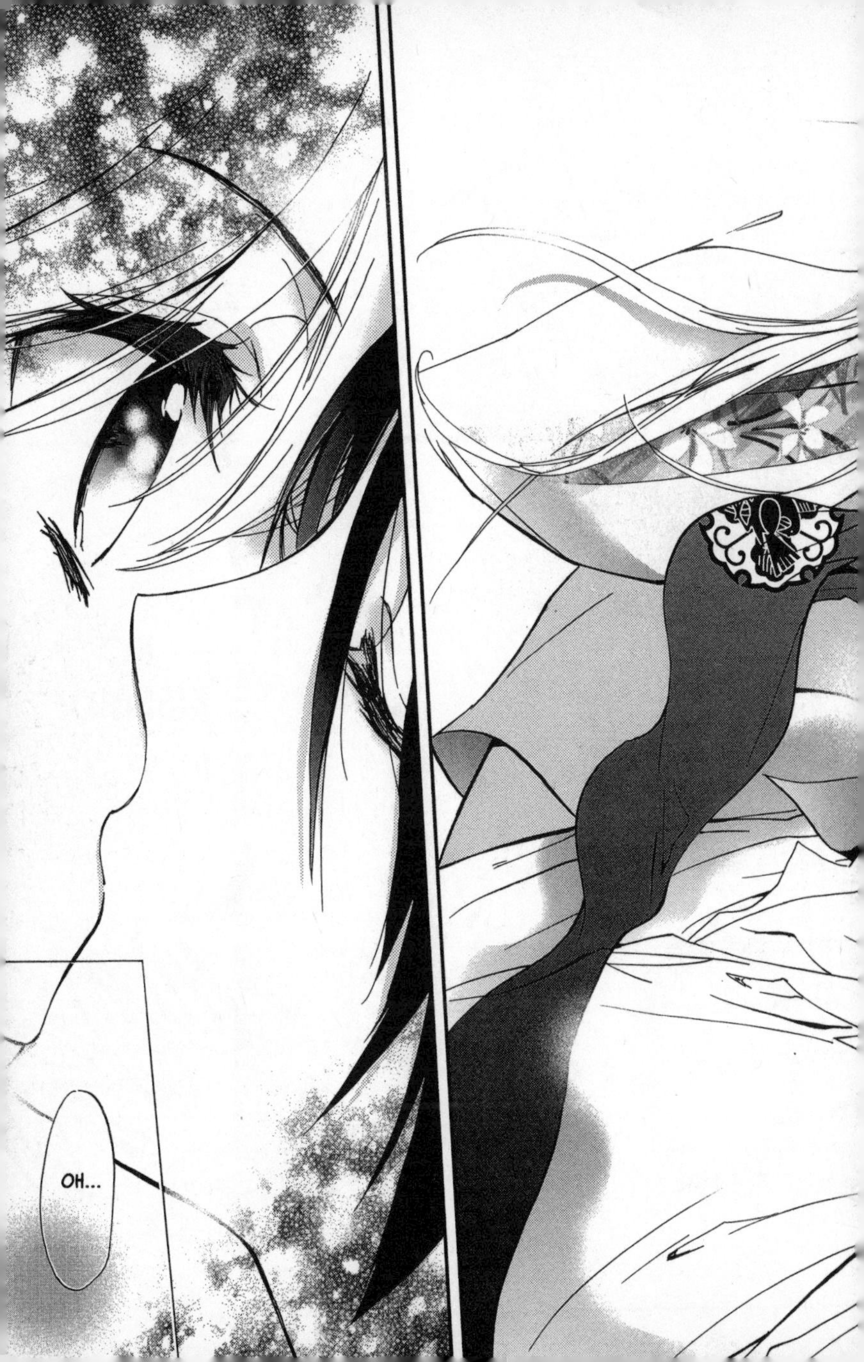
OH...

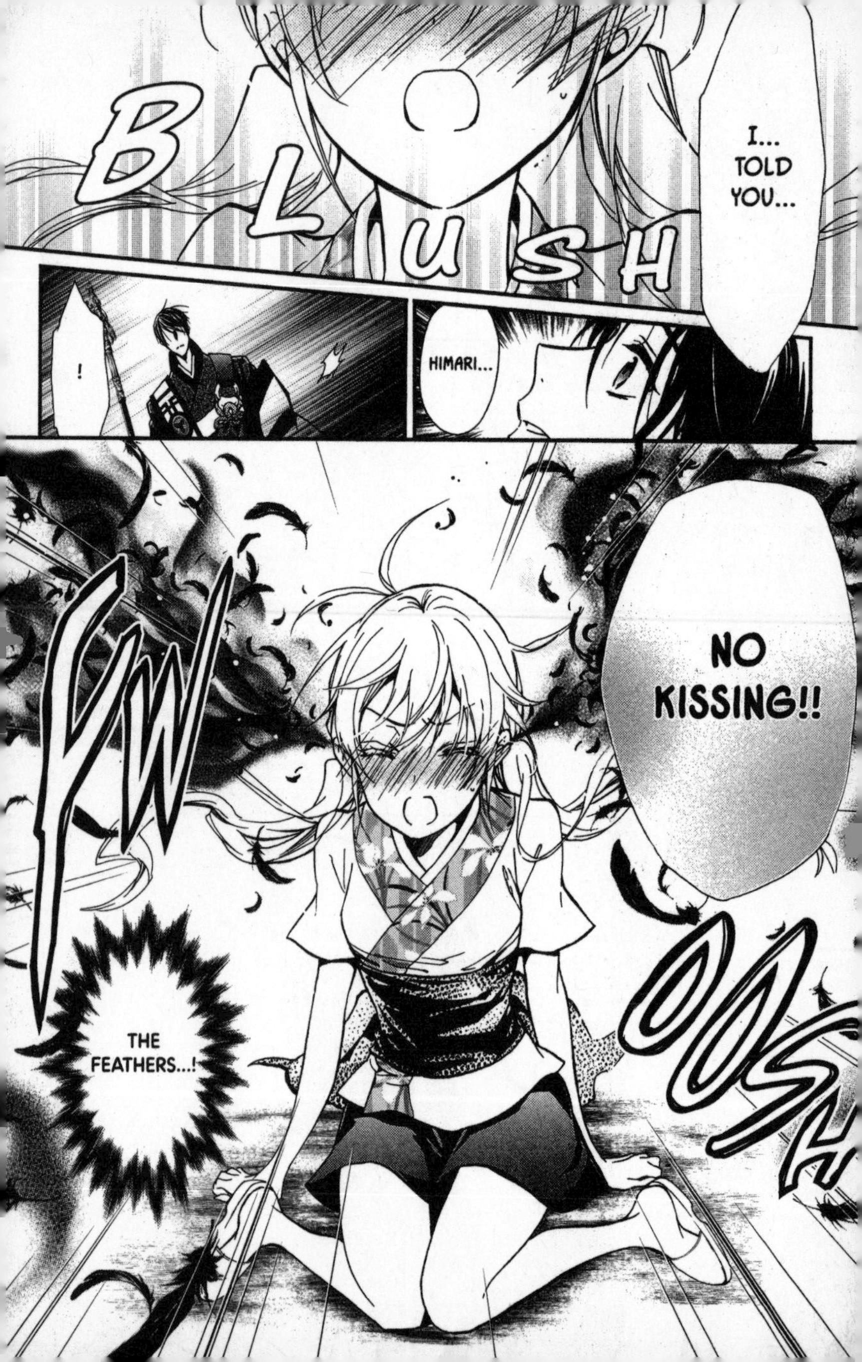
I... TOLD YOU...
BLUSH
HIMARI...
!
NO KISSING!!
WOOSH
THE FEATHERS...!

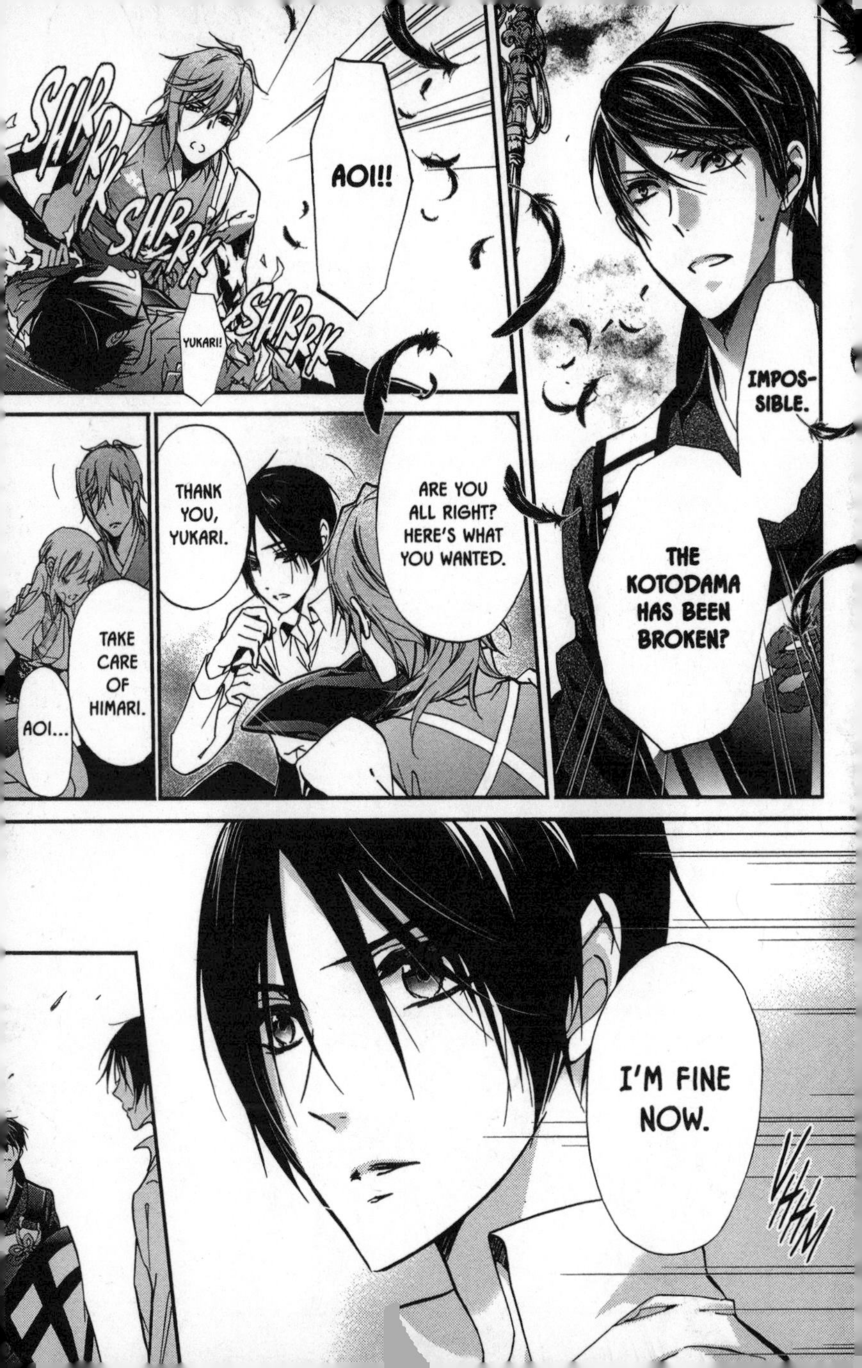
IMPOSSIBLE.
THE KOTODAMA HAS BEEN BROKEN?
AOI!!
SHRRK
SHRRK
YUKARI!
SHRRK
ARE YOU ALL RIGHT? HERE'S WHAT YOU WANTED.
THANK YOU, YUKARI.
TAKE CARE OF HIMARI.
AOI...
I'M FINE NOW.
VHHM

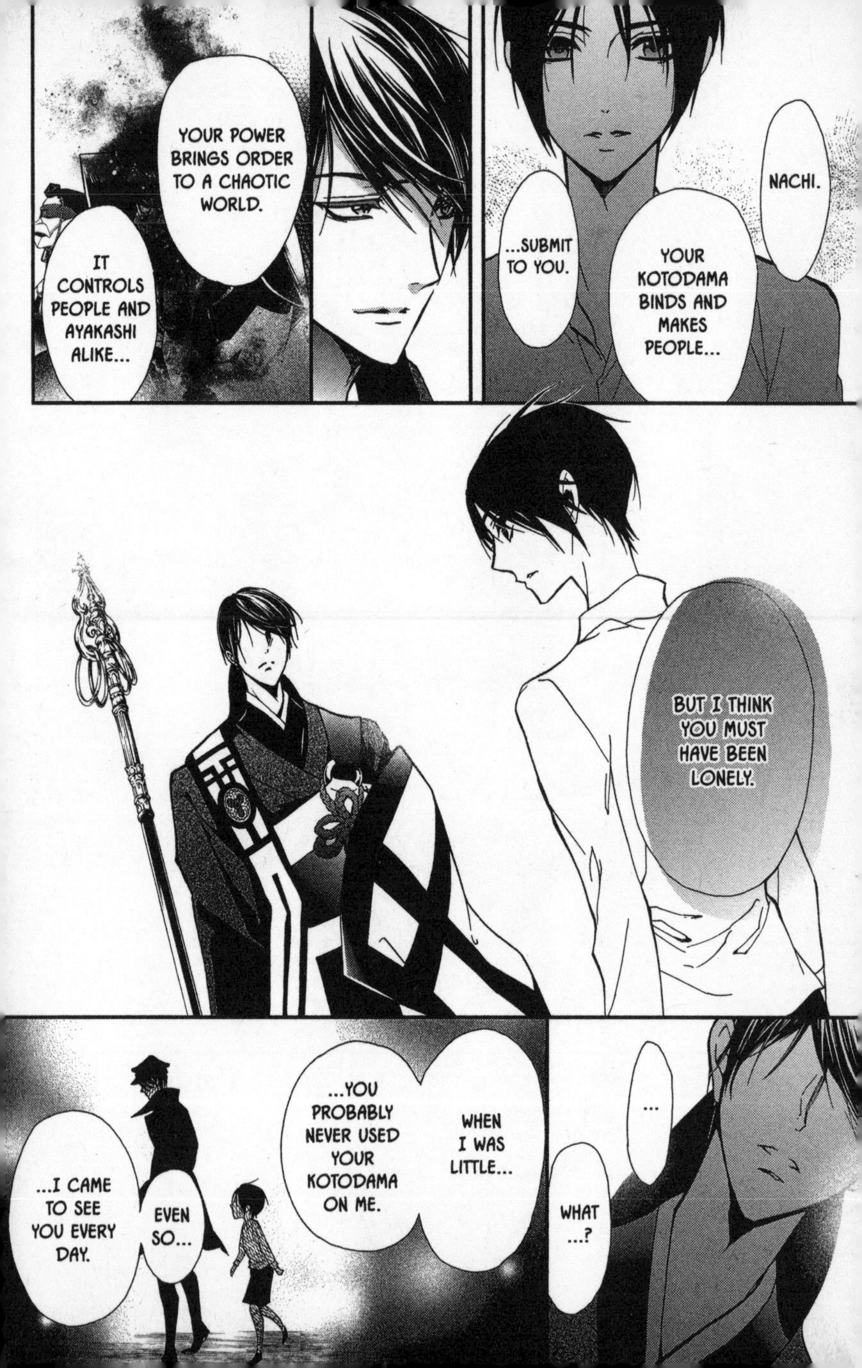
NACHI.
YOUR KOTODAMA BINDS AND MAKES PEOPLE...
...SUBMIT TO YOU.
YOUR POWER BRINGS ORDER TO A CHAOTIC WORLD.
IT CONTROLS PEOPLE AND AYAKASHI ALIKE...
BUT I THINK YOU MUST HAVE BEEN LONELY.
...
WHAT ...?
WHEN I WAS LITTLE...
...YOU PROBABLY NEVER USED YOUR KOTODAMA ON ME.
EVEN SO...
...I CAME TO SEE YOU EVERY DAY.

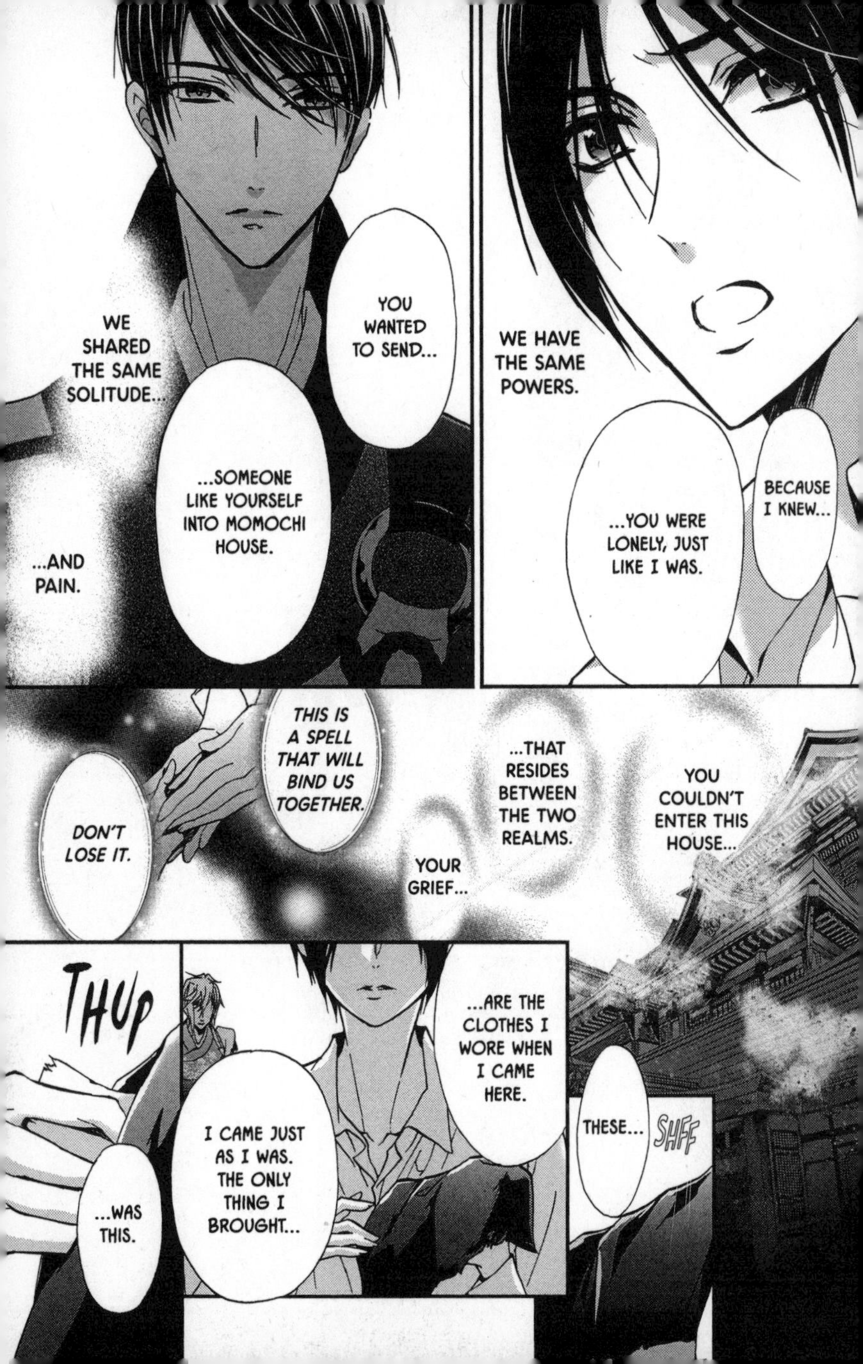
WE HAVE THE SAME POWERS.
BECAUSE I KNEW...
...YOU WERE LONELY, JUST LIKE I WAS.
YOU WANTED TO SEND...
...SOMEONE LIKE YOURSELF INTO MOMOCHI HOUSE.
WE SHARED THE SAME SOLITUDE...
...AND PAIN.
YOU COULDN'T ENTER THIS HOUSE...
...THAT RESIDES BETWEEN THE TWO REALMS.
YOUR GRIEF...
THIS IS A SPELL THAT WILL BIND US TOGETHER.
DON'T LOSE IT.
SHFF
THESE...
...ARE THE CLOTHES I WORE WHEN I CAME HERE.
I CAME JUST AS I WAS. THE ONLY THING I BROUGHT...
THUP
...WAS THIS.

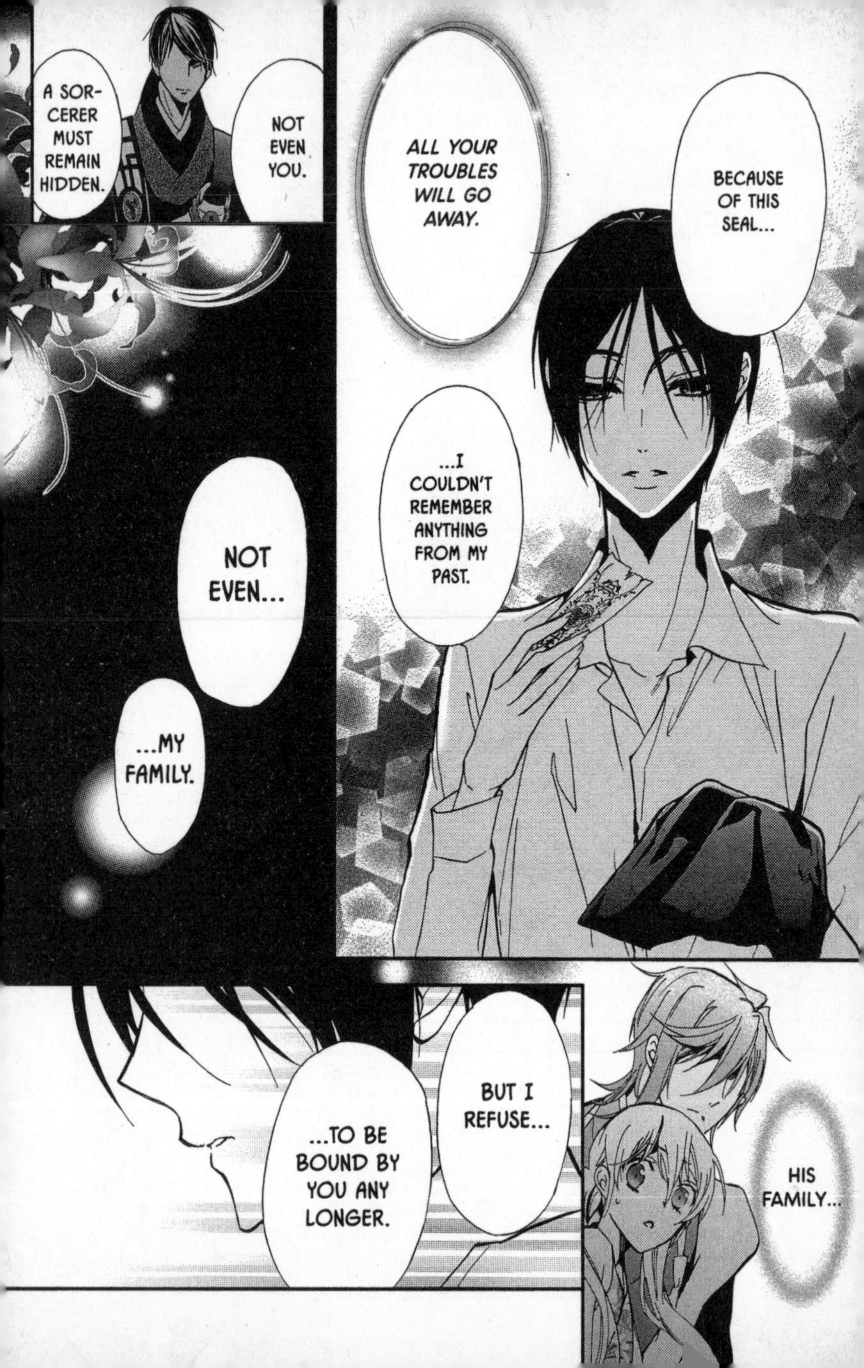
BECAUSE OF THIS SEAL...
ALL YOUR TROUBLES WILL GO AWAY.
...I COULDN'T REMEMBER ANYTHING FROM MY PAST.
NOT EVEN YOU.
A SORCERER MUST REMAIN HIDDEN.
NOT EVEN...
...MY FAMILY.
HIS FAMILY...
BUT I REFUSE...
...TO BE BOUND BY YOU ANY LONGER.

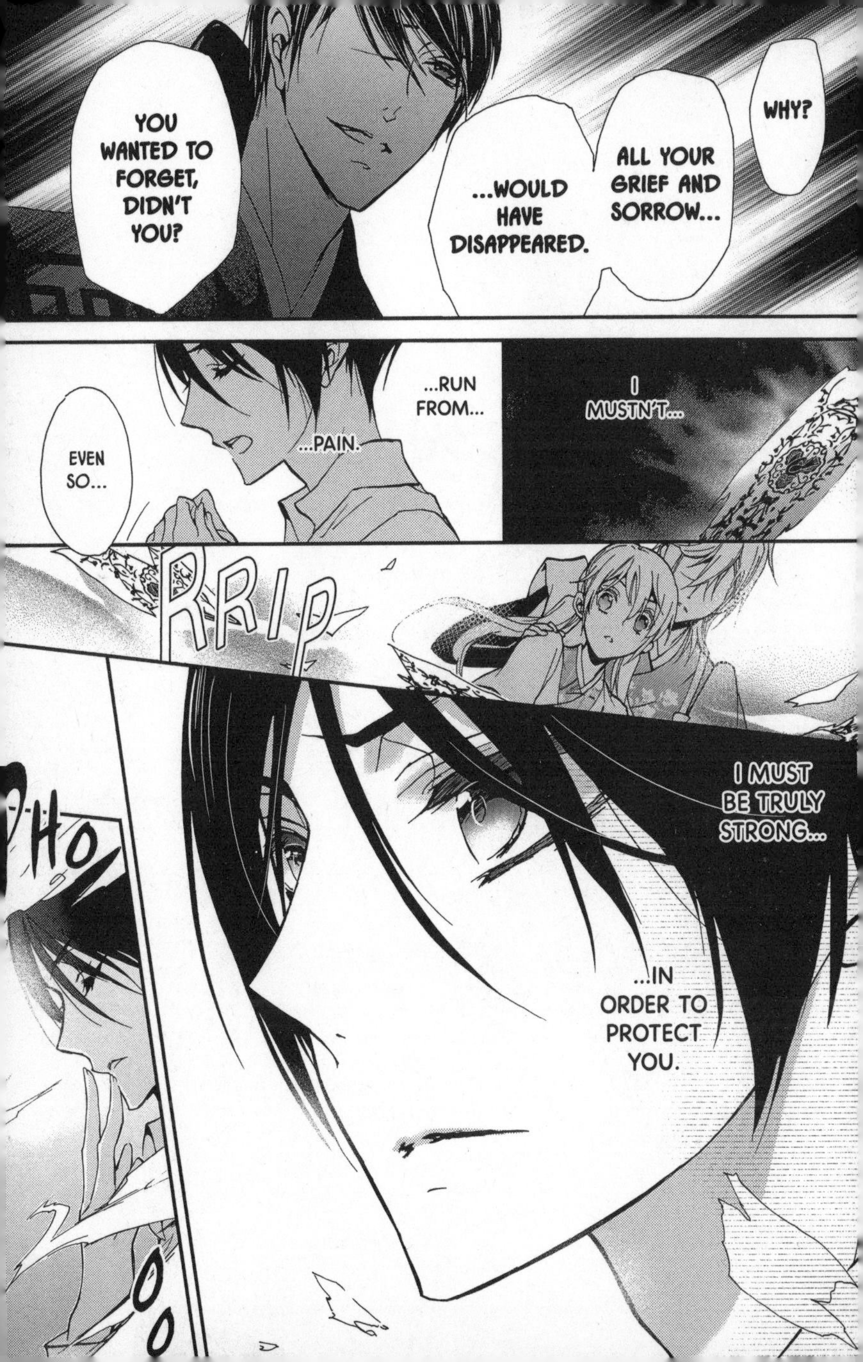
WHY?
ALL YOUR GRIEF AND SORROW...
...WOULD HAVE DISAPPEARED.
YOU WANTED TO FORGET, DIDN'T YOU?
I MUSTN'T...
...RUN FROM...
...PAIN.
EVEN SO...
RRIP
I MUST BE TRULY STRONG...
...IN ORDER TO PROTECT YOU.

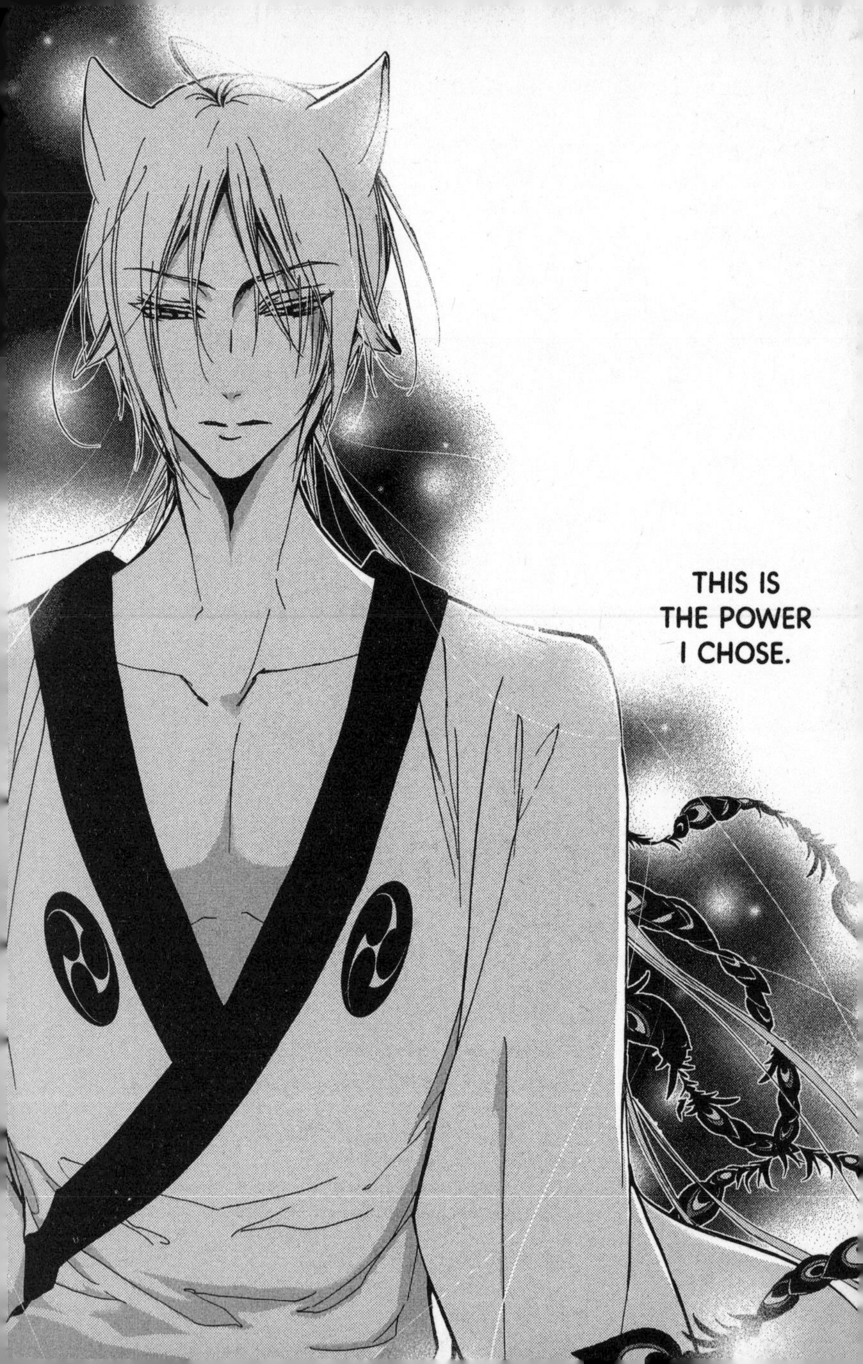
THIS IS THE POWER I CHOSE.

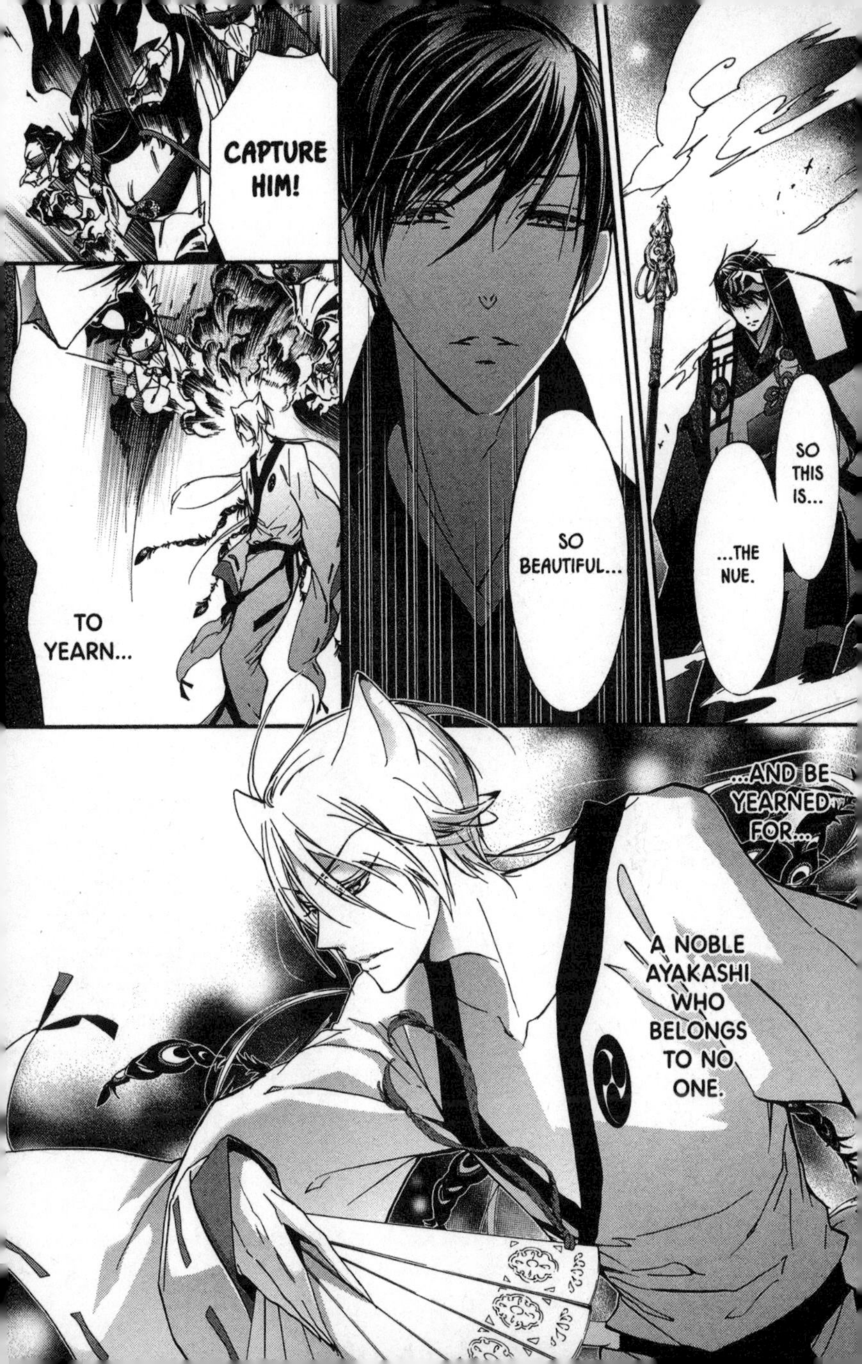
SO THIS IS...
...THE NUE.
SO BEAUTIFUL...
CAPTURE HIM!
TO YEARN...
...AND BE YEARNED FOR...
A NOBLE AYAKASHI WHO BELONGS TO NO ONE.

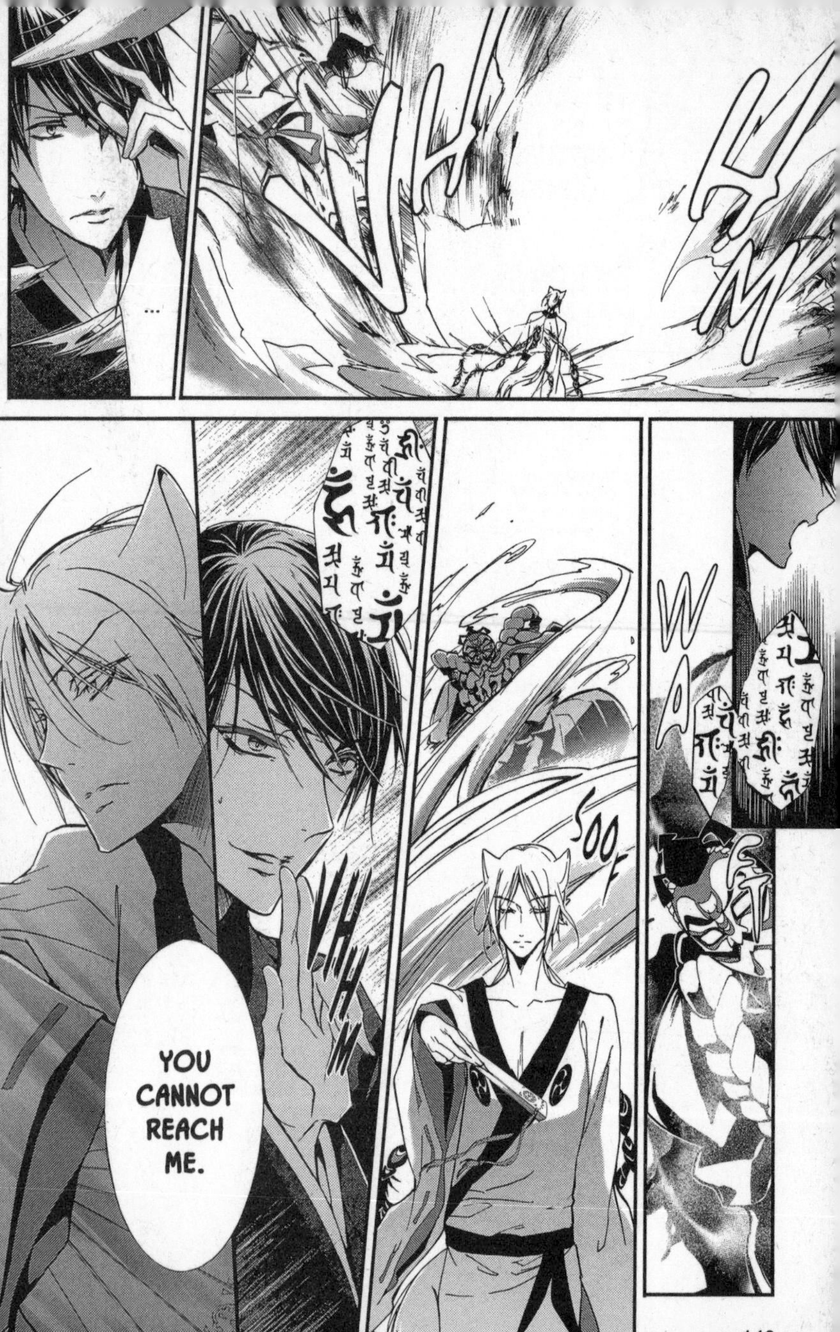
VHHM
...
WA
FFT
SOOF
VHHM
YOU CANNOT REACH ME.

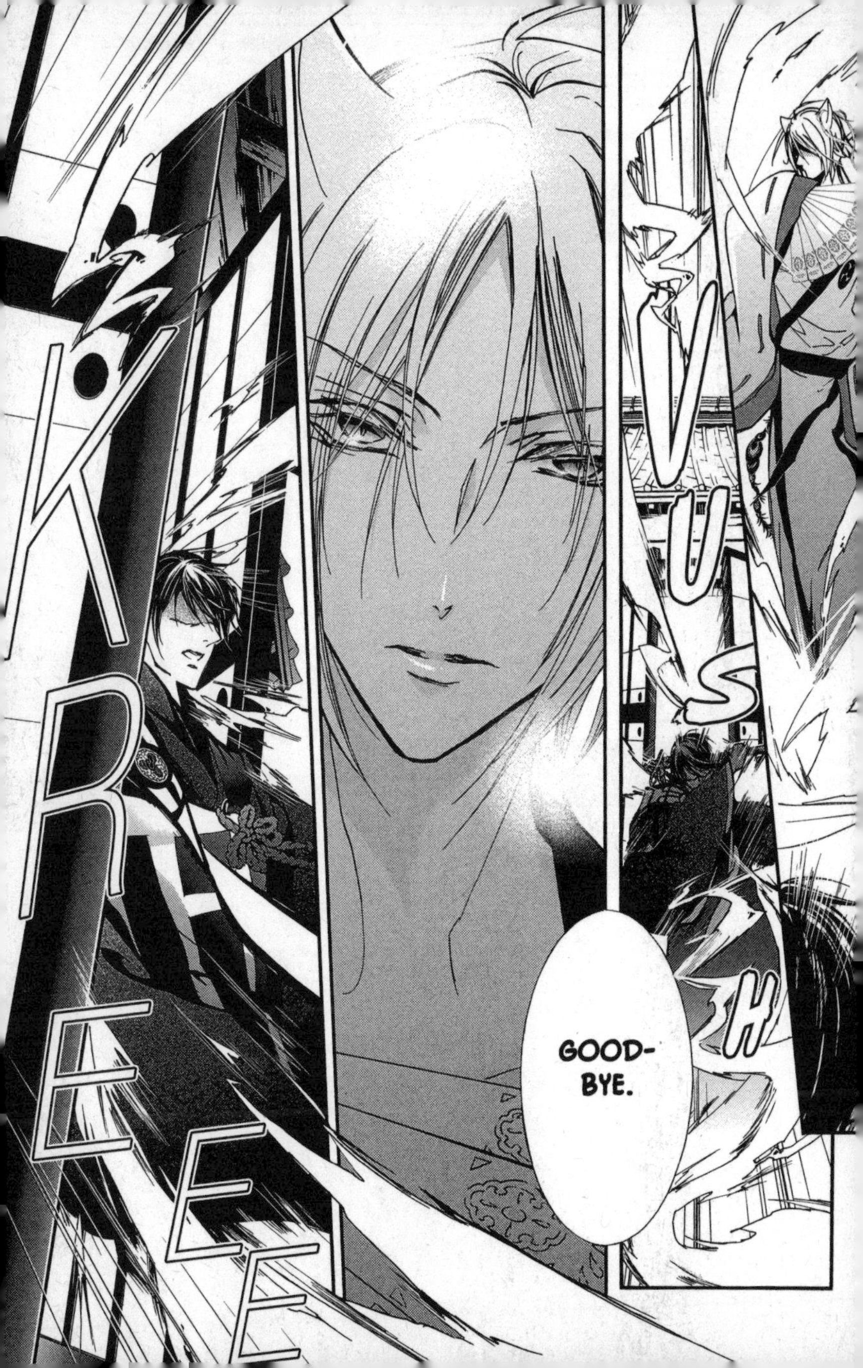
VUSH
GOOD-BYE.
KREEE

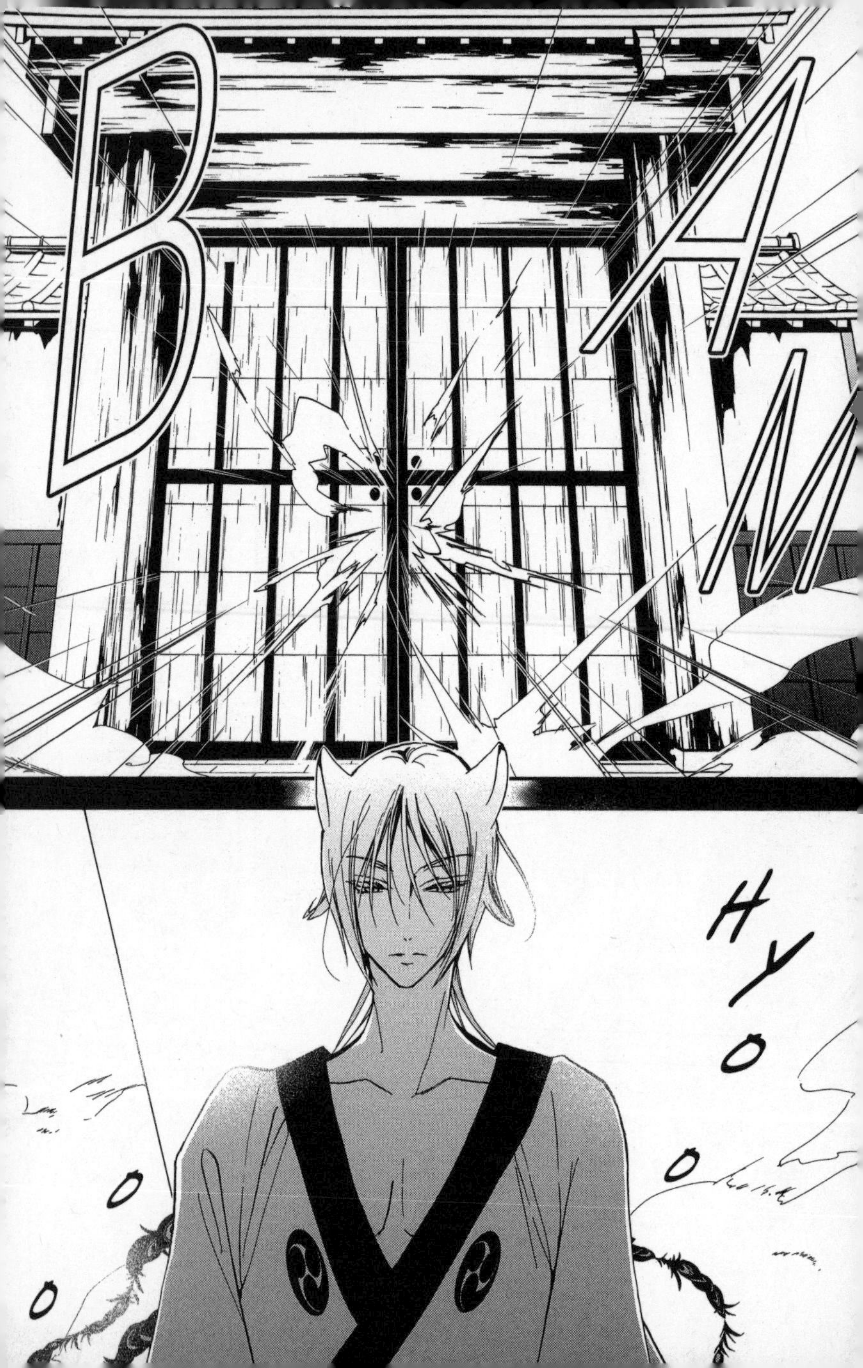
BAM
HYOOOO

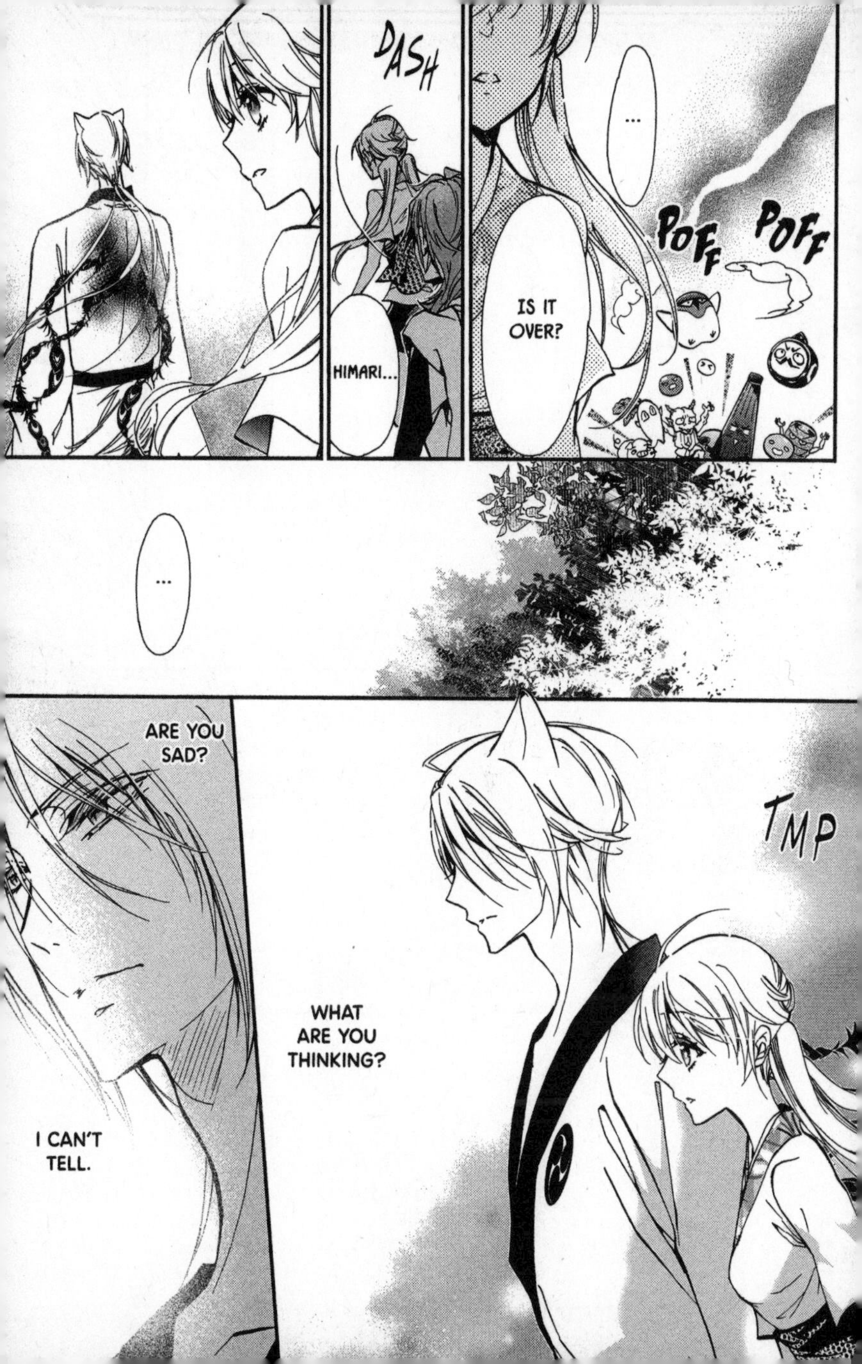
...
POFF POFF
IS IT OVER?
DASH
HIMARI...
...
TMP
WHAT ARE YOU THINKING?
ARE YOU SAD?
I CAN'T TELL.

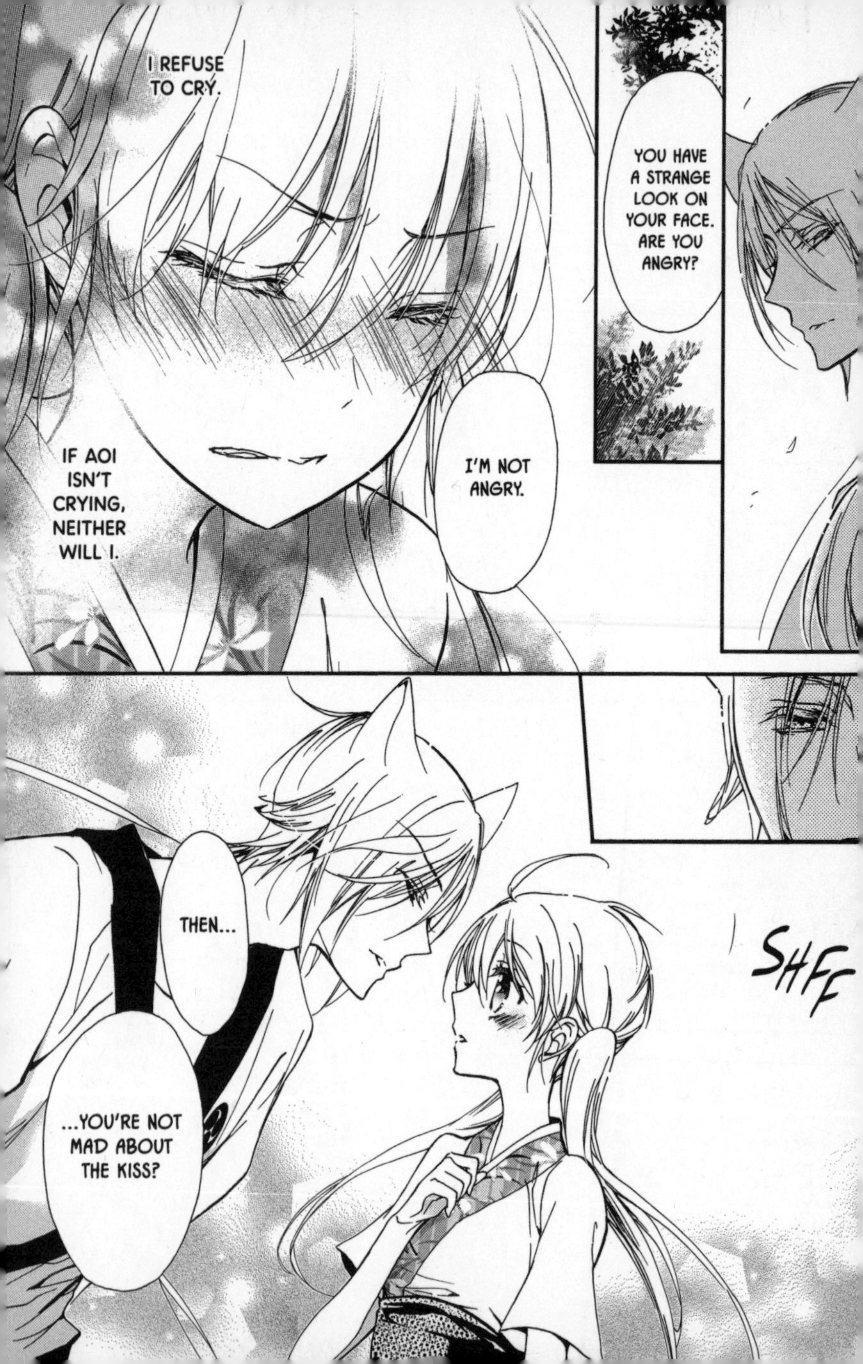
YOU HAVE A STRANGE LOOK ON YOUR FACE. ARE YOU ANGRY?
I'M NOT ANGRY.
I REFUSE TO CRY.
IF AOI ISN'T CRYING, NEITHER WILL I.
SHFF
THEN...
...YOU'RE NOT MAD ABOUT THE KISS?

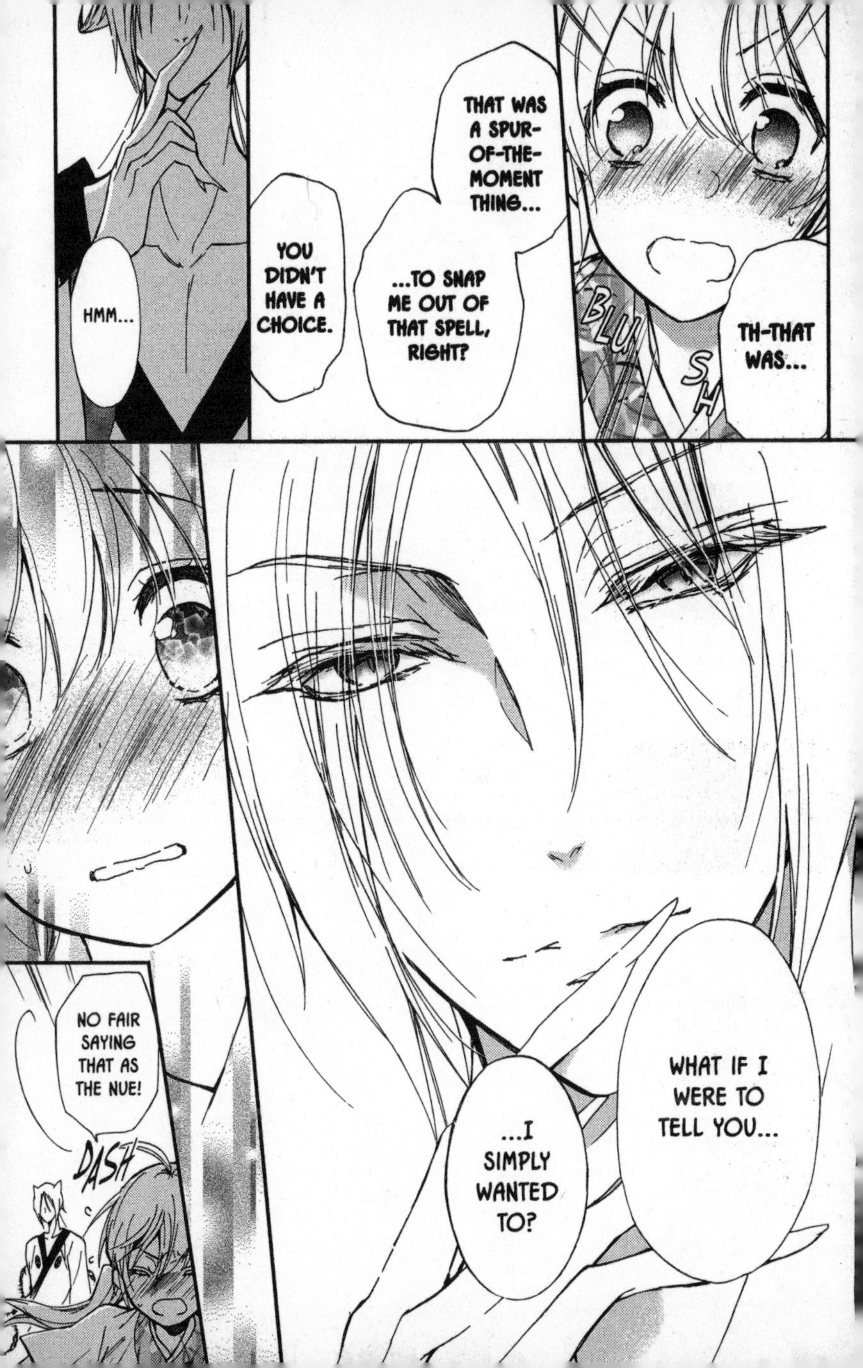
BLUSH
TH-THAT WAS...
THAT WAS A SPUR-OF-THE-MOMENT THING...
...TO SNAP ME OUT OF THAT SPELL, RIGHT?
YOU DIDN'T HAVE A CHOICE.
HMM...
WHAT IF I WERE TO TELL YOU...
...I SIMPLY WANTED TO?
NO FAIR SAYING THAT AS THE NUE!
DASH

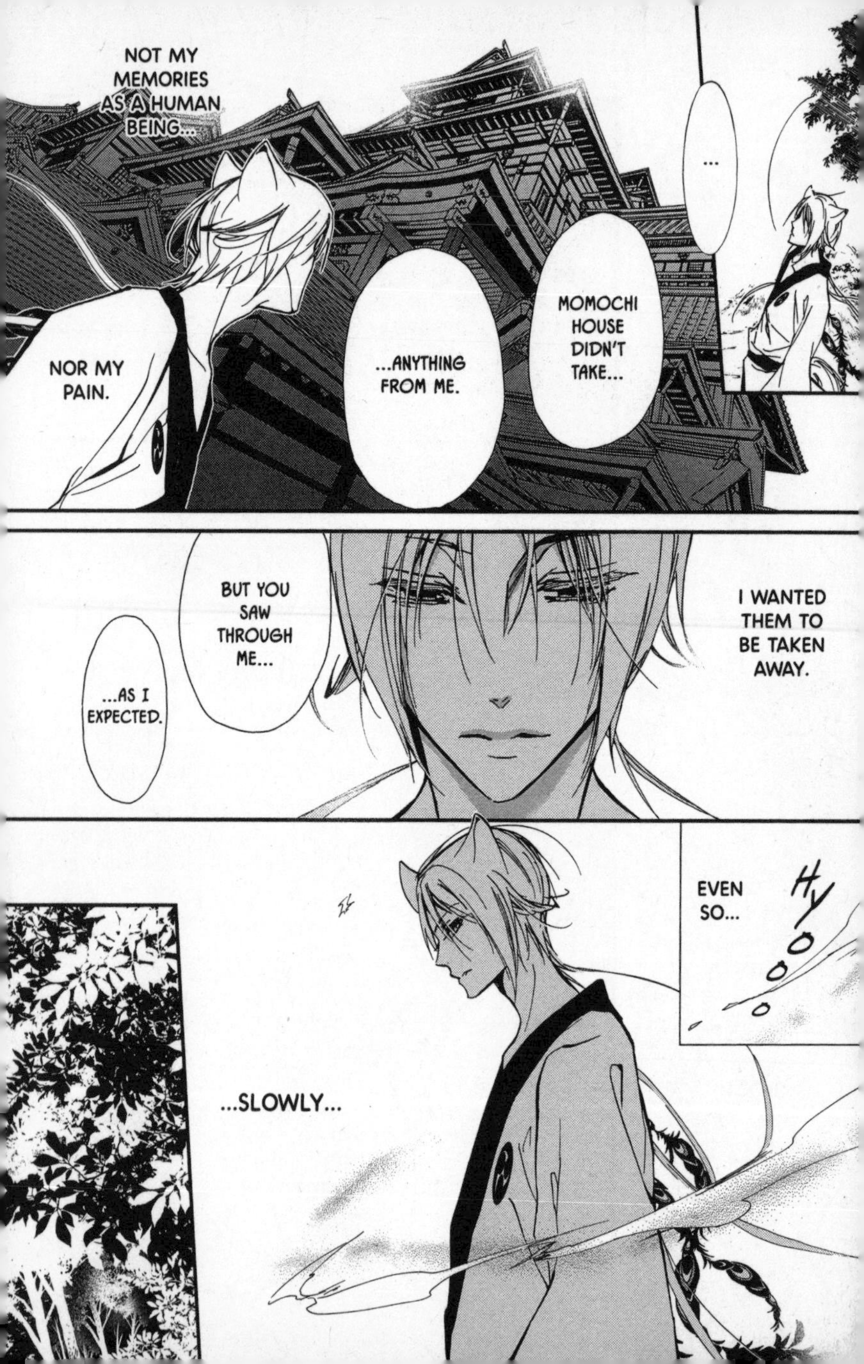
...
MOMOCHI HOUSE DIDN'T TAKE...
...ANYTHING FROM ME.
NOT MY MEMORIES AS A HUMAN BEING...
NOR MY PAIN.
I WANTED THEM TO BE TAKEN AWAY.
BUT YOU SAW THROUGH ME...
...AS I EXPECTED.
EVEN SO...
HYOOOO
...SLOWLY...

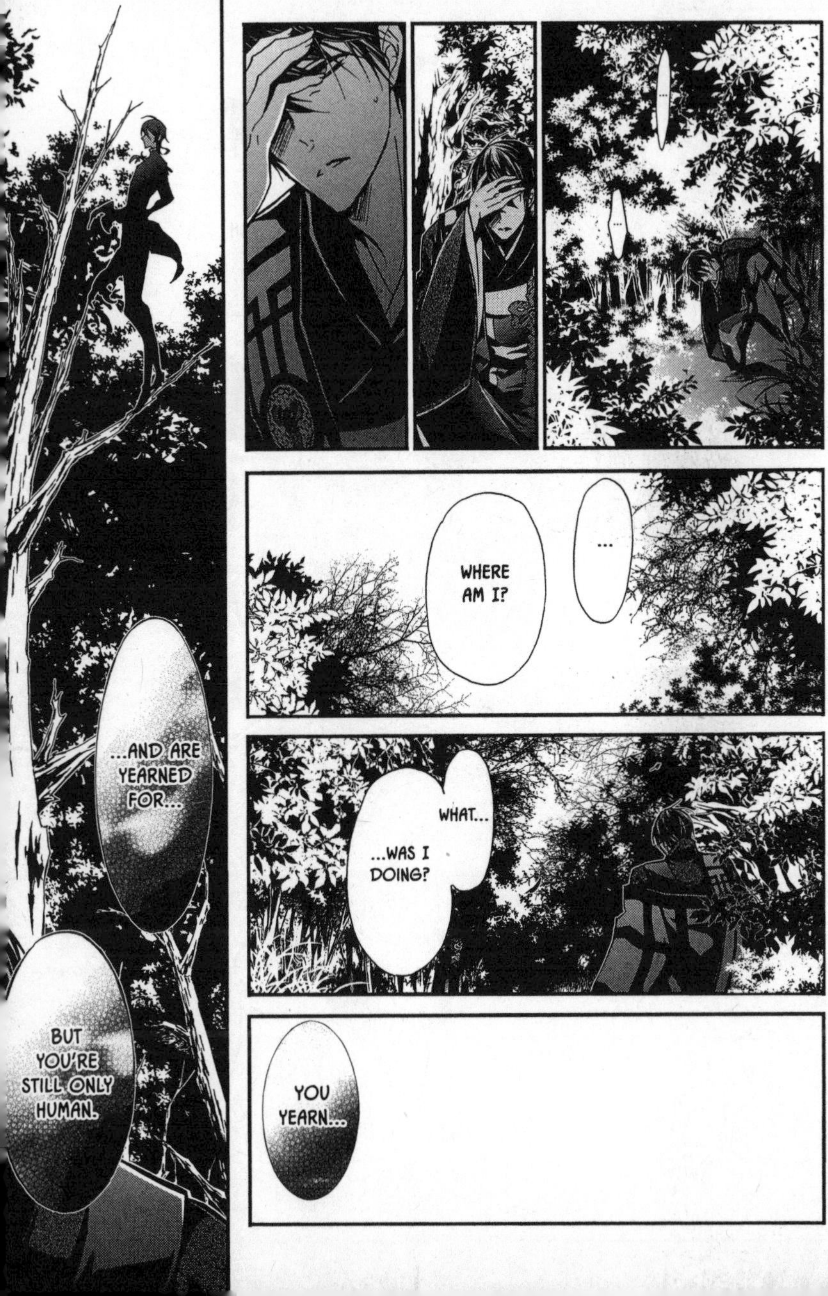
...
...
...
WHERE AM I?
WHAT...
...WAS I DOING?
YOU YEARN...
...AND ARE YEARNED FOR...
BUT YOU'RE STILL ONLY HUMAN.

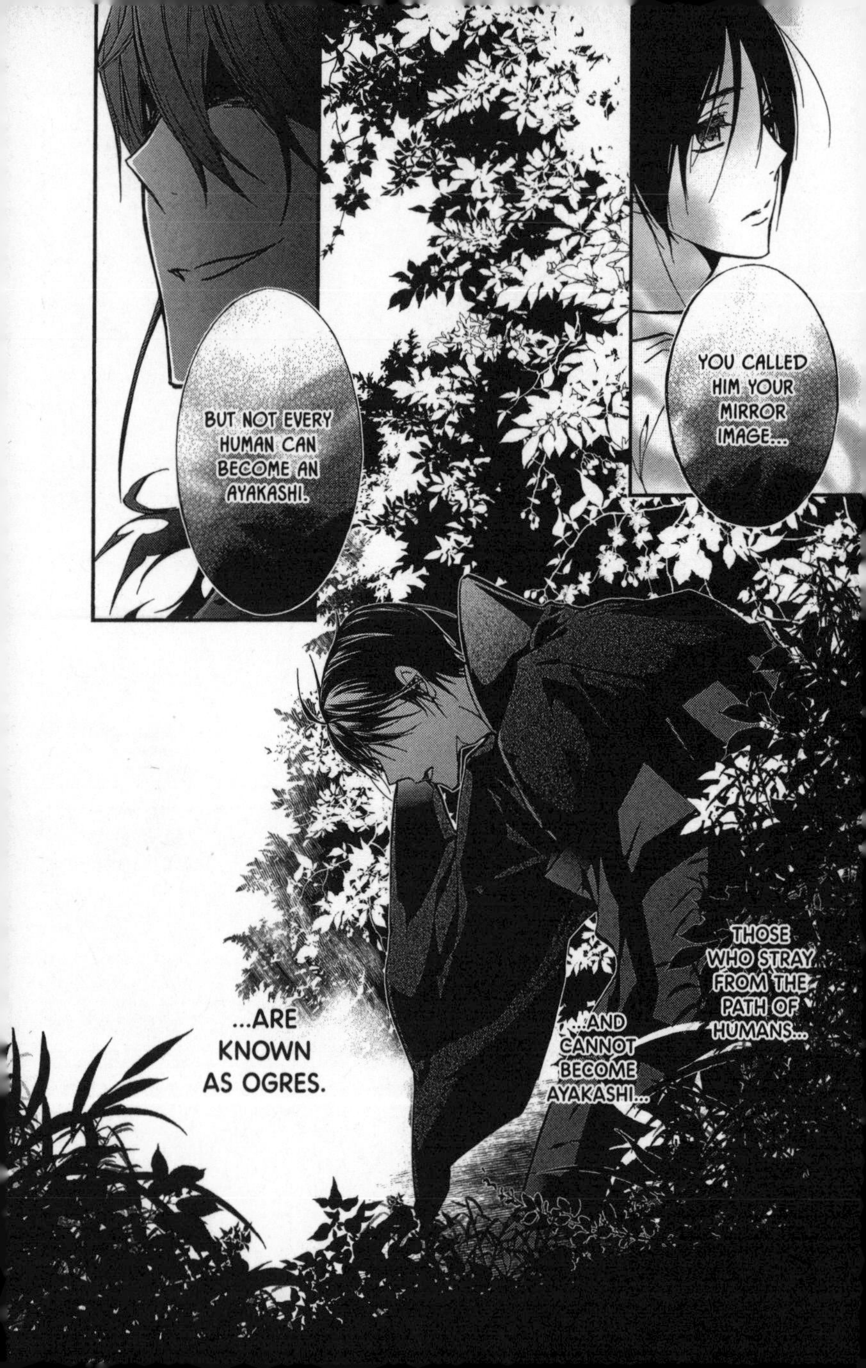
YOU CALLED HIM YOUR MIRROR IMAGE...
BUT NOT EVERY HUMAN CAN BECOME AN AYAKASHI.
THOSE WHO STRAY FROM THE PATH OF HUMANS...
...AND CANNOT BECOME AYAKASHI...
...ARE KNOWN AS OGRES.

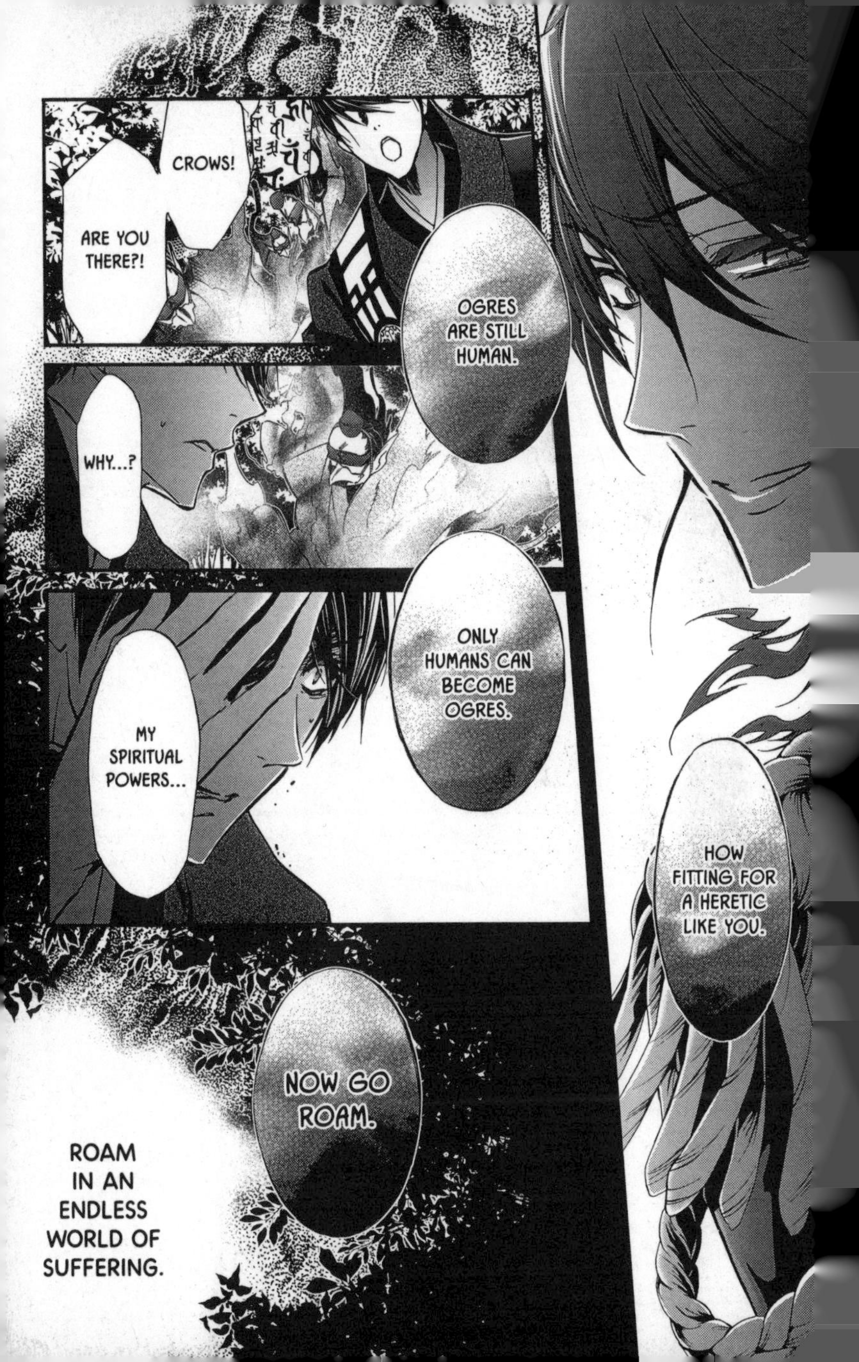
OGRES ARE STILL HUMAN.
ONLY HUMANS CAN BECOME OGRES.
HOW FITTING FOR A HERETIC LIKE YOU.
NOW GO ROAM.
CROWS!
ARE YOU THERE?!
WHY...?
MY SPIRITUAL POWERS...
ROAM IN AN ENDLESS WORLD OF SUFFERING.

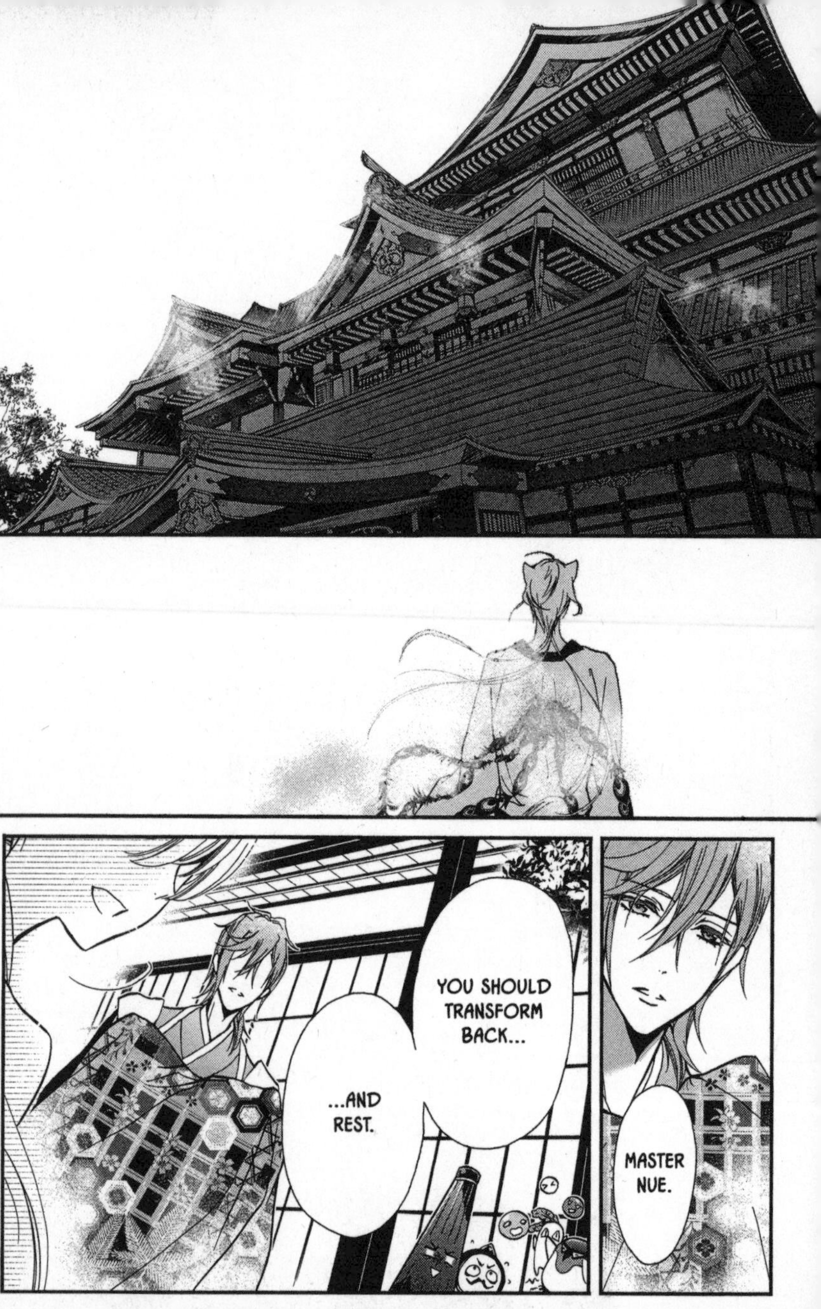
MASTER NUE.
YOU SHOULD TRANSFORM BACK...
...AND REST.

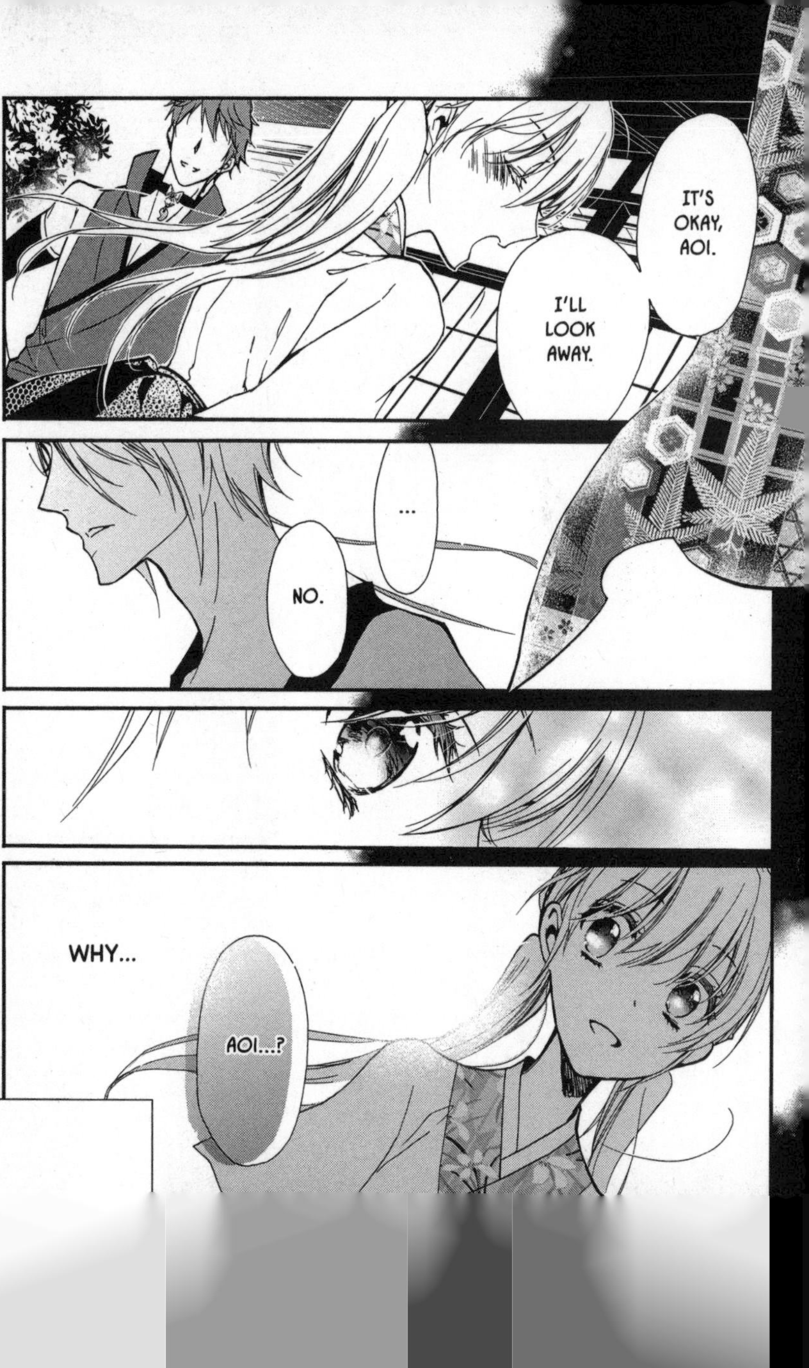
IT'S OKAY, AOI.
I'LL LOOK AWAY.
...
NO.
WHY...
AOI...?

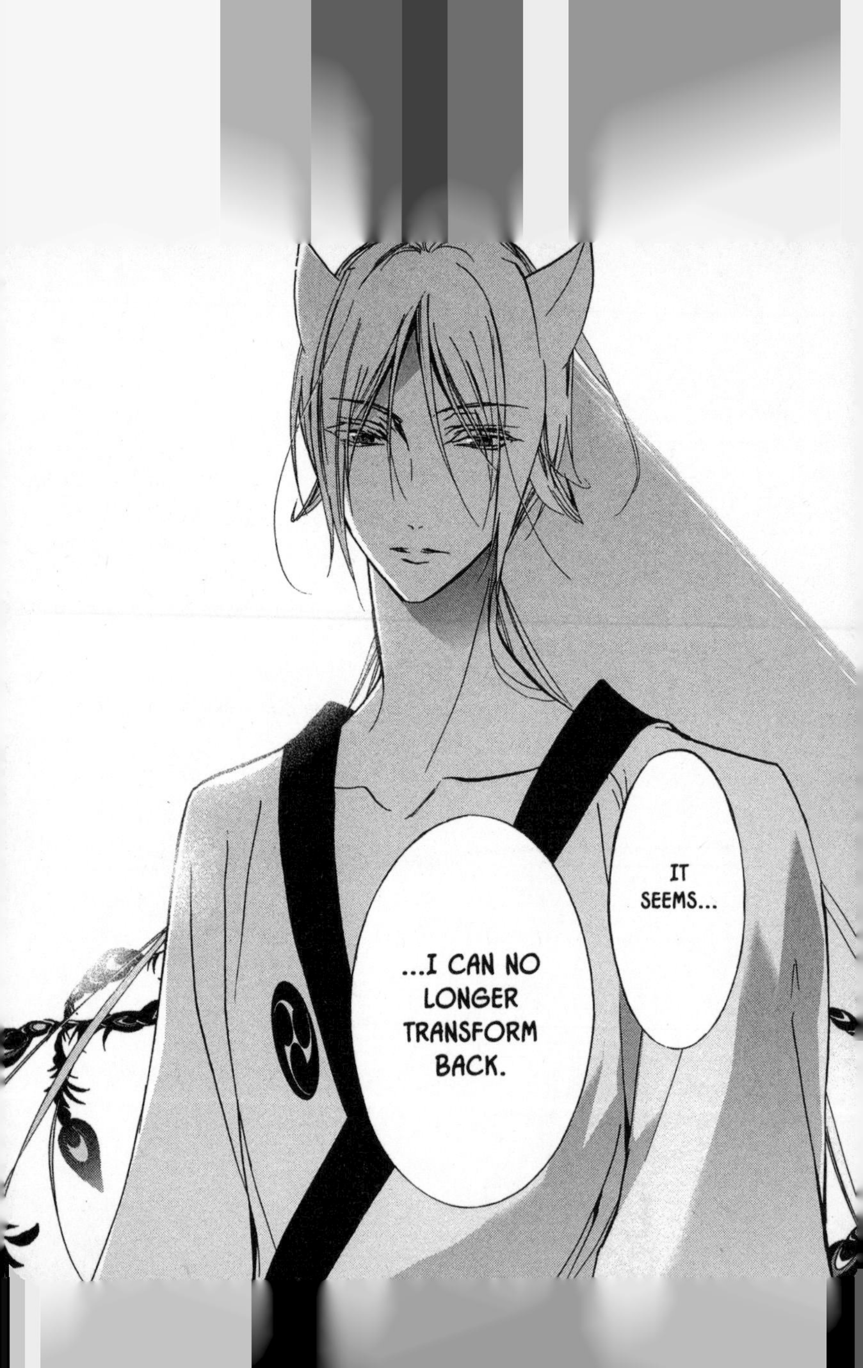
IT SEEMS...
...I CAN NO LONGER TRANSFORM BACK.

The
DEMON
PRINCE
of MOMOCHI
HOUSE

the
DEMON
PRINCE
of MOMOCHI
HOUSE

■ This is Volume 7. Aoi's story now begins to unfold. There is an old saying that children belong to God until they are seven years old. Up until this point, his story has been veiled in ambiguity.

Even some phrases in daily life have sinister nuances. For example, *ojamashimasu* ("thank you for having me") contains some frightening kanji. (*Ja* means "evil" and *ma* means "demon.") If you trace the roots of nursery songs, children's games and seasonal customs, you will often find they are related to demons and evil...

These uniquely Japanese customs are born of our desire to come to terms with such things. I like them.

The undefined categorization of "ayakashi" is the same. Something that exists where there is nothing.

That's what I'd like to portray...

■ Well, well! *The Demon Prince of Momochi House* is going to become a stage play! When I first heard the news, I couldn't believe it. It was unimaginable to me, and I was filled with excitement and curiosity. The color spread at the beginning of this volume was a manifestation of the joy I felt at that time. ♪
Since then, the cast was announced, the script was written, the music was created (J-rock!) and rehearsals began. A 2.5 dimensional world of *Momochi House* is emerging and it is so exciting! I'm so happy that I'll be able to see this brilliant play with all you Momochi fans. Thank you to all who were involved in this endeavor and for your continued support!

Aya Shouoto
Summer 2015

The
DEMON
PRINCE
of MOMOCHI
HOUSE

< STAFF >
NORIE.O / AYA.M / MAIKO.Y
KAZUKO.M / KANAE.S / NAOKO.K

The
DEMON
PRINCE
of MOMOCHI
HOUSE

Momochi House Illustration Gallery

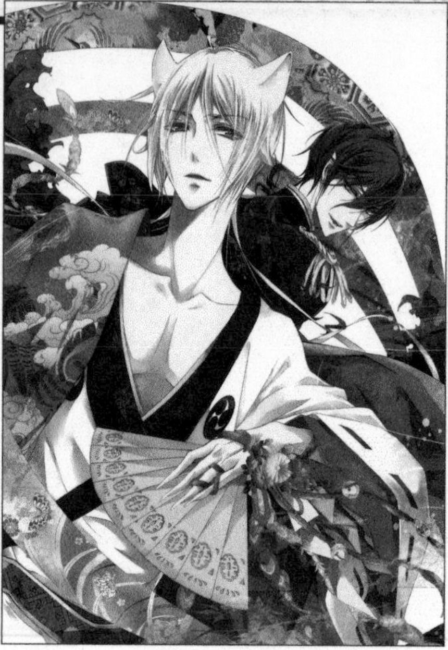

Asuka Magazine Cover, December 2014

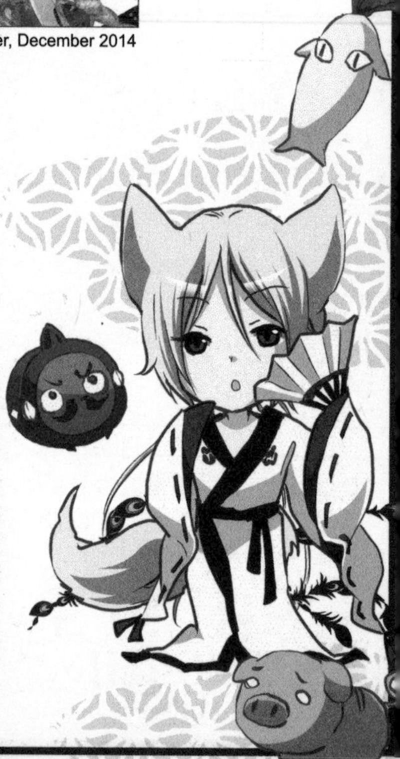

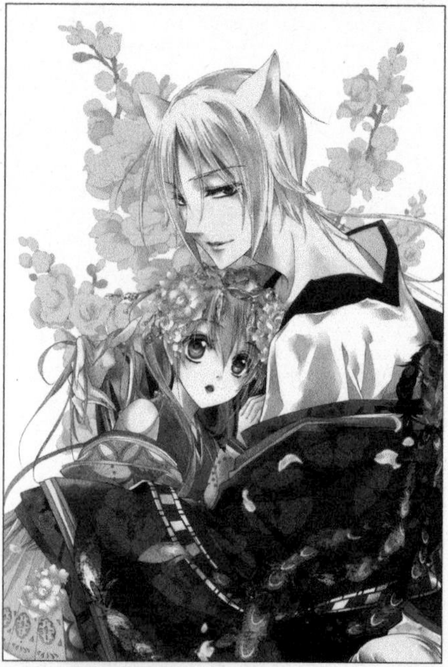

Asuka Magazine Cover, April 2015

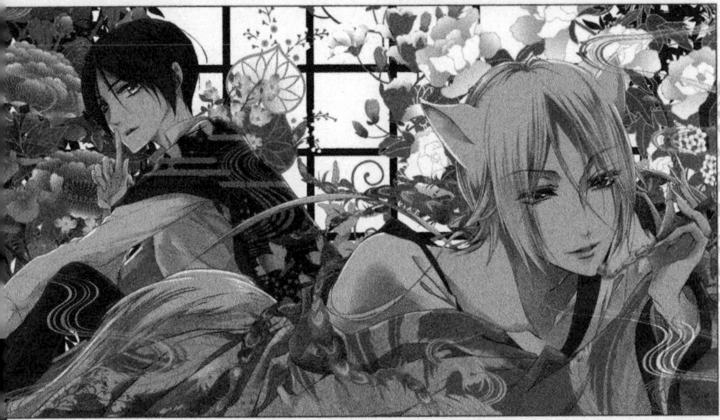

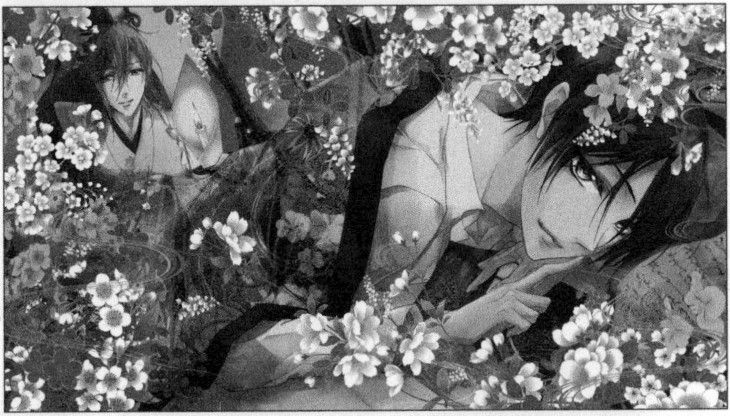

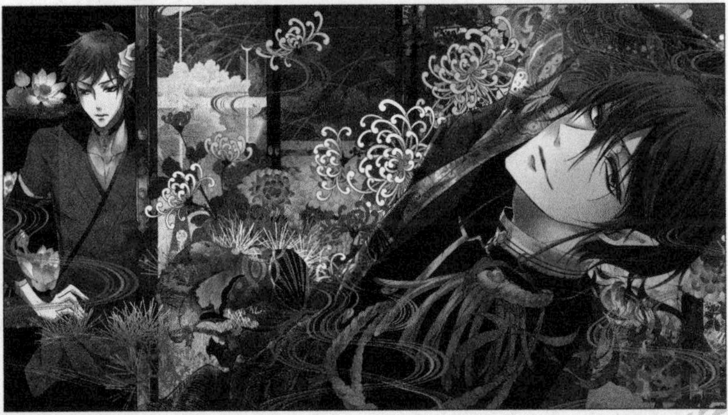

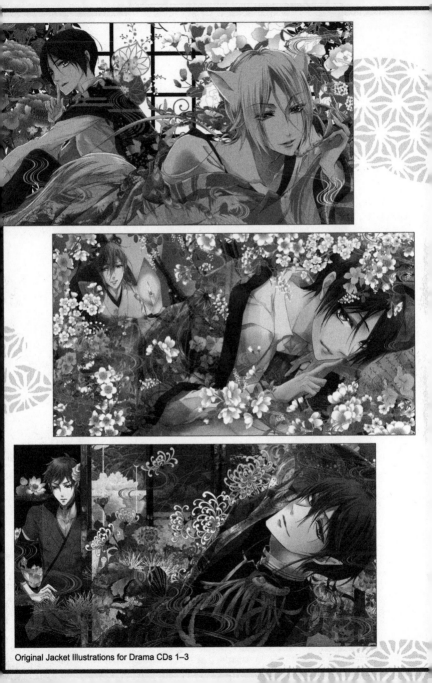

Original Jacket Illustrations for Drama CDs 1–3

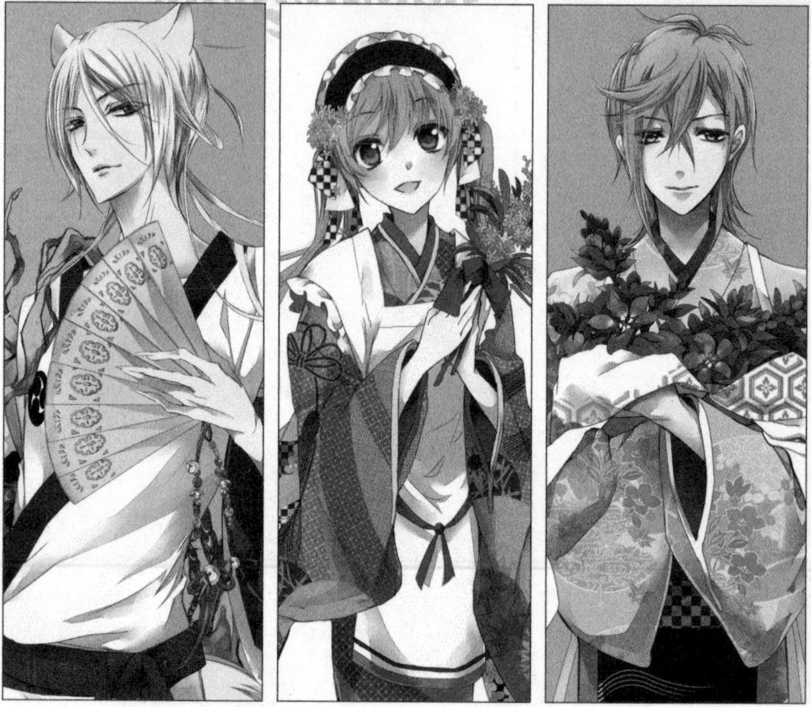

Original Merchandise Illustrations (Incense)

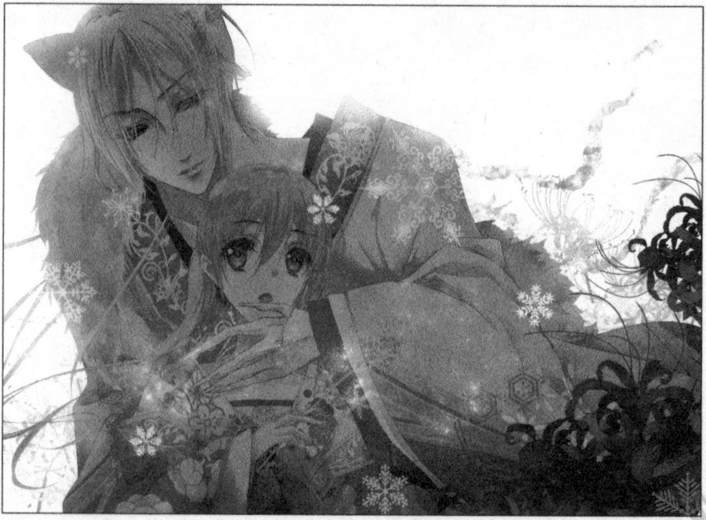

Asuka Magazine Supplement Illustration Collection, January 2015

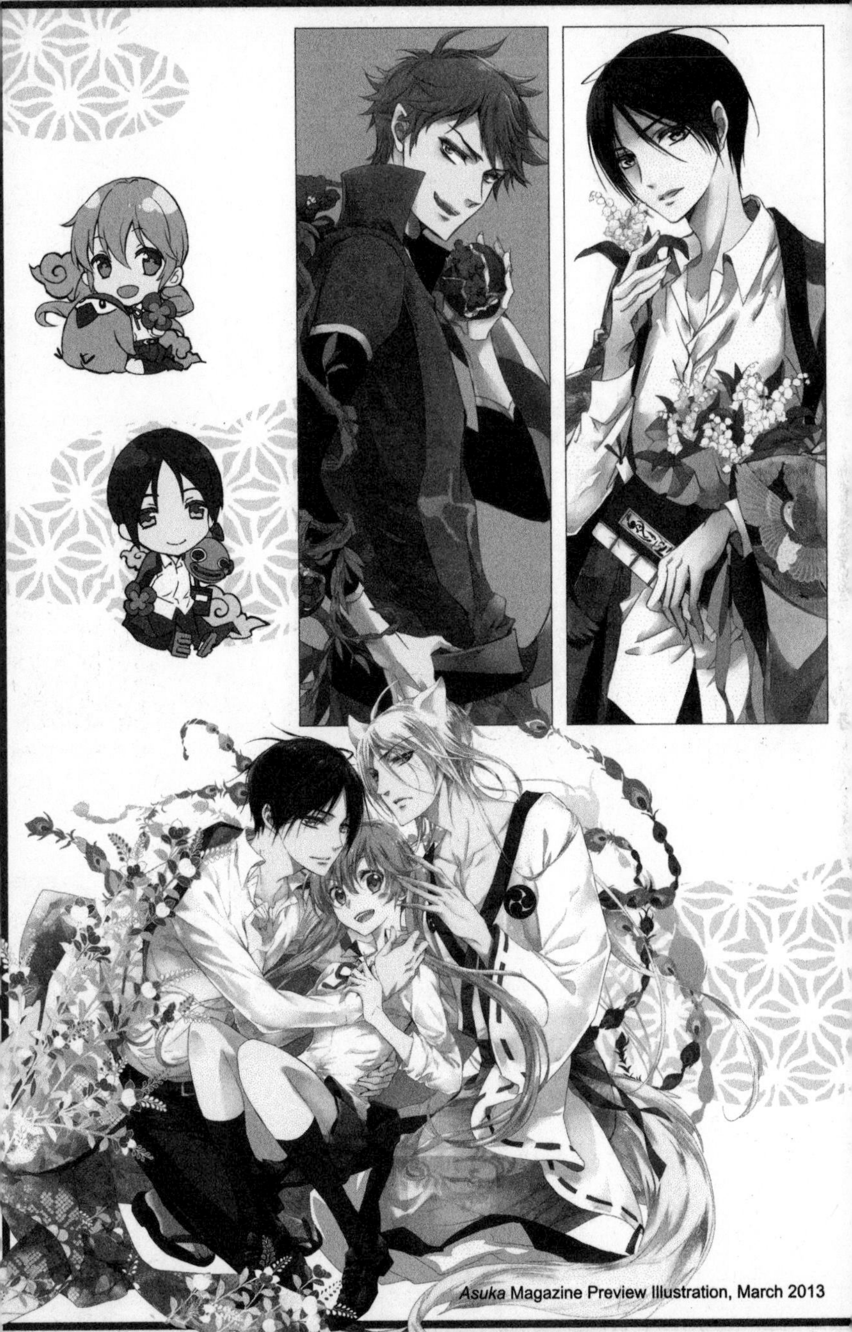

Asuka Magazine Preview Illustration, March 2013

Momochi House is being adapted for the stage! In celebration, I drew Nue on the cover striking a pose as if he were a theatrical actor. Drawing Nue is always a challenge because his ears, which are essential, are hard to see depending on the design. And you only ever catch a glimpse of his tail...

-*Aya Shouoto*

Aya Shouoto was born on December 25. Her hobbies are traveling, staying at hotels, sewing and daydreaming. She currently lives in Tokyo and enjoys listening to J-pop anime theme songs while she works.

The Demon Prince of Momochi House

Volume 7
Shojo Beat Edition

Story and Art by **Aya Shouoto**

Translation JN Productions
Touch-Up Art & Lettering Inori Fukuda Trant
Design Fawn Lau
Editor Nancy Thistlethwaite

MOMOCHISANCHI NO AYAKASHI OUJI Volume 7
© Aya SHOUOTO 2015
First published in Japan in 2015 by KADOKAWA CORPORATION, Tokyo.
English translation rights arranged with KADOKAWA CORPORATION, Tokyo.

The stories, characters and incidents mentioned
in this publication are entirely fictional.

Printed in the U.S.A.

Published by VIZ Media, LLC
P.O. Box 77010
San Francisco, CA 94107

10 9 8 7 6 5 4 3 2 1
First printing, January 2017

www.viz.com

www.shojobeat.com

Behind the Scenes!!

STORY AND ART BY BISCO HATORI

From the creator of **Ouran High School Host Club**

Ranmaru Kurisu comes from a family of hardy, rough-and-tumble fisherfolk and he sticks out at home like a delicate, artistic sore thumb. It's given him a raging inferiority complex and a permanently pessimistic outlook. Now that he's in college, he's hoping to find a sense of belonging. But after a whole life of being left out, does he even know how to fit in?!